Language and Hegemony in

READING GRAMSCI
General Editor: Joseph A. Buttigieg

Also available

GRAMSCI, CULTURE AND ANTHROPOLOGY
AN INTRODUCTORY TEXT
Kate Crehan

# Language and Hegemony in Gramsci

Peter Ives

Pluto Press

LONDON • ANN ARBOR, MI

**Fernwood Publishing**

WINNIPEG, MANITOBA

First published 2004 by Pluto Press
345 Archway Road, London N6 5AA
and 839 Greene Street, Ann Arbor, MI 48106
www.plutobooks.com

Fernwood Publishing
Site 2A, Box 5 8422 St. Margaret's Bay Rd.
Black Point, Nova Scotia B0J 1B0
and 324 Clare Avenue
Winnipeg, Manitoba R3L 1S3
www.fernwoodbooks.ca

British Library Cataloguing in Publication Data

A catalogue record for this book is available from the British Library

ISBN (Pluto) 0 7453 1666 2 hardback
ISBN (Pluto) 0 7453 1665 4 paperback
ISBN (Fernwood) 1 55266 139 3

Library of Congress Cataloging in Publication Data
Ives, Peter, 1968–
        Language and hegemony in Gramsci / Peter Ives.
            p. cm. — (Reading Gramsci)
        Includes bibliographical references.
        ISBN 0–7453–1666–2 — ISBN 0–7453–1665–4 (pbk.)
            1. Gramsci, Antonio, 1891–1937—Views on sociolinguistics.
        2. sociolinguistics. I. Title. II. Series

        P85. G72I93 2004
        335.43'092—dc22                                             2004006313

National Library of Canada Cataloguing in Publication
Ives, Peter R., 1968–
        Language and hegemony in Gramsci / Peter Ives.
        Includes bibliographical references.
        ISBN 1–55266–139–3
            1. Gramsci, Antonio, 1891–1937—Knowledge—Linguistics.
        2. Gramsci, Antonio, 1891–1937—Contributions in political science.
        3. Communism and linguistics. 4. Language and languages—Political
        aspects. 5. Political science. I. Title.

        HX298.7.G73I85 2004
        335.43'092                                                  C2004-902139-7

10  9  8  7  6  5  4  3  2  1

Designed and produced for Pluto Press by
Chase Publishing Services, Fortescue, Sidmouth, EX10 9QG, England
Typeset from disk by Newgen Imaging Systems (P) Ltd, Chennai
Printed and bound in the European Union by
Antony Rowe Ltd, Chippenham and Eastbourne, England

# Contents

# Reading Gramsci

*General Editor: Joseph A. Buttigieg*

Antonio Gramsci (1891–1937), little known outside communist circles at the time of his death, is now one of the most frequently cited and widely translated political theorists and cultural critics of the twentieth century. The first wave of interest in Gramsci was triggered by the publication, in Italy, of his prison writings, starting with the letters, which appeared in 1947, and continuing with the six volumes of the thematic edition of the notebooks, the last of which was brought out in 1951. Within the space of a few years, hundreds of articles and books were written explicating, analysing and debating Gramsci's concept of hegemony, his revisionist views on the history of Italy's unification, his anti-economistic and anti-dogmatic version of Marxist philosophy, his theory of the state and civil society, his anti-Crocean literary criticism, his novel approach to the study of popular culture, his extensive observations on the role of intellectuals in society, along with other aspects of his thought. Although long dead, Gramsci became more than an object of dispassionate study; the intensity of the discussions surrounding his work and the often heated struggle over his legacy had, and continue to have, a profound effect on the political culture and cultural politics of postwar Italy.

During the late 1960s and the 1970s Gramsci's name and ideas started circulating with increasing frequency throughout Europe, Latin America and North America (and, to a lesser extent, elsewhere too). The various currents associated with Eurocommunism and the 'New Left' that accompanied the swell of interest in what came to be known as 'Western Marxism' contributed immensely to Gramsci's rise to prominence during this period. In the anglophone world, the publication, in 1971, of Quintin Hoare and Geoffrey Nowell Smith's superbly edited *Selections from the Prison Notebooks* made it possible for scholars to move from vague and general allusions to Gramsci to serious study and analysis of his work. Gramscian studies were further bolstered by various editions in diverse languages of the pre-prison writings – which, among other things, drew attention to the valuable essay on the Southern Question – and by the publication, in Italy, of Valentino Gerratana's complete critical edition of the *Quaderni del carcere* (1975).

Gramsci's influence became even more pronounced in the 1980s with the spread of cultural studies, the growing fascination with the question of 'power', and the greater attention that scholars from different disciplines were devoting to the relations among culture, society and politics. The rapid decline of interest in Marxist thought following the events of 1989 had no effect on Gramsci's 'fortunes'. By that time, as Stuart Hall was among the first to point out, Gramsci had already 'radically displaced some of the inheritances of Marxism in cultural studies'. Indeed, Gramsci's ideas have come to occupy a very special position in the best known of post-Marxist theories and strategies by the political left. Furthermore, the ubiquitous concern with the concept of civil society during the past 15 years has rekindled interest in Gramsci's reflections on the subject. Likewise, many of the issues and topics that currently preoccupy a broad spectrum of academic intellectuals – subaltern studies, postcolonialism and North–South relations, modernity and postmodernity, the relation between theory and praxis, the genealogy of Fascism, the sociopolitical dimensions of popular culture, hegemony and the manufacturing of consent, etc. – have motivated many a reading and rereading of Gramsci's texts.

In the 50 years since Gramsci first became an 'object' of study, his theories and concepts have left their mark on virtually every field in the humanities and the social sciences. His writings have been interpreted, appropriated, and even instrumentalized in many different and often conflicting ways. The amount of published material that now surrounds his work – John Cammett's updated *Bibliografia gramsciana* comprises over 10,000 items in 30 languages – threatens to overwhelm even the trained scholar and to paralyse or utterly confuse the uninitiated reader. Yet the sheer size of the Gramscian bibliography is also an important indication of the richness of Gramsci's legacy, the continuing relevance of his ideas, and the immensity of his contribution to contemporary thought. In many respects, Gramsci has become a 'classic' that demands to be read. Reading Gramsci, however, is not quite an easy undertaking; his most important writings are open-ended, fragmented, multidirectional explorations, reflections and sketches. His prison notebooks have the character of a cluttered, seemingly disorganized intellectual laboratory. The well-trained scholar, no less than the first-time reader, would welcome an expert guide who could point to the salient features of Gramsci's work and bring into relief the basic designs underlying the surface complexity of different parts of his massive oeuvre. Similarly, a critical exposition of the most important existing treatments of Gramsci's works, together with a discussion of the potential usefulness of his insights to certain current lines of inquiry in the humanities and social sciences, would enable readers of Gramsci to appreciate better why (and in what ways) his ideas have a bearing on discussions about some of the most pressing social, cultural and political issues of our time.

The multifaceted character of Gramsci's writing and the rich diversity of critical and theoretical work it has inspired cannot be treated effectively in a single, comprehensive study. A series of monographs, each dealing with a specific aspect of his work (but also cognizant of the many threads that link its various parts), would be a much more useful companion to the reader who is seeking to become better acquainted with Gramsci's legacy. Each volume in the 'Reading Gramsci' series is devoted to a theme that is especially prominent in Gramsci's work or to a field of study that has been strongly influenced by his ideas.

# Acknowledgments

I would like to thank Joseph Buttigieg for his tremendous support and assistance. He suggested the idea for this book and was very helpful, especially in its earliest phases. Roger van Zwanenberg and the editorial board at Pluto Press offered invaluable advice when I was defining the project. Julie Stoll and everyone else at Pluto have been patient and delightful to work with. James Martin was kind enough to read some of my roughest draft chapters and provide useful advice. A work such as this depends on the vast body of research on Gramsci and the community of scholars who conduct such work. More scholars than I can name provided inspiration and a conviction that such a project is worthwhile. On a personal level, they include Derek Boothman, Renate Holub, David McNally, Barbara Godard and Marcus Green. I would also like to thank my students at Simon Fraser University and the University of Winnipeg. They were the unwitting guinea pigs for some of these arguments (and they helped me recognize that others were not worthy of inclusion). My colleagues in the Department of Politics at the University of Winnipeg provided friendship and support especially Byron Sheldrick, Joan Grace and Jim Silver. My greatest thanks goes to Adele Perry and Nell Ives Perry for their patience, companionship and energy. I dedicate this book to Theo Ives Perry who has yet to learn language. I hope that he, Nell and their generation will grow old in a world considerably more just than our current one.

\* \* \*

Lawrence & Wishart granted permission to quote extensively from *Antonio Gramsci: Selections from the Prison Notebooks*, edited and translated by Quintin Hoare and Geoffrey Nowell Smith, © 1971, and *Further Selections from the Prison Notebooks*, edited and translated by Derek Boothman, © 1995. Georges Borchardt granted permission to quote from *Letters from Prison*, edited and translated by Lynne Lawner, © 1973. The quote from *The Portable Nietzsche* (edited and translated by Walter Kaufmann, © 1954 by The Viking Press, renewed © 1982 by Viking Press Inc.) is used by permission of Viking Penguin, a division of Penguin Group (USA) Inc. The Board of Regents of the University of Winnipeg provided financial support for the index compiled by Graham M. Smith.

# Abbreviations

# Introduction

## Language and hegemony in Gramsci

This book provides an interdisciplinary introduction to the ideas and writings of Antonio Gramsci, an Italian Marxist born in Sardinia in 1891 who died shortly after being released from Fascist prison in 1937. It is aimed at readers with diverse interests including Marxism, critical theory, cultural studies, postmodernism, multiculturalism, nationalism, colonialism, postcolonialism, new social movements, deliberative democracy and globalization.

There are two reasons why I use language as an entrance point into Gramsci's political and cultural theory, which was developed primarily in the notes that he wrote while in prison. The first and most important reason is that since his death, language has become increasingly a central topic within political, social and cultural theory. Many of the trends that have dominated the humanities and social sciences in the twentieth century have been called 'linguistic turns' or have in some way focused on language, discourse or deliberation. The second reason is based on my own more particular interpretation of Gramsci's writings, which is that his interest in the politics of language was a defining influence on his entire thought. Not all scholars agree with this second point.[1] So, like any introduction, this one includes the author's own perspective. While my goal is in part to convince readers of this second argument about how to read Gramsci, my primary purpose is to introduce him to a wide interdisciplinary audience in a form that makes his ideas pertinent to current social, cultural and political theory.

Some of the most influential social and political theorists of the twentieth century have been concerned with language: Ludwig Wittgenstein, Ferdinand de Saussure, Martin Heidegger, Jacques Derrida, Michel Foucault, Jürgen Habermas and Noam Chomsky. In addition to academic movements from psychoanalysis to poststructuralism and deliberative democracy, many of the last century's social and artistic movements paid considerable attention to language. These include dadaism, feminism, antiracism, postcolonialism, multiculturalism and identity politics. An important body of scholarship also connects the phenomena of language with the revival of ethno-nationalism.[2] It is in this context that Gramsci's own development of 'hegemony' – a concept with which he first became familiar while studying linguistics – has become so influential. Indeed, even those who have most explicitly argued for a move 'beyond' Marxism and its categories have retained the concept of hegemony, as we shall see in Chapter 5. Gramsci's notion of hegemony has been accepted across many academic disciplines and in non-academic, mainstream discussions.

I am certainly not suggesting that Gramsci's interest in language is his only contribution of importance, nor that those who turned to Gramsci's writings did so expressly because of his approach to language. Quite the contrary, most of the non-Italian literature on Gramsci neglects his writings on language and de-emphasizes his early studies in linguistics. What I am proposing is that by focusing on language, Gramsci's ideas can be introduced in a manner underscoring their continued relevance and importance. This approach provides the theoretical framework to understand Gramsci's many insights into the politics of culture, the institutions and operations of power in democratic regimes and the interaction of the requirements of capitalism with the maintenance of consent and legitimization of elected governments.

## The pervasiveness of Gramsci's hegemony

Before Gramsci, the term 'hegemony' was more or less limited to meaning the predominance of one nation over others, especially within relatively friendly alliances. Significantly due to his writings, hegemony is now used to describe the intricacies of power relations in many different fields from literature, education, film and cultural studies to political science, history and international relations. In a nutshell, Gramsci redefined hegemony to mean the formation and organization of consent. But as we shall see, this is not an adequate understanding of Gramsci's notion of hegemony, which contains a richer and more complex theorization of consent and its relation to coercion.

How has Gramsci's influence spread so widely? Why have there been over 14,500 publications on Gramsci in 33 different languages throughout every field in the humanities and social sciences? Why have the prison notes of a relatively obscure Italian communist reached well beyond Marxist circles?

Of course, there are many answers to these questions. Gramsci was imprisoned by Mussolini and thus he is an ideal martyr, a revolutionary Marxist who was not tarred by the brush of Stalinism. He was one of the earlier Marxists to reject the economic reductionism of many of the Marxists of his time. Thus, unlike other Marxists who omitted the importance of culture and non-economic aspects of society, Gramsci provided a much broader social and cultural portrayal of modern society. He helped found the Communist Party of Italy, the successor of which became one of most successful Western communist parties. All these points go some way towards explaining Gramsci's past influence. But with the fall of the Soviet Union, the demise of the Italian Communist Party, and the new historic circumstances of the twenty-first century, will Gramsci's name fade into history?

If the number and breadth of recent publications regarding Gramsci is any barometer of the future, his legacy is far from over.[3] As this book illustrates, Gramsci's lasting importance derives substantially from his insightful and wide-ranging analyses of the politics of culture and operations of power in industrialized democratic capitalist countries. This poses a major question of whether the stagnation of industrialization in the so-called 'Western World' and post-industrial developments make Gramsci's writings obsolete. Or, as this work hopes to show, does the advent of computerization, all the various trends that are called 'globalization', and the 'new information-based economies' compel us to take an even closer look at Gramsci's insistence on the importance of culture in the maintenance of democratic capitalism even if viable alternatives seem remote?

Gramsci is best known for his analyses of the political importance of cultural and social institutions. Politics, for him, cannot be conceived exclusively in narrow terms of the state and government but must encompass the wide range of human activity often seen as non-political, such as our everyday beliefs and behaviour, from the books we read and the films we enjoy to our religious feelings and perceptions of the world. It is Gramsci the theorist of cultural politics who garners attention not only from progressive activists and academics on the Left but even from the unlikely quarters of the Right. For example, Rush Limbaugh, the extreme right-wing American talk show host, discusses Gramsci in relation to what has been dubbed the 'culture wars' in the United States in the 1990s. He even argues that the Right must learn Gramsci's lessons.[4]

Gramsci's insistence on the political importance of cultural matters led him to write about such things as why Italian peasants more often read French novellas than Italian ones. He wrote newspaper articles about how the demise of theatre in Turin was connected to more widespread economic and cultural factors, not simply the technological advantages of cinema. For Gramsci, to understand the complex social issues that lie at the heart of the general population's political beliefs and activities, one must take account of the ways in which our everyday world and daily experiences are organized. The schools we attend, the organizations we belong to and the way we spend our free time are of central political importance. Gramsci's ideas have been seen as useful in sorting out some of these complexities.

But this does not fully answer the question of why we should be interested in what Gramsci had to say about the reading habits of Italian peasants or obscure politicians and intellectuals in Italy near the beginning of the last century. Why read Gramsci's writings, especially since most of them are notoriously fragmentary, unfinished notes written under harsh prison conditions making them difficult for most readers to understand? Cannot we forego the arduous process of trying to interpret his sketchy notes, which he never had the chance to prepare for publication? Why not just take heed of his simple point that culture is important for political and social analysis? Why have his writings resonated in so many different academic disciplines throughout the twentieth century and what insights do they contain for the twenty-first century?

This book is based on one of several answers to these questions: his approach to language.[5] Other introductions offer different answers highlighting the historical context of Gramsci's thought, the philosophical traditions in which he was writing or the academic and political debates that have arisen about interpreting his work. Focusing on language – a topic that has preoccupied social and political thought since his death – illustrates Gramsci's relevance to contemporary theories and analyses across an array of intellectual disciplines. Just as Gramsci's own writings are not restricted to one field and his influence has a particularly broad scope, the topic of language has also been approached from an interdisciplinary perspective. This book highlights such interdisciplinarity by summarizing key ideas within structuralist linguistics, philosophy, political science and cultural studies for readers less familiar with these specific disciplines. It will help to overcome the disciplinary obstacles that face many readers trying to understand Gramsci and his legacy.

## Approaching language and hegemony

Gramsci was able to combine two approaches to language in a unique way that spoke to broad trends in Western society and various more specific concerns and uses of language. He pays great attention to language as a political issue, for example, to government policy around language, educational language curricula and everyday language practices. He combines this with the rich metaphorical power of linguistic concepts as tools to help analyse political circumstances, specifically the role of culture in shaping people's beliefs, behaviour and even their voting patterns. Chapters 1 and 5 summarize some of the ways in which other prominent thinkers in the twentieth century use similar linguistic metaphors and concepts. These two chapters also note the differences between Gramsci's approach to language and that of others. Chapters 2, 3 and 4 highlight Gramsci's more unique concern with the actual process of the standardization of the Italian language and its political implications. From such a perspective, his use of linguistic metaphors does not become as abstract and esoteric as that of many other social theorists who, also realizing the metaphorical power of linguistic concepts, make what has been called 'the linguistic turn'. Because he is ultimately concerned with political questions, such as how Fascism took hold and why his own counter-hegemonic movement failed, he expands narrow linguistic concepts to be of great use for social and political analysis.

Chapter 3 outlines the complexities of the concept of hegemony, including some of the debates over its interpretation. It also illustrates how Gramsci's method is at least a partial explanation for why he never gave a clear definition of the term 'hegemony'. Among all the different possible meanings for the term, one common element is that it helps explain why large groups of people continually acquiesce to, accept and sometimes actively support governments – and entire social and political systems – that continually work against their interests.[6] In other words, can we say a society is free of domination if the government or state is not using overt coercion and physical force to dominate its subjects? Gramsci would answer, no. And hegemony is a central concept in analysing such domination.

We will discuss the Marxist concept of 'class' and Gramsci's role in debates about class reductionism in detail in Chapters 4 and 5. Suffice it to say that he was primarily concerned with class relations. He accepted Marx's argument that class position is defined by one's role in the economy. Do you work in a factory owned by others and receive a wage? Do you farm land belonging to someone else? Or do you own land or a factory? In other words, in the 1920s and 1930s in Italy, Gramsci was most concerned with the question, how did the bourgeoisie or capitalist classes, who were after all a small minority, rule over the large peasantry and working class? For various reasons, including changing economic circumstances, failures of Marxist political movements, and criticisms of Marxist and class analyses by feminists, environmentalists, postmodernists and others, the question of class, its definition and its relation to consciousness or identity, is of central importance to Gramsci's legacy and continued relevance. Chapter 5 engages with the work of Ernesto Laclau and Chantal Mouffe, two 'post-Marxists' who criticize the notion of 'class' and find Gramsci lacking because of his adherence to it. Laclau and Mouffe are of central importance because they epitomize a broader trend of moving away from economic analysis and moving towards linguistic, or discourse analysis. As they describe their progress beyond Gramsci, they draw on ideas about language inaugurated by Ludwig Wittgenstein and Ferdinand de Saussure. By looking at Gramsci's own writings on language, the reader will be better able to assess Laclau and Mouffe's position and that of other theorists of 'new social movements'.

The Italian linguist Franco Lo Piparo has pointed out that the role of language and its diffusion throughout different populations served as an important metaphor for Gramsci in explaining similar political dynamics. Language is spread predominantly not by government or state coercion, military or police action, but by speakers accepting the prestige and utility of new languages, phrases or terms.[7] Yet the idea that we have totally free choice over the language we use, the words we speak, is clearly misleading. People select vocabulary by gauging their audience and use the style and conventions that they hope will most effectively communicate their message or achieve their desired results. Sometimes this means indicating deference, understanding or camaraderie with listeners. This may involve a degree of ignoring – or showing a lack of respect for – people we are speaking about. This is especially common, even if inadvertent, when we are talking with some people about others. To use a contemporary term, it may involve 'othering' people – that is making generalizations that serve to emphasize differences between 'us' and 'them'. For example, by complaining about 'immigrants', a speaker can create a commonality between themselves and whoever they are talking with (assuming they do not take themselves to be 'immigrants' even if they have actually immigrated) and cast a diverse array of people who happen to have immigrated as 'other', that is different. We may adopt phrases, terms, attitudes or even languages even if they are awkward for us, because we know they will be met positively. As we shall see, such dynamics are central to Gramsci's notion of hegemony and he provides an array of concepts to help investigate them, such as his notions of 'common sense', 'organic intellectuals', 'subalternity' and 'normative versus spontaneous grammars'.

The decisions about how we speak are clearly affected by institutional resources including the existence of grammar books and dictionaries (often government subsidized), government-sponsored training of teachers and many other policies that affect language use. Such questions were being examined by linguists with whom Gramsci studied. In describing the geographic and social centres from which language change originated and radiated they used 'hegemony' (or *egemonia* in Italian) along with 'attraction' (*fascino*) and 'prestige' (*prestigio*). These theories had a profound influence on Gramsci's thought.[8]

His use of language as a metaphor enables him to develop the rich concept of hegemony that addresses the crucial and complex tension to paraphrase Marx, between, our being constrained by our historical conditions, and yet being human agents capable of mobilizing and organizing to change our world. Expressing this tension in the terms of contemporary social theory, Gramsci's focus on language helps address how our subjectivity is constituted by forces external to us, and yet, at the same time, we as subjects make choices that collectively determine our lives.

## Overview

Chapter 1 provides an overview of the role of language within contemporary social theory including summaries of Ferdinand de Saussure, structuralism, Ludwig Wittgenstein and Marxist accounts of language. Chapter 2 gives some essential background for Gramsci's life, with special attention to language issues. This chapter highlights two specific contexts. The first is what in Italy is called *la questione della lingua*, the Language Question or Language Problem. While Italy was politically unified in 1861, it was far from being a culturally or socially cohesive nation. One of its major obstacles was that there was hardly a coherent Italian language common to the new Italian citizens. While commentators have expressed amazement at the fact that in France in the 1840s only about 40 per cent of the population spoke French, in Italy the situation was far more drastic. Historical linguists have estimated that only a small fraction (some estimate about two and a half per cent, others about twelve per cent) of Italians spoke the 'standard' language, making the entire question of what 'standard Italian' was a question with significant political and social ramifications. Indeed, there were rampant debates throughout the end of the nineteenth century about how best to 'standardize' the language and spread it throughout the nation. The language issue was integrally related to other questions of national unity and how to rectify, decrease or mediate all the various divisions that separated Italy into its regions and social classes. This is a part of the historical background that Gramsci finds is at the heart of the Fascist success in exploiting regional and class interests to come to power.

The second specific context dealt with in Chapter 2 is connected to *la questione della lingua*. It is the general situation of Italian and European linguistics in the 1910s when Gramsci was a student at the University of Turin. I will outline how linguists used the concept of hegemony and its synonyms which, as the later chapters demonstrate, became central for Gramsci's development of the term in the direction of political and cultural analysis. There are two additional reasons to consider the state of linguistics in Italy during this period. The first is that the Italian linguists, especially G.I. Ascoli, who had a significant influence on Gramsci, were involved in *la questione della lingua*. The second is that Gramsci's professor of linguistics, Matteo Bartoli, was engaged in a heated polemic against the Neogrammarians, with whom Saussure's early career was intermeshed. Thus the issues raised by Saussure's creation of structuralist linguistics, discussed in Chapter 1, are quite close to those that Gramsci was grappling with both as a student and later as a political thinker. If we are to ask how Gramsci's work is relevant in disciplines that have been very much influenced by structuralism, it makes sense to have a careful investigation of the milieus and debates from which both emerged. This will set the stage for the issues of structural determination and human agency to be addressed throughout the rest of the book, especially in Chapter 5.

Chapters 3 and 4 explain Gramsci's major political concepts such as hegemony, organic intellectuals, war of manoeuvre, passive revolution and subalternity. These chapters lay out Gramsci's theory of politics and culture with the added enrichment of the contexts of language provided in Chapters 1 and 2. Chapter 3 addresses the most central concept of hegemony by using Gramsci's discussion of grammar and language as a model for different types of hegemonic formations. This illustrates how he derives central ideas from linguistics and explains his important notion of 'common sense' and his Marxist or historical materialist conception of knowledge and history. Chapter 4 builds on Chapter 3, encompassing the concepts of 'passive' revolution, war of manoeuvre/position, civil society, state, national–popular collective will and historical bloc. The central issue here is how

Gramsci understands the relationship between coercion and consent.

Gramsci employs language to think through how human agency is related to structure. We will see how the structures of language are used to understand that as individuals we do have creative freedom and, as Marx says, we create our own history, but not under the conditions of our own choosing.[9] In other words, we are not able to do this in a total vacuum or with no constraints. Just as a speaker can form new sentences which are understandable even though they have never been heard, individuals and collectivities create new realities. But speakers are not totally free to speak in whatever way they wish. If we do not substantially conform to how other people speak, to the language structure that already exists, we simply will not be understood. Or our basic point might be conveyed, but it will be accompanied by a whole host of other meanings and ideas that we did not necessarily intend to be communicated. For example, if I use racist language and refer to a black man as a 'boy', you may well understand who I am referring to. But you will also learn that I have a bigoted world-view. Or if I do not speak grammatically, my meaning might come through fine, but my lack of education and social class may also be communicated.

Gramsci's discussions of grammar provide a nuanced appreciation for such dynamics and how they can be used metaphorically to understand how coercion and consent operate, which is central to his theory of hegemony. Chapter 5, the final chapter of *Language and Hegemony in Gramsci*, engages with contemporary social theory and cultural criticism. By highlighting the importance of how language is characterized in current debates about postmodernism, new social movements and globalization, this chapter illustrates Gramsci's continued relevance. Ironically, those who argue that Gramsci is outdated give opposing reasons. Some see Gramsci as inescapably tied to Marxist–Leninist orthodoxy; others, such as Ernesto Laclau and Chantal Mouffe, see him as a crucial passage along the way to post-Marxism. In this way, Laclau and Mouffe make Gramsci a precursor to their theory of radical democracy, which is heavily influenced by the poststructuralism of Michel Foucault and Jacques Derrida.

Laclau and Mouffe's work has become central and far-reaching within political and social theory. But their narrow reading and what I will suggest are one-sided criticisms of Gramsci prohibit Gramsci's possible contribution to such debates. From their perspective, post-Marxism has surpassed Gramsci's insights and overcomes what Laclau and Mouffe see as his inability to transcend the very economism that he attacks. By using poststructural theories of language and discourse as comparisons, this chapter suggests that Gramsci provides an insightful way to rethink the dichotomy between matter and language, between materialism and idealism, that Marxism – and Gramsci in particular – strove to overcome.

In addition to an extensive discussion of Laclau and Mouffe's post-Marxism, this chapter addresses more general themes within semiotic, poststructural and deconstructive theory to show how Gramsci's perspective remains insightful especially in our postmodern, so-called 'information age' where work increasingly involves linguistic activity and language is increasingly commodified. It will address neo- and postcolonial concerns over the politics of language, consciousness and culture within new global hegemonic formations and possible sites of resistance.

The book is organized to provide flexibility for different audiences. I have tried to write each chapter so that it can be read out of order, or on its own. The exception to this is Chapter 4, which should be read after Chapter 3. The chapters are ordered for the reader with little background in either Gramsci or contemporary social theory. This order is also appropriate for those with a degree of knowledge about Gramsci, but less familiarity with postmodernism or poststructuralism. Those more eager to get to Gramsci's ideas can skip Chapter 1 and return to it as necessary. Readers familiar with the major ideas of Saussure and Wittgenstein or who are primarily interested in the relationship between Gramsci and poststructuralism could begin with Chapter 5 and then proceed to Chapters 2, 3 and 4. Those with knowledge of contemporary social theory but little knowledge of Gramsci may start with Chapters 3 and 4 and then read Chapters 2 and 5.

# 1
# Language and Social Theory: The Many Linguistic Turns

This chapter provides an overview of some of the most influential approaches to language that have greatly informed social, political and cultural theory in the last hundred years or so. Thorough accounts of any of the specific thinkers or movements discussed would constitute books in themselves. The goal here is to provide the theoretical background and context to Gramsci's ideas about language. This framework will create a basis of comparison to consider how Gramsci utilized language within his political analysis and especially when developing the concept of hegemony. After a brief discussion of the changing role of language in society, this chapter summarizes some of the central ideas of the Swiss linguist, Ferdinand de Saussure (1857–1913), who founded structuralist linguistics. The adoption of Saussure's ideas in anthropology and the other social sciences is often called the 'linguistic turn'. As will be explained below, while this label captures important trends, it can also obscure the extent to which such influence is as much a 'structuralist turn' (that is, a specific approach to language) as it is a turn towards language per se. After noting how Saussure's structuralism was adopted in the social sciences, the chapter considers the 'linguistic turn' in philosophy, and especially the influence of Ludwig Wittgenstein (1889–1953). The chapter concludes with a brief examination of the enigmatic relationship between Marxism and language.

## Language, production and politics in the twentieth century

The larger question of why ideas about language were so central to social theory and philosophy in the twentieth century is a fascinating one that we can only touch on here. It is essential to put this aspect of intellectual history in its social, economic and historical context. Karl Marx criticized German philosophy in the mid-nineteenth century for being mired in a world of words and ideas to the neglect of the real world of material production in factories. Marx noted that philosophy tended to be dominated by abstract thought and did not take enough heed of the important social and economic conditions and rapid changes taking place with the industrial revolution. But the twentieth century witnessed a trend in economic production processes and products that has eroded any such obvious opposition between the world of ideas, words and language on the one hand, and the world of manual labour, physical production and commodities on the other. Such erosion has not occurred, as Marx had hoped, because the proletarian struggle helped overcome the alienation of intellectual from manual labour. Rather, there have been drastic changes in the nature of important commodities and especially changes in the processes of the production of all commodities, brought about by computer technology, increased world-wide transportation and the globalization of many market places (as Marx argued, this was predictable, since capitalism demands a continual transformation of production processes). Changes in production processes including (but not limited to) technological innovations such as electronics and computerization blur the distinction between manual labour and mental activity.[1] The end of the twentieth century witnessed sweatshop-like factories for 'offshore' workers whose products were the input of data into computer systems. Many occupations have been deskilled with the implementation of technology.[2] For example, people employed in making food in restaurants instead of being skilled chefs became minimum-wage unskilled burger flippers. The labour processes in fast-food restaurants have been modelled on assembly lines, where technology is used as much for control of the workforce as for increased efficiency.[3]

   To take a very different example, the price of two pairs of running shoes produced in the same factory might vary five-fold if one has the Nike swoosh and the other does not. That Nike swoosh itself is the product of countless workers in advertising firms. But what we are buying is not so much the physical characteristics of that Nike symbol, but its symbolic effect, its meaning. Many of the workers who produced that meaning, including the secretaries and mail-room employees, are exploited in ways not altogether dissimilar from Marx's industrial working class or proletariat. They usually have little control over how they work and are at the mercy of their employers from whom they receive a wage. They fit several important aspects, although not all, of Marx's description of the proletariat as those who do not own the means of production and, thus, have to sell their labour power in order to survive. With the so-called 'feminization' of clerical work and many other occupations involving language skills, such as teaching, it is untenable simply to divide physical activity of the factory floor as being laborious and exploitable from mental activity of the office cubicle or schoolroom as being inherently thoughtful, uplifting and non-exploitative.

In addition to such changes in production processes that complicate the relationship between language use and physical labour, the issue of ideology within the development of democratic societies has also put language at centre stage. Especially in his development of the concept of hegemony, Gramsci grappled with the advent of mass democracy, including mass political parties, which were still relatively young in his time. Since his death, the democratic phenomenon of increased suffrage and the legitimation of state power based on mass politics has continued. In a century that witnessed the rise to power of Adolf Hitler and Benito Mussolini, both receiving substantial support from within societies that had been democratic, the question of ideology became paramount. Because many democratic governments are now at least formally accessible to all their citizens (over a certain age), the persistence of closed, elitist circles that control most of the economic and political power is a pressing and sometimes seemingly inexplicable fact. Gramsci's ideas have been useful for many attempting to analyse how power operates within these democratic societies. His notion of hegemony addresses some of the phenomena that the concept of ideology describes but adds to ideology a focus on institutions and daily practices as well as ideas and belief systems.

One cannot think about the developments of democracy relating to language and ideology in the twentieth century without keeping in mind that the European nation-state really came to the fore in the nineteenth century. That century saw the actual political unification of Italy and Germany. The previously unified nation-states of France, Britain and the United States embarked upon massive projects aimed at socially and economically consolidating their populations, including language 'standardization', national education systems, transport and communications networks. These all contributed to the confluence of the political state with the cultural nation, sometimes more effective, sometimes less. And while the simple equation of nation-state with language has rarely been successful, the role of language-related policies in nation building is a hallmark of nineteenth-century Europe.

The twentieth century witnessed a proliferation of the European-style nation-state throughout the globe. But it has also seen a dissolution of the assumptions upon which nation-states are founded. Now we are faced with many questions often discussed under the label of 'globalization'. Is the nation-state still capable of having an important impact on its citizens' lives in the face of multinational corporations, global stock markets and international trends in production and consumption? What is the role of non-state 'nations' such as Northern Ireland, Scotland and Quebec, or the Basques, Inuit, Cree, Mohawk, Maori and Laps? With the 'English only' movement in the United States, the increasing use of English by the global elite and the general failure of the equation of one nation-state, one language, what is the role of national or public languages in democratic societies? These questions facing us today are rooted to a large extent in the dynamics of language and community that Gramsci was dealing with in Italy between 1911 and 1937. For these reasons, to understand Gramsci's writings about hegemony and be able to use them to help us analyse and act in our world, it is best to focus on Gramsci's theory of language. The first step in such a process is a brief overview of various diverse intellectual trends that have all been labelled at one time or another 'the linguistic turn'.

## The many 'linguistic turns'

It would be overly simple and reductionist to suggest that the political and technological changes discussed above directly caused the paradigm shifts in various disciplines that have been labelled 'the linguistic turn'. While the dadaist's 'sound poems' explicitly question whether life has meaning in the modern, disenchanted world, the impetus for changes in academic methods are more difficult to decipher. It is easy to understand that large numbers of women entering the work force would have a direct influence on our use of language, with terms such as 'chairman' and 'fireman' changing to 'chairperson' and 'firefighter'. But the increase of women's wage labour is not the only reason why academic feminists have examined the complex implications of masculine structures of language and masculine hegemonies.[4] It is difficult to connect the political, social and economic changes directly to the different 'linguistic turns' that occurred in various academic disciplines.

Moreover, it is too simple to characterize the 'linguistic turns' in Anglo-American analytic philosophy, the social sciences, history and literary studies as all belonging to the very same movement or trend.[5] Nevertheless, these paradigm shifts occurred within social, political and economic contexts, and there are clearly some similarities among them. Such commonalities include (1) an emphasis on the interrelated character of phenomena under investigation, (2) the idea that the source of knowledge is rarely to be found in the individual qualities of objects or elements themselves, but instead in the relationships among objects being studied, and (3) the emphasis on how language itself is not a passive representation of reality or our own lives but rather contributes to how we live and make choices.

## Saussure's structural approach to language

In the social sciences, the 'linguistic turn' amounts to the impact of a paradigm first offered by the linguist Ferdinand de Saussure. Near the end of his life, Saussure broke with the tradition of linguistics in which he had been trained and had conducted most of his career. In a series of lectures delivered between 1907 and 1911 (the year Gramsci entered university and began studying linguistics), Saussure proposed a new basis for the science of language. His death in February 1913 prevented him from presenting these ideas as a published work. Instead, *The Course in General Linguistics* was assembled posthumously, mostly culled from his students' lecture notes and a few of his own. It has become a central text and has had a dramatic impact on linguistics and the social sciences at large.

Much of European linguistics at the time of Saussure's death focused on tracing the history of word forms and attempting to determine the patterns in these changes. This is called diachronic change. To overly simplify one example, diachronic or historical linguists noted that many incidences of the 'f' sound in English and German are conversions of the 'p' sound in Latin (*pater* as in paternity changed to 'f' as in 'father'). In short, linguistics was a historical science aimed at understanding how word forms had arisen and how they were related to one another across different languages and over time.

In his lectures, Saussure argued that such an approach could never be truly scientific because it could never isolate language as a decisive object of study. There were not clear enough boundaries between individual utterances or acts of speech, which might be idiosyncratic, and the actual patterned nature of language that enables people to produce meaning. Instead, he proposed a clear division between the historical development of a given language and the actual structure of how a language operates as a system. He argued that because we can use language without knowing anything about its historical development, the scientific study of language must primarily investigate how language operates at any given time, not a language's history. He called this idea of language as a system of signs its synchronic dimension to distinguish it from the diachronic, or historical, dimension.[6]

Saussure's other major contention for linguistics was that in order for it to be a science it had to analyse not individual utterances of language, that is speech (or what he called *parole*), but the system of language (what he called *langue*).[7] While Saussure understood that speech was an inherent aspect of language itself (and even language as a synchronic system), he argued that for linguistics to separate itself from other sciences such as psychology, anthropology and philology,[8] it must take the systemic element of language as its primary focus. In other words, there must be an analytic separation between how language is used in practice – *parole* – and its structure, that is how its elements are related to one another – *langue*. (One of the little ironies of history is that linguistic structuralism based on this demarcation of 'objects of study' was incorporated into anthropology and the other social sciences whose domains are not language.)

Saussure's analysis of language as a system consisted of breaking down that system into signs each of which was made up of two parts: the sound pattern and the concept. The sound pattern, or what he called the 'signifier', is the actual sound as it is heard.[9] The concept, or what he called the 'signified', is what is meant by that signifier, or that idea denoted by the sound pattern. A sign is the union of a signifier and signified.

One of his most important, and controversial, points is that there is no necessary or natural relation between the signifier and the signified. Instead, the signifier is only conventionally or arbitrarily related to the signified. The words 'dog' in English, *Hund* in German and *chien* in French are all signifiers with the same (or similar)[10] signifieds. There is nothing, he argued, about the concept of 'dog' itself that relates to why we call it a 'dog', *Hund* or *chien*. Even the examples of onomatopoeia do not contravene Saussure's notion of arbitrariness. The English signifier for a dog's bark may be 'bow-wow' or 'arf-arf', whereas in French it is *ouâ-ouâ* and in German *vau-vau*. Saussure did not deny that many words or signs have a non-arbitrary nature within a given language system. Some are motivated, to use the linguistic term, or related (i.e. non-arbitrary) partially in their relation to other words or signs. For example, the American English word, 'flashlight' is not totally arbitrary in its relation to 'flash' and 'light'. While the word 'torch' could easily suffice, as it does in England, its 'motivation' or the causes for whether it successfully signifies must contain some way to distinguish it from a non-electric 'torch'. The German *Taschen–lampe* meaning flashlight or torch is more closely motivated by *Tasche* meaning pocket and *Lampe* meaning lamp. In short, signifiers are motivated by their relations with other signifiers, not by the relations within the sign between signifier and signified.[11]

Saussure did not explicitly discuss how signs are related to what is often called the referent, or the objects in the 'real' world that correspond to the signified. It is important to realize that for Saussure, the signified 'dog' is the concept, idea or meaning 'dog', not an actual dog that is being referred to. He clearly rejected the notion that a sign or word simply corresponded to an object, idea or referent. But his unambiguous rejection of this idea of language as nomenclature – language as a collection of words (primarily nouns) that stood for things (objects) – was not replaced by a theory of the link between the term 'dog' and those objects designated by that term outside of the sign system. He did not give an explanation for the philosophical process of relating different objects, individual dogs, or breeds of dogs, to general categories such as 'dog'. This omission is reasonable given his attempt to distinguish linguistics as a science from philosophy. But it has created much controversy over the philosophical and political implications of the structuralism that he inaugurated.

Saussure's focus was on how signs, the signifier–signified couples, are related to each other, that is how signifiers are related to other signifiers and how signifieds are related to other signifieds. So, in the case of signifiers, the crucial aspect of both written and verbal signifiers is that they are distinguishable from other signifiers. For example, everyone speaks slightly differently and may accent a given word in a manner quite different from other speakers. Usually this does not impede our understanding unless we confuse it with a different word. The important aspect of me uttering the word 'boy' is that you do not confuse it with 'toy' or 'joy' or 'bay' or 'pay'. That is, you understand my meaning because 'b' is different from 't' or 'j' and 'o' is different from 'a'. Thus, even though our discussion may not include 'toy's or 'bay's (signifieds) our understanding takes place within a language, a system of signs, in which the place or meaning of the signifier 'boy' is defined by its structural relation to – and separation from – other signifiers.

This is equally true, and perhaps philosophically more profound, of signifieds. For Saussure, linguistics was to examine not how signifieds represent some world outside of language, that is how a concept represents a thing, but rather how signifieds relate to and define each other. In other words, he saw the fundamental question as how a given signified exists within a structure of signs. For example, while we could roughly translate the English terms 'river' and 'stream' with the French *rivière* and *fleuve*, respectively, what they actually signify in each language is different. The distinction between 'river' and 'stream' in English is related strictly to size (and may vary relative to one's geographic context; what might be a river in a dry climate would only qualify as a stream in a wet region with more rivers). In French, a *rivière* flows to the ocean and this is what distinguishes it from a *fleuve* which may flow into a *rivière* or another *fleuve*.[12] In this way, we see that the concepts being signified are defined in relation to each other within the system of language. It is the relations among signifieds that divide up the conceptual field.

These propositions led Saussure to the conclusion that '[t]he mechanism of a language turns entirely on identities and differences'.[13] The fact that language is a structure means that its elements are defined not by their own innate qualities or characteristics but by their place within the system. He uses two metaphors to explain this: chess and trains. If we lose the black king while playing chess, we can replace it with some other object that is not black and bears no resemblance to a king. The only qualities of this object that are important besides it fitting in the chessboard squares, are that we can distinguish it from the other pieces. That is, we could not use a pawn as a replacement. We would confuse it with the other pawns that are not the king. Likewise, we regularly refer to the train that leaves a station daily at five o'clock as 'the five o'clock train' and do not bother with the fact that each day it is physically a different train.

The fact that Saussure's linguistics analyses language by relating its various elements to each other rather than to some realm external to language has given rise to innumerable debates. Many of these debates centre on how Saussure, or structuralism in general, depicts the relationship between the structure under investigation and other phenomena. Specifically, this has led to questions about whether Saussure or structuralism are relativistic, or maintain that there is no 'real', or non-linguistic world in which 'truth' or 'reality' is maintained beyond language. Some argue that language is so vital for framing our perception of the world that it makes no sense to talk about a 'real world' or 'truth' outside of language. Others argue that we can see language as the medium of interpretation without denying that there are other ways to access 'reality' and that the structure of 'reality' outside language is still of paramount importance. This is a central issue for Marxism since it claims to be a 'materialist' theory rooted in examining how we produce those things that we need to survive. Marx and Marxists criticize other theories for being 'idealist' because they are not based on the material reality of daily life. Rather, Marxists argue, 'idealist' theories are abstract ideas often important only to a minority of wealthy people (precisely because they have the luxury to neglect how their physical needs are met). But Marx also placed great emphasis on the process of human history and the role of humans in creating their history. As we shall see in Chapter 4, Gramsci has his own very specific position on these questions.

Despite many problems that Saussure's writings raise, his basic paradigm – the idea that the social sciences should focus on structures and the synchronic interrelation of the elements – had a profound impact on a wide range of disciplines, most especially anthropology, sociology and social theory. Structuralism rejected previous traditions that tried to determine the content or essence in distinct phenomena. Instead structuralists showed how it is the relations among elements that define those elements and give them the characteristics that are important. In this sense, there are important similarities with the 'linguistic turns' in philosophy and literature. Moreover, Saussure's structuralism contained the idea that underneath the actual manifestation of phenomena was a 'hidden' structure. Because Saussure saw individual utterances as secondary to, and generated by, the system of language (which was not obviously apparent), the actions of individuals came to be seen as mere superficial occurrences, whereas real understanding came from uncovering the underlying structures.

## The structuralist turn towards language

Given that Saussure was a linguist, it would be odd to consider his work as part of a 'linguistic turn', that is, a turn towards language. It is only with the importation of Saussure's ideas into other disciplines that it makes sense to discuss the 'linguistic turn'. Even then, it is important to realize that what is being discussed with this label is not a generic turn towards language, but a turn towards specific understandings of, and methods for studying, language. Thus, in the social sciences what is called 'the linguistic turn' should more properly be understood as a turn towards synchronic and structuralist theories of language. One of the unfortunate ramifications of the label 'linguistic turn' is that it tends to obscure the role of language within the social sciences before this so-called turn. It falsely implies that before the turn towards language, language was not in the picture.

Claude Lévi-Strauss was one of the key anthropologists to import Saussure's ideas to the study of culture and society. Rather than describe the history of any particular culture, compare it to other cultures or relate it to some ultimate or universal meaning outside of that society, Lévi-Strauss looked at the elements of cultural systems as signs that created a structure in which meaning is produced. Whether anthropologists focus on myths, status or rituals, structuralist anthropology examines how the various elements make up a system in which each element is defined through its relation to the other elements and especially through the distinctions between elements. Lévi-Strauss emphasized the binary tendency in how these elements are related; for example, hot/cold, raw/cooked, sacred/profane, familial/non-familial. He detailed how various cultures were organized around such underlying structural relationships.

Through Lévi-Strauss and others, Saussure's focus on language was combined with Emile Durkheim's founding of sociology as the study of 'social facts', giving sociology and anthropology a wide-ranging structuralist character. Durkheim's distinction between physical facts that exist in the natural world and social facts that may not be tangible outside their existence in human minds and activities fits well with Saussure's ideas. Durkheim emphasized that 'social facts' are indeed 'real' and can be studied objectively and scientifically. Saussure's notion of language, as an object that can be isolated scientifically and studied by linguistics, was non-material, was that of a structure that did not actually exist as a physical entity, but that was necessary for the actual speaking of individuals. Similarly, Durkheim argued that while an entity like 'anomie' is not a physical or tangible entity, it is an objective 'fact' that is necessary to explain social phenomena like suicide rates.

These ideas of structures and synchronic systems were also central to structural–functionalism and behaviourism, which developed especially in the United States. It is important not to over generalize, and this is not the place to explore the intricate connections and differences of such approaches. However, it should be noted that Talcott Parsons and other systems theorists also emphasized the synchronic over the diachronic dimension and focused not on qualities of separate elements of society and culture, but rather on their relations.

In quite a different field, the psychoanalyst, Jacques Lacan also derived considerable impetus from Saussurean structuralism. He proclaimed that the unconscious is structured like language and, thus, linguistics provides important tools for psychoanalysis.[14] But unlike Saussure's notion of language as a system, Lacan's structures of consciousness are unstable, because the elements, signifiers, of the unconscious are no longer part of the conscious discourse of signs. Rather these signifiers are floating elements that are primarily visual. Lacan understands human subjectivity and sexual pleasure as constituted not around a positive identity or simple pleasure. As Elizabeth Grosz summarises, 'sexuality is pleasure marked by a lack, this lack is not given, but an effect of signification. It is for this reason that sexuality, desire, is marked by the search for particular meanings.'[15] Laclau and Mouffe, as we shall see in Chapter 5, extend this analysis to the terrain of social-identity formation, arguing that political consciousness is structured around a 'lack', or an 'empty signified'. Central to Lacan's work was the use of Saussure's understanding of the signifier in describing the 'phallus' (a structural element) as distinct from the 'penis' (a physical body part) as being central to the structure of human subjectivity, desire and power. The seminars that he delivered in Paris starting in the 1950s were particularly influential and attended by a wide circle of French intellectuals, including Jean-Paul Sartre, Simone de Beauvoir, Maurice Merleau-Ponty, Roland Barthes, Louis Althusser, Luce Irigaray and Julia Kristeva.

Louis Althusser developed structural Marxism within this French context of structuralism heavily influenced by Saussure and later semioticians like Louis Hjelmslev and Emile Benveniste. While Althusser looked to Marx's texts – and especially *Capital*'s synchronic analysis of how capitalism functions as a system – his theories have many commonalities with non-Marxist structuralism. He argues that the primary importance of Marx is his theory of value, which shows how value lies not in objects or commodities themselves but rather in their relations to other commodities and money. As with Saussure's study of language, Althusser emphasizes that Marx's theory of value is synchronic rather than diachronic and in order for it to operate it must be seen as a system, that is, its structure must be the locus of explanation. As we saw above with Saussure, Althusser emphasized the hidden nature of the structure of capitalism that Marxism was to reveal. He also emphasized the key role of ideology and institutions that sustain capitalism, hiding its secret structure. Althusser's scientific Marxism is aimed at stripping away the ideologies that keep the structures of capitalism hidden, including those institutions that he calls 'ideological state apparatuses', such as school systems, religious institutions, legal structures and even the family.[16]

Althusser shares with many intellectuals influenced by Saussure the notion that human beings are not the authors or subjects of social processes and behaviour but rather they are 'effects' and supports of the structures and relations of social formations. It is in this sense that Althusser is critical of Humanism[17] and has been criticized for denying Marx's emphasis on human agency, a criticism often levelled at any social theory that takes Saussure's view of language as a model. As we shall see in Chapters 4 and 5, one of Gramsci's great strengths and attractions is his emphasis on agency and the potential of human organization to create political change even if it takes a very long time and much groundwork. Nevertheless, Gramsci shares some aspects, but not all, of Saussure's approach to language.

Michel Foucault has also been very influential in the social sciences for his questioning of the human subject and his emphasis on language and especially discourse. He adamantly rejects the labels 'structuralism' and 'poststructuralism', does not embrace Saussure's theories, and is quite critical of Marxism. Nevertheless, his work is often seen as an important part of the 'linguistic turn' in history and the social sciences. Although Foucault did not write a lot about methodology itself, his work has been emulated and has made a large impact on history and the social sciences. By studying 'discourses' he means tracing the rules that govern statements, practices, classificatory schemas and, in general, objects of analysis that share a set of discursive rules. Foucault's influence has stretched well beyond the social sciences and history to studies of literature. Chapter 5 provides a more thorough explanation of Foucault's notion of discourse in comparison with Gramsci's ideas about language and grammar.

## Philosophy's 'linguistic turn'

The label 'linguistic turn' has been applied to other academic trajectories not explicitly related to Saussure. Most notably in analytic philosophy rooted mainly in Britain and the United States (Anglo-analytic philosophy), the trend of linguistic philosophy, including what is called ideal-language philosophy, ordinary-language philosophy and speech-act theory, have been described as part of the 'linguistic turn'.[18] Philosophers such as Rudolf Carnap, A.J. Ayer, Gustav Bergmann, Gilbert Ryle and J.L. Austin take the general position that philosophical problems are often (or always) problems created by misunderstandings created by how we use language. Such problems can be solved, or shown not to exist at all, by either changing our language and how we describe ideas or by better understanding what we mean by the language we already use. The former view, that we must change our language, is taken by Gustav Bergmann, who argued that philosophers must create language capable of being precise enough not to create philosophical problems. What became known as 'ordinary-language philosophy' took the rather different position that regular languages – whether English, German or Hindi – are already 'ideal' in Bergmann's sense, that is, they themselves do not create philosophical problems. Rather, it is philosophers who create philosophical problems by misunderstanding how ordinary language is used.

The enigmatic philosopher Ludwig Wittgenstein was the original impetus for many of these different approaches to language. Although he had a background in the history of European philosophy, or what is called Continental philosophy, as a student and professor at Cambridge he made scarce reference to the history of philosophical ideas or thinkers. Yet, especially his later work shows a unique combination of Anglo-analytic and Continental perspectives. It is worth discussing Wittgenstein in some detail given the influence he has had on theorists including Laclau and Mouffe, as is elaborated in Chapter 5.

Wittgenstein wrote his first book, *Tractatus Logico-Philosophicus*, in the trenches during the First World War. Published in 1921, it is heavily influenced by the ideas of Wittgenstein's teacher Bertrand Russell and the mathematician and philosopher Gottlob Frege. It tries to show how every meaningful sentence must have a logical structure, and thus, philosophical problems were produced by sentences which either had no real meaning or whose logic was obscured. Not unlike structuralism, this led to a method of trying to uncover the structure that lay below the apparent confusion. Wittgenstein's early work maintained that the world consists primarily of facts, the concatenation of simple objects. If language is meaningful, it should be able to be broken down into 'atomic' sentences that correspond to these facts. Sentences that could not be analysed this way must be meaningless.

While many of his readers were fascinated with the implications of these ideas for symbolic logic, Wittgenstein took the paradoxical conclusion that if you really understood the *Tractatus* you would have to discard it as senseless. This is because its propositions did not relate to the concatenation of simple objects, i.e. they were not propositions of fact. In effect, the only fields of inquiry based solely on such meaningful statements seem to be empirical investigations found in the natural sciences. Sentences concerned with aesthetics, ethics and all that is central to human life are philosophically meaningless, thus his puzzling conclusion 'What we cannot speak about we must pass over in silence.'[19]

After a period of years during which Wittgenstein returned to Austria to be a schoolteacher and embarked on a number of wide-ranging philosophical speculations, in 1936 he began the work that would become his most famous, the *Philosophical Investigations*. In a thorough rethinking and, many argue, refutation of his earlier work, the *Tractatus*, Wittgenstein argued that the question of meaning cannot be sought in the relation between sentences and simple objects. Instead, as he put it, 'the meaning of a word is its use in the language'.[20] This perspective is quite critical of his earlier approach and that of other philosophers. In order to describe how it was that meaning was created through language use, Wittgenstein invented the idea of 'language games'. In ways both similar and different from Saussure, Wittgenstein argues that words become meaningful in their relation to other words within a system, or game, that is a set of rules and practices. But Wittgenstein's language games are not themselves entire systems in Saussure's sense.

Wittgenstein addresses the question of language understood as a complete structure or system using the metaphor of an ancient city: 'a maze of little streets and squares, of old and new houses, and of houses with additions from various periods; and this surrounded by a multitude of new boroughs with straight regular streets and uniform houses'.[21] This presents quite a different picture from Saussure's notion of language as a synchronic structure, and it is at odds with Saussure's *langue/parole*, or abstract system/actual language use. Rather, meaning is much more closely connected with usage.

The metaphor of language as a game has two related elements. One is that, like games, language is based on rules, but these rules vary from game to game (and from language to language) and can even be changed within a game, as long as the players agree. There is a degree of arbitrariness to the rules. However, for the game actually to be played the rules must have some stability. The other element of the game metaphor is that just like the word 'game' the idea of 'language' is not defined by a common essence but those things that qualify as languages share 'family resemblances'.[22] It is futile to try to discover the one thing that underlies board games, card games, ball games, the Olympic games and so on, but it still makes sense to group them by chains of resemblances. Just as in families, of three siblings, two may have similar noses that are very different from the third but the third may have hair or eyes much like one but not the other sibling. This idea of categories not being reducible to an underlying commonality became pivotal for many poststructuralist and postmodern theories. Chapter 5 returns to this notion, which is central to what Laclau and Mouffe call 'chains of equivalence' and is used to theorize potential political alliances among 'new social movements'.

One key difference between Wittgenstein's notion of a language game and games is that, according to Wittgenstein, the rules of language games are created as we use language, as we play the game. We do not create languages by sitting down and defining the rules, and then applying those rules. Rather, like the organization of a city, we know the rules of language games through learning a language. Those rules change as new situations arise or speakers change the rules and other speakers tacitly agree to those changes. For Wittgenstein, it is futile for philosophers (or linguists and social scientists) to try to determine some sort of fundamental, natural or logical set of rules that all language follows. Wittgenstein would reject anything like Noam Chomsky's concept of 'deep structures' that all language share. Instead, language games are human practices created and modified by speakers in conversations.

Moreover, in contrast to Saussure, who did not explicitly address the issue of how signs related to their referents, this is one of Wittgenstein's central themes. While there is still much debate over how to interpret his position on this matter, much of the question revolves around his relation of language to *Weltanschauungen* (German for 'world-views'), or what Wittgenstein himself called 'forms of life'. As he stated, 'to imagine a language means to imagine a form of life'. This was a radical departure from the *Tractatus* since it denied the possibility of a singular, or universal, logical language. Rather, languages are as diverse as the daily practices and experiences in which they are produced and routinized. This suggests that language and thought are intimately bound together instead of thought preceding language, with language being just the outward expression or manifestation of a speaker's thoughts.

It is Wittgenstein's discussions of 'forms of life' and language learning that most closely relate him conceptually to Gramsci. While there is no evidence that there was any influence of one on the other, there is a biographical connection between Gramsci and Wittgenstein. In the Preface to the *Philosophical Investigations*, Wittgenstein noted his indebtedness to Piero Sraffa for stimulating 'the most consequential ideas in this book'.[23] Sraffa was an Italian economist who was associated with John Maynard Keynes, Frank Ramsey and Wittgenstein at Cambridge, where he taught from 1927 to 1931. He had been good friends with Gramsci before Gramsci's imprisonment. During his captivity, Sraffa was one of Gramsci's most important correspondents after his sister-in-law, Tatiana Schucht, especially since Sraffa had helped Gramsci have access to books while in prison. Unless someone finds the notes that Wittgenstein is reported to have taken after each of his weekly discussions with Sraffa, we are unlikely ever to know if there was any clear influence between Gramsci and Wittgenstein.[24] But their writings remain incomparable in form and in what each was aiming to achieve, in that Gramsci was first and foremost a political thinker and Wittgenstein seemed to eschew all such considerations. Nevertheless, there are important similarities between their thoughts about language. And given the wide-ranging impact of Wittgenstein, Chapter 5 discusses how Wittgenstein's emphasis on linguistic practice defining meaning and its connection to 'forms of life' is comparable to Gramsci's social theory.

## The many other 'linguistic turns'

This overview does not, of course, exhaust the disciplines and subdisciplines in which there have been debates about the 'linguistic turn'. Within philosophy there has also been a turn towards linguistic phenomenology, starting with Martin Heidegger and being strengthened in the followers of Maurice Merleau-Ponty. Social historians such as Gareth Stedman Jones and Patrick Joyce, who take a methodological focus on language and discourse analysis, have been said to participate in a 'linguistic turn'. Literary theory in the twentieth century is also characterized by trends inspired by an emphasis on language taken from linguistics, formalism, poststructuralism and deconstruction. Jacques Derrida, poststructuralism and others have inspired shifts away from structure, plot and mechanism towards discourse analysis and an emphasis on the instability of language. Chapter 5 engages with some of the reasons why such literary theories are important in social and political theory, especially Derrida's influence on Laclau and Mouffe. We do not need a comprehensive overview to make the general point and show the variety of ways in which language became a primary concern for a broad range of intellectuals in the twentieth century. The most notable gap in this general propensity is Marxism.

## Marxism and language

Although theorists such as Louis Althusser and Julia Kristeva were influenced by the Saussurean 'linguistic turn' as well as being self-described Marxists, the majority of Marxist thinkers are generally a little inimical to the 'linguistic turn'. As Raymond Williams wrote in 1977, 'Marxism has contributed very little to thinking about language itself.'[25] Part of this is due to the overly simplistic notion that Marxism as a materialist theory should eschew language as that which takes place in the realm of ideas. Some Marxists have even argued that placing emphasis on language makes any theory inherently idealistic.[26] The worthwhile element of such criticisms is the concern over abstract theories that ignore the material exploitation in the world. It is not always clear what such linguistically informed theories have to offer anyone interested in actually changing the world, as opposed to just interpreting it.

There are many exceptions to Marxist hostility towards linguistic theory, most notably the work of Raymond Williams, Valentin Vološinov, Adam Schaff and Ferruccio Rossi-Landi. But they failed to have a large impact on Marxism with regard to the role of language. Similarly, various combinations of Marxism and structuralism or semiotics have made influential contributions, from the cultural studies of Stuart Hall and the Birmingham Centre for Contemporary Cultural Studies to journals like *Screen*. However, even Hall, a prominent follower of Gramsci, never developed a theory of language per se.[27] Many of the criticisms of the Birmingham school's work have drawn out the presumed tension of Marx's emphasis on production as central to class politics versus the linguistic focus on culture and interpretation.[28]

As Chapter 5 investigates, Marxism's problems with approaching language became most apparent in 1985, when Ernesto Laclau and Chantal Mouffe launched their version of *post*-Marxism. One of the ways they separate themselves as post-Marxists from previous Marxism is to insist that their own focus on language – and their use of linguistically informed poststructuralism – is beyond Marxism. While Gramsci and his notion of hegemony play a pivotal role in their book *Hegemony and Socialist Strategy*, they ignore his writings on language and his early linguistics. Instead, they redefine 'hegemony' using concepts borrowed from Louis Althusser, Jacques Lacan and so-called postmodernists – terms such as 'overdetermination', 'articulation' and 'discourse'. Paradoxically, they claim that Gramsci is still too much of an economic reductionist.

Since the advent of the term 'postmodernism' and the proliferation of literature about it, it has had an uneasy relation with Marxism, and much of this tension has revolved around the issue of language. Fredric Jameson's 1973 book, *The Prison House of Language*, described the political pitfalls that, according to him, any linguistically based structuralism is bound to fall into. Terry Eagleton, Perry Anderson, Ellen Meiksins Wood and many other Marxists have waged virulent attacks on postmodernism, poststructuralism and/or post-Marxism based on various arguments of the incompatibility between Marxism and a language-oriented social theory. Laclau and Mouffe articulate what proponents of postmodernism and its Marxist critics had presumed all along, that 'materialism' is necessarily at odds with language since language exists solely in the realm of ideas. We will turn to these debates most explicitly in Chapter 5.

## Conclusion

This chapter attempts to give some of the background needed to place Gramsci in the context of theories of language that proved to be very influential as the twentieth century proceeded after Gramsci's death. There are of course many differences among the various 'linguistic turns' and it is important not to overgeneralize nor conflate diverse traditions and trends. Chapter 5 comes back to the question of how these ideas became central to poststructuralism and what is often labelled, more broadly, postmodernism near the end of the twentieth century.

Sometimes we tend to look back at intellectual developments in a limited manner framed by current debates. One of my hopes is that Gramsci can provide an alternative approach from which to approach the ideas of thinkers like Saussure and Wittgenstein. As we shall see in the following chapters, Gramsci agreed with both of them that language is central to human life and social arrangements (it is not just the manifestation or representation of ideas or thought) and that it creates meaning through the relations among words and word forms. Sometimes polemics about postmodernism suggest that such ideas about language detract from concrete political activism and/or serious empirical economic analysis. Gramsci, being immersed in a different set of academic and political debates, did not view such ideas about language as apolitical or abstract at all. He did, however, theorize language in a way that questions some of the core ideas of both Saussure and Wittgenstein, though he agrees with both on other points. Most importantly, as we shall see, he questioned the type of abstraction or isolation of language from other social activity that Saussure insisted on. He also paid much greater attention than Wittgenstein to the institutional aspects of language (education policies, national language policies and the writing of dictionaries and grammar books) and the power relationships involved in language.

# 2
# Linguistics and Politics in Gramsci's Italy

For Gramsci, language is not an abstract or overly philosophical topic. Unlike many other social theorists, Gramsci's interest in language grew out of practical and everyday experiences as a Sardinian. Linguistic differences and the 'standardization' of Italian was a practical concern that resonated with political overtones. This chapter provides a brief overview of Gramsci's life and the politics of language during his life.[1] It provides some details of the state of the linguistics that he studied in university. My major point is to illustrate how Gramsci's approach to language and its involvement in politics and the exercise of power helped shape his political theory, which Chapters 3 and 4 examine. As we shall see, Gramsci grappled with a complex tension between his mother tongue, Sardinian, and his second language, Italian. His position was far from simple. He argued for a national 'standard' Italian but did not want speakers to relinquish their dialects. While he understood the connection between local vernaculars and parochial world-views, he did not simply connect national Italian with modernization and progress. These tensions between dialects and national language parallel his own political development from a Sardinian outraged by the injustices he witnessed and experienced first hand to a leader of the Italian Communist Party and an inmate of a Fascist prison. In his prison writings, he traced the roots of Fascism in the history of Italian unification and the lack of integration of the masses, especially the southern peasantry (which for him included Sardinian peasants).[2] The history of language in Sardinia and Italy are integrally related to the social and political histories of Italy and Gramsci's home island.

## Gramsci's home, Sardinia

Antonio Gramsci was born on 22 January 1891 in Ales on the island of Sardinia. Sardinia was part of Italy and had been since Italy's unification in 1861. Since the sixth century BC, it had been ruled by various foreign forces including the Carthaginians, the Romans, the Byzantines, then in 1297 (as the Kingdom of Sardinia and Corsica), the Aragonese. With the union of Ferran II of Aragon and Isabel of Castile and the unification of Spain, Sardinia came under the Spanish Crown, with Catalan as its language of administration. After a short period of Austrian rule due to the War of Spanish Succession, it was 're-Italianized' in 1720 under the House of Savoy. Italian became the 'official' language of Sardinia in 1764. The princes of Piedmont even took refuge there during the Napoleonic wars. But this so-called 'Italianization' of Sardinia was far from complete or successful; under the rule of the Piedmontese, the Sardinian dialects, culture and identity retained their prominence. Italian unification did not drastically change this tension between Sardinia and the mainland. Gramsci grew up in a Sardinia rife with political tension and popular rebellion, as it had been in the earlier periods of domination. But, just as in earlier periods, such struggles were ineffective, being met by various combinations of forces supported from outside Sardinia and the co-operation of different elite groups on the island.

In addition to various political and strategic reasons for wanting to rule Sardinia, most of the island's foreign rulers exploited its resources, including its indigenous labour. From the time of Roman rule, this included agriculture, notably grain, and sheep. Later the coal from the mines of Sulcis-Iglesiente became particularly attractive. Due to the lack of fertile soil on this mountainous island, it required extremely hard work to produce anything from the land, work which was forced on the Sardinian serfs. Many Sardinians, including Gramsci, saw the Italian mainland, particularly northern Italy, as continuing this history of foreign rule. This view was reinforced because political and economic power of the new Kingdom of Italy was concentrated in northern Italy, the process of unification in 1861 was led by Piedmont, and its capital, Turin, became the first capital of Italy. The Italian government was seen as making decisions not for the benefit of the majority of the Sardinians, but in the interest of the mainland.

Gramsci would later argue that this dynamic was not particular to Sardinia, but that southern Italy and Sicily were also subject to similar economic and political domination by the North. He made this argument by engaging in a debate called *la questione meridionale* – the 'Southern Question' or 'Southern Problem' – that went back to the movements that led to the political unification of the Italian peninsula and the creation of an Italian nation-state in 1861.

## The Southern Question and the *Risorgimento*

> The bourgeoisie has unified the Italian people in terms of territory. The working class has the task of concluding this work of the bourgeoisie and unifying the Italian people in economic and spiritual terms.[3]

The idea of Italy as an entity, a cultural spirit or some future ideal, has a long history, but before the middle of the nineteenth century the peninsula was divided into different political regimes often under the control of foreign powers, most notably France and Austria. The *Risorgimento*, literally meaning revival or resurgence, was the cultural and social movement of the nineteenth century that led to political unification in 1861 and finally added Venetia and Rome by 1870.

Shortly after political unification, Massimo d'Azeglio coined a phrase about Italian history that would become proverbial: 'Italy is a fact, now we need to make Italians.' This process of making 'Italians', including Italy's political, economic, social, linguistic and cultural dimensions, constitutes much of the context of Gramsci's political and cultural theory. It must also be noted that while Italy is more extreme than other countries, all nation-states have involved similar processes whereby citizens come to think of themselves, to a greater or lesser degree, as Italians, French, Chinese, Canadians or South Africans.[4] In Italy, this process of unification, and the obstacles to it, gave rise to the Southern Question, which arose from the differences between the North and the South – political, economic, cultural and social differences.

Conservatives and reactionaries argued that the South was inherently backward due to the inferiority of southerners – often expressed in biological and racist terms. As Gramsci summarized it, for such reactionaries, 'the South is the ball and chain which prevents the social development of Italy from progressing more rapidly'.[5] Gramsci and others intervened in this debate about the 'Southern problem', arguing that the South had not been perpetually 'backwards' but that its problems and lack of development were in part the result of policies that supported capitalist development of the North and the southern elites' acceptance of the policies that favoured the North. The tariffs of the 1880s were a clear example, since they protected the developing industries of the North but hurt the agricultural exports from the South.[6] Chapter 4 investigates these questions in greater detail, discussing Gramsci's notion of the 'passive revolution' that he used to describe the process of Italian unification. The crucial point here is that Gramsci was very concerned with the tensions between the North and South of Italy and Italian unification. These issues for him were intricately connected to the role of language within politics and culture.

## The Language Question

Together with the Southern Question one of the significant problems facing the newly unified Italy in 1861 was its practical lack of a 'standard' language. It is estimated that in 1861, only somewhere between two and a half and twelve per cent of the new Italian population spoke anything that could be called 'standard' Italian.[7] In other words, the very existence of Italian as a spoken language of daily life is questionable. Literary Italian was primarily a written language of the elite. It was not used by large numbers of people. The spoken languages of 'Italian' were more like a family of Latin dialects with greater and lesser influences from other languages such as the pre-Roman Etruscan, French, Spanish and German.[8] Sardinian was particularly distant from literary Italian. Added to this lack of a 'standard Italian' was the very high illiteracy rate of about 75 per cent throughout Italy. The *questione della lingua*, or the 'Language Question' is connected to the Southern Question, as exhibited by the fact that in Sardinia the illiteracy rate was 90 per cent.[9]

The lack of a truly national language was not unique to Italy. For example, French historians have noted that in the middle of the nineteenth century, French was a foreign language to about half the French citizens, a situation that the government played an active role in changing.[10] But while the Italian case was not exceptional, it was extreme. Many Italians saw this as a deficiency, looking to France as a model of a nation-state and bemoaning their lack of a capital like Paris. The history of Italian unification is also bound up with the relation between the Catholic Church's religious and social authority emanating from Rome and the political authority of the government. But here, we must limit ourselves to the question of language.

Alessandro Manzoni played a key role in Italian linguistic unification.[11] He is best known as the author of *The Betrothed* (*I promessi sposi*), a novel that he first wrote in a language that he created by adding to literary Italian words, phrases and expressions from the 'living' dialects of Lombard, Tuscan, French, Latin and other dialects. He was heavily influenced by the rise of Romanticism, a movement especially prevalent in Germany that praised living vernacular languages over classical and literary languages including Greek and Latin.[12] Manzoni adopted the Romanticist position that literature should be written in the spoken languages of daily life rather than modelled on the beauty and elegance of previous great literature. He praised 'living' languages as opposed to the 'dead' languages of Latin and Greece or the written languages of great literature like Petrarch, Boccaccio and Dante.[13] Against the tradition that demoted Romance languages and dialects to corrupted Latin, Manzoni saw them as rich sources of eloquence and passion. His first published edition of *The Betrothed* began with an introduction explaining that an author should use the language with which she is most familiar, and also one that is known to the readers – such a language did not exist for Italy as a whole.

Manzoni then changed his ideas about language and the best way to overcome Italy's lack of a national language. He decided that the national Italian language should be the Tuscan dialect, specifically that spoken by educated people in Florence – a dialect quite close to literary Italian. He 'translated' *The Betrothed* into this Florentine dialect, publishing a significantly revised edition in 1840.[14] For Manzoni, the unification of Italy provided the opportunity to create a shared language for authors and reading audiences. He wanted this common language to be entirely based on the 'living' language of Florence free of any trace of other dialects or literary Italian not used in Florentine speech.[15]

Seven years after unification, in 1868, Manzoni was appointed to head a government commission on linguistic unification in Italy – to spread good language and pronunciation. His solution to the lack of an effective national language was to adopt the dialect of Florence as the 'standard' national language for the entire country. He proposed subsidizing dictionaries and grammar books of this new standard Italian and that the schoolteachers for all of Italy should be recruited as much as possible from Tuscany, the region around Florence. In various ways, he argued, Florentine could be spread around to all the regions of Italy.[16] While Manzoni's solution was quite influential, it did not conclude the debates on the Language Question, which continued well into the twentieth century.[17] As we shall discuss below, one of Manzoni's major critics was a linguist, Graziadio Isaia Ascoli, who influenced Gramsci and is mentioned numerous times in the *Prison Notebooks*.[18]

The Language Question was an especially acute issue for southern Italy, Sicily and Sardinia, whose languages and dialects were quite distinct from Tuscan.[19] Added to this were the much higher rates of illiteracy and the lack of education in these areas. In 1911, the year Gramsci moved from Sardinia to Turin, the illiteracy rate throughout Italy had been reduced to 40 per cent (from 75 per cent in 1861). In Piedmont, where Turin is located, it was only 11 per cent (from 54 per cent in 1861); whereas in Sardinia, in 1911, 58 per cent of the population were still illiterate (as compared to 90 per cent in 1861).[20] Thus, Gramsci's move from Sardinia to Turin was a move from a predominantly illiterate, poverty-stricken, agricultural society, where even the educated people experienced 'standard Italian' as a second language, to an increasingly educated, urban, industrial and relatively wealthy society where the language situation did not create the same level of dissonance. Like Gramsci, many other southerners and Sardinians immigrated to Turin. Most were to work in newly created factory jobs, especially at the Fiat automobile factory.

## Gramsci's youth

Gramsci's life started in a relatively privileged family in Ghilarza, Sardinia. His father, Franceso Gramsci, born in 1860 in the town of Gaeta between Rome and Naples, was a registrar. As an administrator originally from the mainland, he and his family enjoyed petit bourgeois status and the relative wealth that went along with it. Antonio Gramsci's mother, Giuseppina (or Peppina) Marcias Gramsci was native to Sardinia, from the landowning, petit bourgeois, Italo-Spanish background. Had it not been for the imprisonment of Antonio's father when Nino (as Antonio was called) was seven, the Gramsci family might have continued to live in relative luxury amidst the much less fortunate Sardinians. But, as was not uncommon with the type of job that he held, Franceso Gramsci was susceptible to the results of local political feuds. When his rivals won a local election, a few relatively small improprieties in the registry books were used to suspend him from office and give him a five-year prison sentence. This meant that Antonio Gramsci's early life was one of unexpected economic hardship, shadowed by a fall from prestige, and this perhaps accounts for his quite introspective and solitary character.

The other major contributions to Nino's reclusive character were his hunchback and poor health. The family attributed his hunchback to a fall when he was four that nearly killed him.[21] Such health problems and physical deformity might be seen as purely arbitrary misfortunes, but, as commentators have pointed out, their impact on Gramsci should be seen within the context of a poor agricultural area with less than adequate medical facilities and rough social circumstances where people with any disability or weakness were ridiculed. His physical condition (as an adult he was under five feet and had noticeable bumps on both his back and upper chest) and social position in an impoverished petit bourgeois family combined in creating a boy who felt ostracized by society.

In Sardinia, Nino became familiar with some of the ideas of socialism, especially through his eldest brother, Gennaro. Nino started reading the issues of *Avanti!*, the socialist newspaper, that Gennaro gave him. Gennaro was an active member of the Socialist Party and introduced Nino to its leaders. While Nino did not transform his interest in socialism into party membership, he became an avid reader and kept files of articles by Gaetano Salvemini and Benedetto Croce, both of whom are major topics throughout his writings, especially in the *Prison*

*Notebooks.* He was greatly influenced by Sardinian separatism. He even wrote an article for and tried to obtain a permanent position at the separatist newspaper, *L'Unione Sarda.* This paper had the largest circulation in Sardinia.[22] After having moved to mainland Italy, Gramsci would reflect back on this relationship, describing in 1919 how for the Italian peasantry in general (including Sardinia), '[c]lass struggle was confused with brigandage, with blackmail, with burning woods ... it was a form of elementary terrorism, without long-term or effective consequences.'[23] It was not until Gramsci moved to the industrial centre of Turin that he would attempt to sort out some of this confusion between class struggle and peasant insolence.

One of the themes that would occupy Gramsci's life germinated at an early age: what is the relationship between the struggle of the working class against capitalism and the peasants' poor conditions and rebellion? As we shall discuss later, this was the beginnings of his influential writings on the North–South relationship, the Southern Question and 'subalternity' – meaning the condition of subjection and subordination. While he later came to embrace Marx's argument that the industrialized working class was the group that had the potential to lead a revolution against capitalism, he also remained committed to the argument that any such revolution would fail, in early twentieth century Italy at least, if it did not also include the peasantry and other subaltern social groups. We shall see in Chapter 5 that some contemporary versions of post-Marxism claim that Gramsci 'presupposed' that the working class was the revolutionary subject of history, due to his unwillingness to let go of an 'essentialist' notion that ultimately the economy determines revolutionary possibility. In order to address this question later, here we have to establish the nature of this so-called presupposition. The young Gramsci of 1910 did not even see the working class as *the* revolutionary agent, although he did have an early interest in the very small working class in Sardinia, especially the miners.[24] The question is, for what reasons did Gramsci accept Marx's arguments that the proletariat was the most likely social class around which a progressive hegemony (including other subaltern groups) could be formed? What does it mean that Gramsci saw the Italian proletariat, following Marx, as the leading group or centre of this hegemonic formation? Ernesto Laclau and Chantal Mouffe argue that Gramsci presupposed the role of the working class and that this is one of the serious deficiencies in his thought. As Chapter 5 discusses in detail, they argue that for his ideas to be made relevant to current society, which has a very different class structure from that of early twentieth-century Italy, we must reject this supposed presupposition. Suffice it to say here that it was not until he had moved to Turin and become involved with the Socialist Party that he gained this conviction. Moreover, as we shall see, he seems to have arrived at his faith in the proletariat as the potential leader of revolutionary change from a historical analysis of Italy in the early twentieth century. And even on this point, he insisted that the working class had to make alliances with the peasantry and include them at the centre of the political struggle. Some of our central questions are: To what extent are his methods, concepts and presuppositions open to reassessing revolutionary potential under different circumstances? Do other historical circumstances require different hegemonic formations? Do these always require one economically defined group that leads the others? These questions will be taken up in Chapter 5.

## 'Beyond the Wide Waters'

The key factor for Gramsci's move from Sardinia to mainland Italy was education. Of course, this move is one of the major elements shaping his life. His well-known prison writings as well as his career as a communist reflected his Sardinian roots as they interacted with his life in northern Italy. In 1911, Gramsci won one of 39 scholarships of 70 lire a month offered by the Carlo Alberto College, to enable impoverished students from Sardinia to attend the University of Turin. As was obvious from one of the examinations for this scholarship, which was to write an essay on the contribution of the pre-*Risorgimento* writers to the unification of Italy,[25] the education system was playing an active part in Italian unification. Gramsci came in ninth in the competition, behind another Sardinian, Palmiro Togliatti, who would later become one of Gramsci's communist comrades, outliving Gramsci and taking up the leadership of the Italian Communist Party until his death in 1964. As Gramsci describes in his letters home, he found Turin quite inhospitable, lonely and cold. He was overwhelmed by the amount of traffic and the bustle of the city. Lack of money and his ill health continued to be problems for him.

In his first year, Gramsci chose the Modern Philology course. Gramsci's professor of linguistics, Matteo Bartoli (1873–1946), was one of the first people to break Gramsci's solitude. Bartoli had published on the Sardinian language and argued that it played an important role in understanding the remote derivatives of the Latin vernacular. He was initially interested in Gramsci as one of the few students at the university who spoke Sardinian. Gramsci soon wrote letters home asking for information about Sardinian dialect pronunciation to aid Bartoli's research. Gramsci and Bartoli developed a rather warm friendship.[26]

It was in 1913, when he was still isolated from his fellow students and spending much time with Bartoli and his literature professor, Umberto Cosmo, that Gramsci began to rethink his attachment to Sardinian separatism and its calls of 'National independence for the region' and 'Continentals go home!' This transformation, according to Angelo Tasca, Gramsci's friend, fellow student and later communist comrade, was what finally made Gramsci a socialist. Gramsci witnessed a strike at the Fiat plant and the Sardinian elections in which the peasant masses took unprecedented participation but many of the Sardinian land-owning class had changed their tune from pro-Sardinian to antisocialist. As Fiori describes, it was while still a lonely student spending much of his time with his professors, Cosmo and Bartoli, and experiencing the strike and elections, that Gramsci

> began to see clearly that the real oppressors of the southern peasants, of the small landholders and the lower middle classes of his island, were not the workers and industrialists of the North, but a combination of the industrialists with the indigenous Sardinian or southern ruling class as a whole. The evil was at home, and far removed from the industrial proletariat which he had seen on strike in Turin for ninety-six days earlier that year.[27]

It was Gramsci's experience in Turin combined with his Sardinian background that laid the foundations for his later analysis of how Fascism succeeded and communism failed. Here lie the seeds of why Gramsci's ideas are so useful for people concerned with colonialism. Imperial powers often co-opt and strengthen the power of local elites in order to secure their rule. The history of most colonial projects cannot be understood simply as the rule by one country over the members of another territory but involves complex relations and complicities amongst all those involved.

Gramsci's initial experiences that transformed him from a disgruntled Sardinian into an Italian revolutionary were augmented tremendously by his leadership during the Turin Council Movement in 1919–20, when the workers took control of the Fiat factory. Moreover, he played a primary role founding and leading the Communist Party of Italy. And while I do not wish to undervalue in any way the later periods of Gramsci's life, they should not be seen, as is often the case in Gramscian commentaries, as radical departures from his earlier concerns.

Gramsci remained committed to the importance of the education system, including the teaching of grammar and language skills (discussed in detail below), as one of the most important methods for the social and cultural unification of Italy. Indeed, Gramsci's transformation into an *Italian* communist leader is unthinkable apart from the impact of Italian unification and its ongoing dynamics. We cannot separate his transition into an Italian from the evolution of his political thinking into communism.[28]

## Gramsci's linguistics

We now need to turn to a closer look at the linguistics that Gramsci studied at the University of Turin. This is necessary not just because it provides some details of one part of Gramsci's intellectual background; there are two more important reasons why it is central for introducing Gramsci's work. The first is that Gramsci initially became familiar with a well-developed and complex concept of 'hegemony' as it was being used in linguistics. This point has been overlooked by many Gramsci scholars who routinely point to the roots of hegemony in the Russian Social Democrats, Plekhanov or Lenin, but it has been thoroughly substantiated by Franco Lo Piparo.[29] This does not in any way decrease the importance of these other influences on

Gramsci's development of the term 'hegemony'. But without an understanding of the linguistic background of the term, many of the contributions that Gramsci makes to Marxist theory are lost. Moreover, Gramsci's early study of linguistics helps explain why and how his concepts have been so widely applicable in such diverse fields.

The second reason why Gramsci's studies in linguistics are crucial has little to do with Gramsci's own life, but rather with our situation today. Since Gramsci's death, intellectual life in Europe and North America has been permeated by various preoccupations with language. As discussed in Chapter 1, the many 'linguistic turns' of the twentieth century are not unrelated to changes in the production process and the types of commodities that dominate the global economy. Of special importance here is the linguistics of Ferdinand de Saussure. Saussure developed a synchronic or structural approach that became very influential in anthropology and sociology and then in all the social sciences and humanities under the name of 'structuralism'. Structuralism held such a place in twentieth-century social theory that much contemporary theory is a development of, and reaction to it, including poststructuralism at the heart of what is often discussed as postmodernism. In other words, the writings of Foucault, Derrida, Habermas, Lyotard, Barthes, Judith Butler, Julia Kristeva and many others are all fundamentally informed by the insights of structuralism. Thus, if we want to understand why so many different people from environments permeated by structuralist (and now poststructuralist) concerns and debates were attracted to Gramsci's work, we need to focus on the issues that were 'in the air', so to speak.

## Italian linguistics

Italian linguistics at the beginning of the twentieth century was shaped to a large extent by the Language Question and Italian unification. The linguists who were most involved in these debates approached language in a very different fashion than did the dominant school of linguistics in Europe at the time, the Neogrammarians. We will examine the debate between these two approaches for two purposes:

1. Ferdinand de Saussure developed his structuralist theory from the mileau of the Neogrammarian school. Gramsci's reaction to the Neogrammarians provides significant insight into a Gramscian approach to the issues raised by structuralism and poststructuralism, especially around agency, structure and politics.
2. The Neogrammarians represented to Gramsci the positivist approach to language which he rejected. Gramsci is widely known for his rejection of positivism in economics and politics. Understanding how Gramsci's critique of positivism in the realm of linguistics will allow us to see how he relates his theory of language to his political and economic theory.

But, Gramsci did not simply reject the Neogrammarians' work. Instead, he saw in it some corrections to another school of linguistics prevalent in Italy and Germany, the Idealist school inspired by the philosophy of Benedetto Croce. A discussion of this last school will enable us to see how Gramsci launched a double-pronged critique. He used the Idealist arguments against the Neogrammarians' notion that language was just a collection of words and linguistic forms and its development was not related to the actual speakers and writers who used the language. He also used the explanatory power of the Neogrammarians' historical analyses to show, contra Croce, that the structures of language are central to how people use it.

Matteo Bartoli, Gramsci's professor, followed the basic linguistic approach of Graziadio Isaia Ascoli (1829–1907), a dominant figure in Italian linguistics in the late nineteenth century. Ascoli had achieved fame within European linguistics for his earlier work on the relationship between sound changes in ancient Indo-Iranian and Graeco-Italic. But his most noteworthy contribution to Italian linguistics and Gramsci's thought was his later studies in Romance linguistics and dialectology, through which he developed the theory of the linguistic substratum. In direct opposition to the German school of comparative philology, specifically August Schleicher, Ascoli argued that most linguistic changes could be explained by the impact of traces of historically previous languages that existed in what he called a substratum.

For Ascoli, this substratum included the physiological effects of how sounds are produced in speakers' mouths as well as psychological senses of what sounds correct or pleasing. In this way, Ascoli saw linguistics as a field of study closely related to ethnology, anthropology and biology.

Ascoli used his linguistics to criticize Manzoni's plan for 'standardizing' and diffusing the Italian language. As Gramsci would repeat decades later, Ascoli's main argument was that Manzoni's 'solution' was an attempt to impose an artificial language over the previous languages.[30] These previous languages would constitute a very strong linguistic substratum that would exert continuous pressure on this new, supposedly 'standard' language, changing it in different ways in different regions. Thus, from a pragmatic linguistic perspective, Ascoli argued, such a plan would not be successful.

Bartoli based his work on the more cultural and historical aspects of Ascoli's research, as distinct from some of his other students who emphasized the more biological and physiological claims of his theories. Bartoli begins with Ascoli's notion, also developed in the field of geographic linguistics by the Swiss linguist Jules Gilliéron, that languages tend to be in conflict with one another. Language change, growth and development are seen as the historical result of sociocultural struggle, whether violent or more peaceful. Bartoli extended the notion that when there is competition between two linguistic forms (such as two words, or sounds, or grammatical structures) these forms cannot be coeval. They cannot have developed at the same time from the same circumstances. Rather, one linguistic form must be older than the other.

In other words, as Gramsci argued later in the *Prison Notebooks*, language is not generated spontaneously, or to use the biological terminology that Gramsci picks up, language is not 'parthenogenetic' – produced by itself without contact with other languages.[31] This ties language change to social and cultural history, against the Neogrammarian school which we will discuss below. These basic tenets will also become very important in examining the effect of Saussure and structuralism on social theory in Chapter 5.

In addition, Bartoli argued that the competition between two linguistic forms would eventually result in one succeeding and the other falling out of use. Bartoli developed a method that begins by determining the chronological order of the two word forms in question, and the geographic areas in which they are used.[32] He would then attempt to determine the centres from which the word forms 'irradiated'. In this way, he is combining a synchronic and a diachronic approach to language. If there was no clear evidence for which linguistic form was older, he would apply five general rules. He would look at the relative isolation of the geographic area in which each form was used, the size of the area, the duration of each use of the two forms and the outcome of their interactions, i.e. which word form was still being used. Bartoli's discussion of 'irradiation' of a word form was explicitly connected to the issue of the cultural power of the speakers and he used the contemporary linguistic concepts *fascino* ('fascination' or 'attraction'), *prestigio* ('prestige') and *egemonia* ('hegemony').[33] Thus, Gramsci's initial significant exposure to the concept of hegemony was in the field of linguistics, where it was used to describe how a given population would adopt a particular linguistic form, parts of a language or an entire language from another group of people. The mechanisms of this adoption were not physical coercion, but were related to cultural prestige as well as economic, political, social and at times even military power.

## Bartoli's polemic against the Neogrammarians

The other aspect of Bartoli's academic pursuits that is important here is his polemical criticisms of the *Junggrammatiker*, or Neogrammarians, a group of linguists centred at the University of Leipzig in Germany. While the label *Junggrammatiker* was originally coined as a slight against them, especially given their youth, it became a general label even though they never officially formed a school or association. The main members were Karl Brugmann, Hermann Osthoff, August Leskien and Berthold Delbrück, and they had taken some of the basic tenets of historical comparative grammar to their extremes. They are an important school for several reasons. First of all, they represented a positivist approach to linguistics, which Bartoli, and after him Gramsci, rejected. This is an important link between Gramsci's more general criticism of positivism, and especially vulgar Marxism, and his interest in linguistics and language. Secondly, before launching his structuralist linguistics, Saussure had studied with them, published in their journals and, to a greater or lesser extent, accepted their approach to the study of language. So while the work that Saussure is so famous for, the posthumously published lecture notes entitled *Course in General Linguistics*, explicitly marks a separation from the Neogrammarians, to fully understand its implications we must have some knowledge of the circumstances of its germination. Moreover, there are some important continuities between the Neogrammarian approach and Saussure's.[34] By summarizing these perspectives, we can see how Gramsci's discussions of language contain both implicit critiques of Saussurean-influenced structuralism, as well as an appreciation for the insights of synchronic, structuralist analysis.

In some respects, the Neogrammarians were just developing the ideas of previous comparative-historical grammar or philology, as it was often called. Based on the excitement of the 'discovery' of Sanskrit by European linguists and its similarities with Latin, Greek and other European languages, comparative grammar focused on tracing the historical connections among these languages. This led to the classification of languages into families and provided a general picture of how languages developed and changed in relation to each other. Rasmus Rask (1787–1832), Franz Bopp (1787–1832), Jacob Grimm (1785–1863) – who with his brother is best known for collecting fairy tales – and August Schleicher (1821–68) specialized in systematizing such comparative projects in the area of Indo-European languages. Much of their work centred around explaining 'sound changes', which are regular and patterned ways in which two related languages differ from each other, such as Old English and Old Norse, or Germanic languages. From such comparisons, they described the history of languages as a series of 'sound changes' such as the 'First Germanic Sound Shift'. This was the example used in the first chapter whereby the 'p' sound in Latin (and in a reconstructed proto-Indo-European language) would have been changed, in almost every word, to an 'f' sound (so the 'p' in 'paternalism' from the Latin *pater* or 'father' becomes the 'f' sound as in the modern English 'father', or the German *Vater* or *väterlich*, the German for 'paternal'). The regularity with which such changes are detected led to a whole series of 'laws' to describe such developments. At this stage there were various ideas about how tendencies towards mishearing, imperfect pronunciation or the use of analogy, the desire to be distinct or the necessity of expressing new ideas accounted for such sound changes.

Schleicher was especially concerned with constructing the proto-language from which all the Indo-European languages were supposed to have developed. And from this effort he devised the family tree model. He also argued that the cause of most sound changes was to be found in biological differences between different peoples, an idea that Ascoli and some of his followers accepted to some degree. Bartoli and Gramsci were clear in their rejection of such a biological preoccupation, favouring cultural, political and social explanations.

Based on many successes of these 'sound laws' and various new laws that supposedly explained what had been previously seen as exceptions, Karl Brugmann and Hermann Osthoff in 1878 published *Morphologische Untersuchungen*, which defined the Neogrammarian approach. Of the six basic points, the one that drew the greatest attention was their claim that the 'sound laws' were exceptionless. Whatever linguistic data did not fit existing sound laws was merely due to the fact that the laws explaining them had not been discovered. The reason for the binding nature of sound laws, they argued, was because linguistic change was not due to aspects external to the languages themselves, such as their cultural, social or political environments. Rather, languages changed due to 'mechanical' laws within the languages and their interaction with the psychological necessity of speakers towards regularization of speech. Moreover, sound changes are unconscious to the speakers. Gramsci's rejection of this last point is important to his notion of 'common sense', as we shall see in Chapter 3.

For the Neogrammarians, what was at stake in the exceptionless character of the sound laws was the very possibility of a scientific study of language. As Leskien stated, 'If one admits optional, contingent, and unconnected changes, one is basically stating that the object of one's research, language, is not amenable to scientific recognition.'[35] It is important to note that in the *Morphologische Untersuchungen*, Brugmann and

Osthoff actually stated that linguistics is a form of history as opposed to a form of science. But as the quote from Leskien above illustrates, many of the advocates and detractors ignored this aspect of their methodological statement.[36]

Besides the more explicit theoretical statement of methods and the rejection of an original proto-language that should be reconstructed, the most fundamental difference between the Neogrammarians and earlier comparative historical linguistics was that this exceptionless aspect of the sound laws meant that they rejected various other considerations for explaining sound changes, especially the question of meaning. To the Neogrammarians, the sounds whose changes were being explained could not be related to the meanings of the individual words in which they existed, except in so far as sound change is related to the other sounds within the word. But the social, political or cultural contexts of a word were to be disregarded.

Saussure's notion of language as a (closed) system, discussed in Chapter 1, has significant similarities to that quality of language that, according to the Neogrammarians, made the sound laws exceptionless. That is, all sounds within a language had to be explained by laws internal to language precisely because, the Neogrammarians contended, language functions as a system of sounds irregardless of its external referents or meanings. This system is not a synchronic one bounded by a given language, say English or French, as Saussure's notion of language as a system is. Rather, for the Neogrammarians, the system is a historical development that includes the interaction among different languages and their histories.

But this diachronic system of language is still a 'closed' one where what is to be explained, the sound change, is defined by an initial identity between two sounds, the 'p' and the 'f', for example. These sounds are said to be the 'same' element; but the reason this element has changed is not because the sounds exist within the two words *pater* and 'father' that have the same meaning (or signified, to use Saussure's terminology), or refer to the same set of objects in the non-linguistic world. The Neogrammarians were clear that such recourse to factors 'outside' language was unscientific and also complicated, since meanings change over time as well and are different for different speakers. Rather the identity between the 'p' and 'f' that causes the change to be subject to explanation is that they play the same role within the sound systems of the languages involved. This key idea that we cannot use the relationship between the sound pattern and what it means, the signifier and the signified, to explain how language functions, is usually seen as a unique attribute of Saussure's. In actuality, the idea existed in its diachronic form in the Neogrammarians, to whom Bartoli and Gramsci were responding. Thus, when we examine Gramsci's discussion of language and linguistics in the *Prison Notebooks* in Chapter 3, we shall see that his concepts of 'normative grammar' and 'spontaneous grammar' are explicitly responses to the Neogrammarians, but are implicitly a response to Saussure. Indeed, Gramsci's work foreshadows some of the criticisms of structuralism that led to poststructuralism. But, where much poststructualism further abstracts language and linguistic concepts from the actual use of language in everyday situations, Gramsci retains the explanatory power of the structural approach and redresses its shortcomings, especially in accounting for human agency, by seeing language as fundamentally a human, historical institution.

The basic ideas behind Gramsci's work in this area can be seen already in Bartoli's criticisms of the Neogrammarians. This is best exhibited by Gramsci's own writings, including one of his first letters sent from prison. In this much quoted letter he describes wanting to accomplish something *für ewig*, using Goethe's German phrase meaning 'for eternity'. It is Gramsci's first outline for his prison research agenda. The second idea that he says he wants to pursue is a study of comparative linguistics:

> from the new viewpoint of the neo-linguists opposed to the neo-grammarians. (Are you beginning to dread this letter?) One of the greatest intellectual 'regrets' of my life is the deep wound inflicted upon my dear professor at the University of Turin, Bartoli, who was convinced I was the archangel sent to destroy the neo-grammarians once and for all, since he, being of the same generation as they, was bound by thousands of academic strings to this infamous sect. In his pronouncements, he didn't dare go beyond certain limits of decorum and deference for old funerary monuments of erudition.[37]

Thus, at least according to Gramsci, Bartoli's quite vehement attack on the Neogrammarians was a toned down version of the actual position that they both held. Indeed, before Bartoli had joined the faculty in Turin in 1907, he had been studying in Vienna and Paris,[38] then very much under the sway of the Neogrammarians.

Bartoli coined the term 'neolinguistics' in 1910 in opposition to the Neogrammarians to emphasize his main contention that their method was really only the study of grammar as a collection of words and sounds, not really the study of language itself. Bartoli understood that the Neogrammarians view language only as abstract data that is disconnected from the people who use it and their lives, including social, political and cultural conflict. Sounds and their relationships take on a life of their own. In this way, Gramsci's general criticisms of positivism and naturalism, which will be addressed in Chapter 3, also apply to the Neogrammarians. Bartoli and Gramsci were critical of the separation of phonetics and semantics apparent in the Neogrammarian method. As we have seen, Bartoli's neolinguistics emphasized the cultural, social and political interaction with languages and argues that these account for most linguistic change.

There has been some confusion of Bartoli's neolinguistics with Idealist approaches to linguistics, especially the work of Guilio Bertoni. This is because in 1925, Bartoli and Bertoni co-authored a book entitled *Brevario di neolinguistica* in which Bertoni wrote the theoretical first part and Bartoli wrote the methodological second part. Gramsci is quite scathing in his criticism of Bertoni, explaining how Bertoni's approach is very different from Bartoli's.[39] Bertoni's theoretical work is based upon the philosophy of Benedetto Croce, to be discussed below. Gramsci points out that Bartoli should never have co-authored the book in the first place. Moreover, Gramsci argues that Bertoni's is not even an adequate version of Crocean linguistics.[40]

Where Gramsci and Bartoli agree with both Bertoni and Croce is in their criticisms of the Neogrammarians as overly positivistic and mechanistic. Gramsci and Bartoli seemed ready and willing to use Idealism to show the weaknesses in the Neogrammarian's positivism. But this does not mean they fully accepted the main tenets of Idealism in general, or Idealist linguistics in particular. On the contrary, some of the criticisms that Gramsci raises against Idealism are informed by positivism. As has often been pointed out, in Gramsci's double-pronged critique of Croce and Idealism on one side, and positivistic, vulgar Marxism on the other, he played the two off against each other, pointing out that while seemingly opposite, they often led to the same consequences, that is, a type of fatalism in which people would not organize in order to change their situations.

## Idealist linguistics and Benedetto Croce

The last piece in the picture of the background to Gramsci's linguistics is provided by the pre-eminent figure in Italian intellectual history, Benedetto Croce (1866–1952). Croce was one of Italy's most prominent philosophers and intellectuals. Gramsci himself draws the parallel between his own relationship with Croce and Marx's relationship with Hegel, in which Marx was heavily influenced by Hegel but also engaged in a rigorous critique that ended up 'turning Hegel upside down' to put him back on his feet.[41] There has been much debate about the extent to which Gramsci successfully departed from Croce, or whether he remained fundamentally Crocean, just as many argue that Marx retained Hegelianism. Here we want to focus on the linguistic aspect of this relationship. That is, Bartoli and Gramsci were critical of the approach to linguistics that Croce's philosophy inspired, especially in the works of Karl Vossler as well as Giulio Bertoni, mentioned above. Croce's specific arguments about what language is and how it should be studied are also important here.

Croce argues that there is no division between language and aesthetics: 'the science of art and the science of language, the Aesthetic and the Linguistic, conceived as true and proper sciences are *not* two distinct things but one single science'.[42] Based on his philosophy, language is understood purely as expression. It is just the conglomeration of individual speech acts which are each aesthetic acts of the speaker. Karl Vossler, elaborating on Croce's perspective, uses the analogy of the weather. Just as a climate is a generalization of usual weather conditions, and not actual meteorological phenomena, so too,

Vossler argues, language is a generalization that only approximates the real phenomena of speech. Just as climate does not really exist at a given moment in time but is an abstraction across time, Vossler argues, language is also an abstraction that never really occurs.[43]

From such a perspective, Croce and his linguistic followers argue that the aesthetic acts that constitute language are never themselves repeatable. Each time a speaker utters an expression, it is a unique aesthetic act. To argue otherwise, according to Croce, would be to falsely separate the content of an expression from the act of speaking:

> The Linguistic has itself discovered the principles of the irreducible individuality of aesthetic entities when it has asserted that the word is what is actually spoken, and that no two words are really the same; thus eliminating synonyms and homonyms and demonstrating the impossibility of correctly translating one word into another, or a so-called dialect into a so-called language, or a so-called mother tongue into a so-called foreign language.[44]

Such a position is clearly at odds with the approach of Ascoli, Bartoli and Gramsci described above. But it is also totally different from the Neogrammarian approach. Indeed, it is such an extreme attack on the positivism that defines language as an objective structure that changes over time due to its own laws, that one can imagine why Bartoli or Gramsci might use some of its philosophical arguments to highlight the problems with what the Neogrammarians understand language to be.

### Summary of various approaches to language

The Neogrammarian position:

- Language is an object of study that changes in time according to its own laws; these laws can be determined by the comparative method, focusing on sound changes.

Croce and the Idealist linguistics position:

- Language cannot be the object of study for linguistics since it is itself an abstract generalization constituted by the sum of individual expressive acts of speech or writing.

Bartoli and Gramsci's position:

* Language cannot be separated (as with the Neogrammarians) from the culture, society and history of its users.

* Language changes and develops not due to its own internal laws or the physiology or psychology of its users, but when different languages (dialects or phases of a language) come into contact with each other. Language change is the result of the inherent conflict between the languages once they have come into contact.

* Linguists can still analyse language change over time since language does exist beyond just the individual speakers' uses of a language. Indeed, the use of language requires that it has a relatively stable structure and consistency in its phonetics, syntax and semantics.

The following chapters illustrate how important these ideas about language were to Gramsci's development of his unique concept of hegemony in his prison writings. While this was the culmination of his interest in language and politics, these themes were interrelated well before Gramsci was imprisoned. Turning to Gramsci's assessment of Esperanto will illustrate that he began to see this interconnection as early as 1918. Esperanto (meaning 'the hoping one') is an artificial language based on words common to the main European languages. It was created by a physician, Ludwig Lazarus Zamenhof, in Warsaw in 1887. Zamenhof and advocates of Esperanto argue that it can be used to facilitate international communication, help overcome ethnic conflict and lead to greater human co-operation around the world.

### Gramsci and Esperanto

Well before Gramsci began to elaborate his specific theory of hegemony, he wrote about the importance of language to politics using precisely the ideas about language discussed above. On 16 February 1918, Gramsci published a short article in *Il Grido del Popolo*, 'A Single Language and Esperanto'. As David Forgacs and Geoffrey Nowell Smith have pointed out, he used the issue of Esperanto as a vehicle 'to make a more or less explicit attack on the backwardness and superficiality of the [Socialist] party's approach to cultural questions'.[45]

Gramsci's article was the summary and concluding remarks to a small debate that had developed between him and the editors of *Avanti!* (the Italian Socialist Party's official newspaper). As editor of *Il Grido*, Gramsci had earlier published a letter in support of the promotion and study of Esperanto by the Italian Socialist Party (PSI). He had attached an editorial note criticizing the letter.[46] The previous year, Cesare Seassaro proposed to the Milan section that the Party fully adopt Esperanto.[47] The editors of *Avanti!* took up Gramsci's point, agreeing with him in theory but rejecting it in practice. They argued that Esperanto could be quite useful for socialism.[48] Gramsci penned an anonymous reply describing himself as a student 'preparing my thesis on the history of language, trying to apply the critical methods of historical materialism to this research as well'.[49] Gramsci clearly saw his academic interest in linguistics as connected to his political role in the proletarian movement.

Gramsci summarizes his perspective on Esperanto, and more importantly *la questione della lingua* and the entire question of the Socialists' approach to cultural questions. In a passage that remains pertinent to current discussions of English as a global language, Gramsci writes:

> The advocates of a single language are worried by the fact that while the world contains a number of people who would like to communicate directly with one another, there is an endless number of different languages which restrict the ability to communicate. This is a *cosmopolitan*, not an international anxiety, that of the bourgeois who travels for business or pleasure ... [50]

While distinguishing between bourgeois cosmopolitanism and proletarian internationalism, Gramsci does not write off the entire language problem as unimportant to politics. Quite the contrary. He opens his article emphasizing that the problems of a single language are related to larger cultural problems and 'all man's historical activity'. Moreover, it is useful to 'accustom people's minds to grasp this unity in the many facets of life....'[51] He then provides a brief historical overview of the development of language questions, tracing this development through the Enlightenment and the nineteenth-century Italian debates. He summarizes the disagreement between the classicists, who look

to fourteenth- and sixteenth-century literature for a model of a
true, beautiful Italian language, and Alessandro Manzoni's advocacy of the living dialect of Florence. He then criticizes
Esperanto by extending Graziadio Isaia Ascoli's arguments against
Manzoni to Esperanto. His basic argument against both
Esperanto and Manzoni is that they are attempts to artificially
impose a language created arbitrarily without the participation
and activity of the speakers and writers of the language.[52] He
contends that Ascoli had proved

> that not even a national language can be created artificially,
> by order of the state; that the Italian language was being
> formed by itself and would be formed only in so far as the
> shared life of the nation gave rise to numerous and stable
> contacts between various parts of the nation; that the spread
> of a particular language is due to the productive activity of
> the writings, trade and commerce of the people who speak
> that particular language.[53]

Gramsci goes on to argue that such a process can only happen
spontaneously and from the bottom up as opposed to the
top-down formulations of both Esperanto and Manzoni. If
Manzoni's plan of imposing a 'living' dialect of Florentine on
Italy was unsuccessful, why should socialists suppose that Esperanto
(with far less prestige or what we may call cultural capital and
actual financial and political backing of the Italian government)
could be successful in an international context? But as Gramsci's
tone makes clear, his point is not just an empirical question of
whether Esperanto or Manzoni's plan will work. Rather, as he
elaborates in great detail in his prison writings, this is a political
argument that the imposition of a national language (or dominant ideology) created by a small elite cannot, given their life
experiences and view of the world, be made to fit the lives and
experiences of others with very different social, class and geographic conditions. To do so is an attempt to suppress their cre-
ativity, productivity, intelligence and ultimately their humanity.
And while hopefully the failure of such an imposition and the
resistance against it will be productive, revolutionary and effective, the danger is that resistance will be ineffective, leading to
perpetual frustration and perhaps irresponsible vandalism and
violence. This is one of the central elements of Gramsci's notion

of hegemony, one that has caused significant trouble for interpreters.[54]

There are several points of importance about Gramsci's argument in this piece, especially since Esperanto becomes an important metaphor in the *Prison Notebooks*. As Lo Piparo argues in relation to the prison writings:

> The metaphoric use of the terms 'language,' 'esperanto,' 'neolalism,' 'lexicon,' for explaining phenomena that are found beyond the strictly linguistic domain is an indication of the intellectual itinerary of Gramsci. In language, in its synchronic functioning and in its history, a microcosm is implicitly recognized, a fundamental component of a more vast and complex social reality.[55]

Gramsci develops this pre-prison critique of Esperanto into a full blown metaphor for artificiality, the plans of an elite being imposed on subaltern classes and their subsequent failure. There are profound parallels between this analysis of Esperanto and his analysis of the Southern Question and critique of the *Risorgimento* as a 'passive revolution' (see Chapter 4). They are all processes whereby subaltern people submit to top-down impositions of specific policies and more general world-views or ideologies, which are in conflict or friction with their own lives, experiences and interests. They are signs of Italy's ongoing lack of a 'national popular collective will'.

In comparing Manzoni's plan to the promotion of Esperanto, Gramsci is offering a more severe critique of Manzoni and the contemporary national language. Where Manzoni had stressed the Romanticist attraction to 'living' language that could be expressive, beautiful, creative and productive, Gramsci argues that, in effect, for most speakers, it is no different from the 'dead' classical literary Italian or a purely artificial language. What is 'living' for the Florentine bourgeoisie is imposed like a dead language on the rest of Italy, especially the southern peasantry.

In the *Prison Notebooks*, Gramsci uses Esperanto in a similar way in his cultural analysis of the importance of theatre on Italian national culture. Analyzing Pirandello's works, he argues that some succeed while others fail in 'getting in tune with the public', because literary language remains 'a largely cosmopolitan language, a type of "Esperanto", limited to the expression of partial notions and feelings'. He uses this as a measure of national cultural unity, which in Italy is lacking.[56]

Moreover, Gramsci uses Esperanto as a metaphor to represent the scientific positivism and naturalism that he is so opposed to, especially because it leads to passive acceptance and parochialism rather than critical engagement to new and different ideas:

> For the Esperantists of philosophy and science, everything that is not expressed in their language is a delirium, a prejudice, a superstition, etc.; making use of an analogous process to what is found in a sectarian mentality, they transform what should be a mere historical judgement into a moral one or into a diagnosis of a psychiatric order.[57]

Gramsci uses the comparison of what he calls 'primitive' people who refer to their own society with the general term for humans but to other societies using words such as 'barbarian', synonymous with 'dumb' or 'stammering'.

One may question his use of Esperanto in such a way. Proponents of Esperanto are often avid translators open to many different points of view and their support for Esperanto is based on its usefulness in cross-cultural communication. But for Gramsci, the idea of a universal language, created outside of its use in people's daily lives, is bound to neglect and pass over their experiences, feelings and especially their participation in the very creation of language and meaning. Thus, just as Marx shows that the problem of capitalism is not the immoral intentions of individual capitalists, but rather the structural nature of the system of capitalism regardless of intentions, so too, Gramsci argues that despite the good intentions of advocates of Esperanto, or Manzoni's approach, the implications are detrimental to subaltern consciousness and freedom.

For these reasons, Gramsci uses Esperanto to represent the most abstract and formulaic aspects of positivism and naturalism. Gramsci is highly critical of what he labels 'sciences-as-fetish', in which the methods from the physical sciences are deemed 'science' par excellence and used as the criteria for other areas of inquiry, especially those dealing with society.[58] Such 'Esperantic' approaches, according to Gramsci, are not only inaccurate, but most fatally they deter people from being 'critical' and 'historical' – both perspectives that Gramsci finds central to

Marxism and the workers' struggle. Chapter 3 describes Gramsci's criticisms of Nikolai Bukharin and positivistic Marxism as being too close to economism. Gramsci explicitly utilizes Esperanto and the idea of 'philosophical Esperantism' as part of this attack.[59]

There is one more positive aspect of Esperanto, or its attractiveness, that Gramsci mentions in another article. In an article in *Avanti!* from 14 June 1920, Gramsci repeated one of his consistent arguments that the proletarian revolution must be a 'total revolution' and that '[t]ogether with the problem of gaining political and economic power, the proletariat must also face the problem of winning intellectual power... it must also think about organizing itself culturally'.[60] In this context he raises the subject of Esperanto again:

> The existence of Esperanto, although it does not demonstrate much in itself and has more to do with bourgeois cosmopolitanism than with proletarian internationalism, shows nevertheless, by the fact that the workers are strongly interested in it and manage to waste their time over it, that there is a desire for and a historical push towards the formation of verbal complexes that transcend national limits and in relation to which current national languages will have the same role as dialects now have.[61]

In classic Gramsci style, even though he rejects the whole idea of Esperanto, he still looks to it as a phenomenon that indicates some positive potentiality.

Thus, while hegemony seems absent from this discussion of Esperanto in 1918 and in the *Prison Notebooks*, as with the term 'hegemony', Gramsci uses 'Esperanto' to connect his cultural and political analysis of how ruling classes are able (or unable) to impose their visions of the world and propagate general ideologies that do not represent subaltern classes, to his philosophical and epistemological critiques of positivism and his concern with scientific and philosophical methodology and knowledge production. Gramsci's 1918 critique of Esperanto is a building block on which he develops his major themes of the 'popular collective will' and its role within hegemony.

## Conclusion

This chapter makes five main points. The first is that the history of Italian unification, including the 'standardization' of Italian, is central to Gramsci's entire framework. It is the basic historical background to several of his key concepts discussed in the next chapters, including the Southern Question, subalternity, the passive revolution, organic intellectuals, civil society and hegemony. Second, Gramsci was familiar with the term 'hegemony' as used by linguists as a synonym for the terms 'prestige' and 'attraction' to describe how certain populations adopt and adapt the linguistic forms of other social groups. We shall see the political implications of these ideas of 'prestige' and 'attraction' in Chapter 3. They are important to how Gramsci uses 'hegemony' to understand the relations of coercion and consent. While consent is sometimes defined as an antonym to coercion, as the absence of coercion, actual operations of power rarely separate them so clearly. Often, the very fact of having power means you do not have to use it, a point that both Machiavelli and Hobbes noted. The most effective way to maintain control is often to create consent, which is easier if you hold the potential use of force in reserve. As we shall see in Chapter 3, at one point Gramsci defines the state as 'hegemony protected by the armour of coercion'.[62]

Point three: Gramsci engaged in a critique of positivist science in the field of linguistics in his university and pre-prison years that mirrors, and helps constitute, his better-known general critique of positivism, especially within Marxism and the economic determinism of the Second International. The fourth point is the other side of point three, that his thorough critique of the Idealism of Croce, which he embarks on in his prison writings, also has linguistic roots in his rejection of Idealist linguistics dating back from his student years.

The last point is the culmination of the previous ones, arising from what Gramsci learned about how to approach the study of language. His view of language and its study is a model that became very useful to him as he developed his Marxist political theory. It is useful precisely because of the major lesson he learned from Bartoli and Ascoli: language is inextricable from culture, politics and society. This is precisely why he found it so useful for social and political analysis, as we see in his early discussions of Esperanto. The next chapters examine in much greater detail how Gramsci developed these linguistic notions into his influential theory of hegemony. This background in Gramsci's linguistics also distinguishes him from Noam Chomsky, Jürgen Habermas and many others who see in language or its structures some autonomous essence or element that makes it unique and separate from other fields of social inquiry. Gramsci took from Bartoli and Ascoli the idea that the history of any given language is the history of its contact, interaction, conflict and mixing with other languages. That is, language does not grow and develop spontaneously, of its own accord. This, as we shall see, is also central to his discussion of 'spontaneity' in general, which is directly related to how he understands the political categories of coercion and consent.

# 3
# Language and Hegemony in the *Prison Notebooks*

The term 'hegemony' has a long history before Gramsci. Derived from *hegemon*, literally meaning leader, and its Greek root, ηγεμονία, hegemony traditionally signifies some combination of authority, leadership and domination.[1] In Ancient Greece, it was usually distinguished from domination precisely in that the *hegemon* had only limited control or influence and the subject retained much autonomy. Thus, in the fifth century BC, Athens had a hegemony over the other city-states in central Greece. The other city-states were autonomous but followed the military, political and cultural leadership of Athens. *Hegemon* describes the leader of an alliance rather than the capital city of a state or the ruling country of an empire. This notion of hegemony did include an aspect of military supremacy as well as of cultural superiority and leadership. But the source of hegemony was not the direct threat of overt coercion.

These two features, military predominance and cultural prestige, are evident in much of the term's history, including its usage in Russian social democratic circles from the 1880s onwards. Georgi Plekhanov developed the term 'hegemony' to combat economism (the position that economic laws beyond human control dictate future social and political developments). To address the Russian situation in the late nineteenth century of a small and weak proletariat facing an autocratic aristocracy not threatened by the weak bourgeoisie, Plekhanov wrote about the need for a class hegemony. Drawing explicitly from Engels' work, *The Peasant War in Germany*, Plekhanov argued that such conditions compelled the Social Democratic leaders to broaden their political struggle even if that meant accepting that their economic goals would not be met immediately. Lenin, picking up from Plekhanov, added to this link between hegemony and consciousness a greater sense of the questions of alliance building – specifically the relatively small proletariat leading the peasantry and using its material dissatisfaction to fuel a revolutionary struggle. For Lenin, hegemony was a concept used to theorize how the proletariat could secure power through an alliance with the peasantry against not only the Czarist state but also the more liberal and bourgeois forces.[2]

Our question is, what did Gramsci contribute to the concept of hegemony and how did he change it into a term that has had much greater prominence in social, political and cultural theory? Why has Gramsci's name become almost synonymous with the term hegemony, when Lenin's and Plekhanov's uses of the term remain relatively obscure? How was the domain of 'hegemony' expanded from international relations and revolutionary politics to analyses of education, literature, films, popular culture, ideology and the administrative organization of everyday modern (and postmodern) life? How does Gramsci's hegemony go beyond strategic questions of alliance building across different political movements (or 'new social movements')? Are there limits or disadvantages to such wide usage of the term 'hegemony'? What does it mean when Gramsci's hegemony is referred to as a theory of the organization of consent?

As we shall see, it may be suitable to start one's understanding of Gramsci's hegemony as the organization of consent. But that is not sufficient, and it also has the danger of falsely separating and opposing coercion and consent. One of Gramsci's greatest contributions is his investigation of the complex relationships between coercion and consent in democratic capitalist societies. He was continually perceptive about how the possibility or threat of coercion and subtle uses of it are often integral to shaping and organizing consent.[3]

## Approaching the *Prison Notebooks*

It was not until Gramsci was imprisoned and began his famous *Prison Notebooks*, that he really developed a *unique* concept of hegemony. As we have seen in the previous chapter, Gramsci had espoused many of the ideas about language, culture, political power and resistance that would become integral to his notion of hegemony. But he did not incorporate them into what is now understood as his conception of hegemony until his prison writings. Arguably, even the *Prison Notebooks* fail to articulate clear, unambiguous definitions for most of their essential concepts: hegemony, passive revolution, wars of position/ manoeuvre, intellectuals, subalternity, historical bloc and civil society. Instead of defining concepts, the *Prison Notebooks* contain investigations that use these concepts. Gramsci does not tell us what such concepts mean in a consistent and precise way. Rather he shows us how he uses them to analyse various historical situations. It is almost as if he is practising Wittgenstein's dictum, 'the meaning of a word is its use in the language', rather than some stated definition prior to its use.[4]

Similarly, Gramsci rarely invents new terms or concepts but instead works with previously existing terminology that his readers will be familiar with from other authors or contexts – 'intellectuals', 'hegemony', 'civil society' – and transforms them. As Anne Showstack Sassoon has noted, '… he uses ordinary or traditional words to signify something new and, further, he often uses a word both in a traditional way and in a novel and sometimes an almost absurd manner'.[5] Much of Gramsci's analytic process is the 'subversion', to use Sassoon's term, of given language and concepts by stretching and altering them. Chapter 4 illustrates how he transforms the term 'passive revolution' that he derives from Vincenzo Cuoco and how he adopts military expressions such as 'war of manoeuvre'. This chapter discusses another military metaphor central to his thought; 'subaltern', originally meaning 'of subordinate military rank'. We shall also see how Gramsci transforms Benedetto Croce's notion that everyone is a philosopher.

On one hand, Gramsci's use of language in this way can make his writings quite difficult to understand. Terms like 'war of manoeuvre' or 'subaltern' may not be from a jargon that you are familiar with. Moreover, as Sassoon describes, sometimes it is difficult to figure out whether Gramsci is using the term in the usual sense or in his own new and expanded sense. On the other hand, this method of refusing to coin new jargon – 'neolalism' is the term Gramsci uses – is a prescient strategy that fits Gramsci's political argument very well. Just as he does not want rural peasants to adopt a language imposed on them from somewhere else, he does not want readers to adopt a new set of terms that are defined outside of their usage. Kate Crehan notes this characteristic of

Gramsci's writings: 'Paradoxically, the new, however revolutionary it may in fact be, must (if it is to be intelligible) be expressed,
at least initially, in existing language and concepts.'[6]

Gramsci then works to alter such concepts, organizing them,
making them richer in meaning, comparing them to other concepts, and using them in other 'language games', to borrow
Wittgenstein's term. And this process does not occur in abstract,
philosophical reasoning, but with historical examples and concrete situations. Our difficulty is that many of these situations
are not concrete to readers with little knowledge of Italian history.
But the pragmatic nature of Gramsci's method comes through
nevertheless.

Gramsci's major goal in writing this way was to understand
how he and the Italian communists had failed and the Fascists
had succeeded in gaining and maintaining power. Thus we will
search in vain in the *Prison Notebooks* for definitive and static
answers to the questions that our society faces. When we read
Gramsci we should look instead for examples of how to carry
out thorough and useful analysis.

The other obvious reason for the difficulty in reading
Gramsci's *Prison Notebooks* is that they were written under the
very difficult conditions of a Fascist prison and he never had the
chance to finish them or put them in a form for publication. In
various published selections of these notebooks, editors and
translators have attempted this work. Other scholars have
argued that Gramsci's theory cannot be made consistent in all
its parts but remains fundamentally incoherent.[7] From this perspective, Gramsci may be an important figure in the history of
political and social thought, but his ideas are not very relevant
nor useful for understanding current social and political forces
or movements. Moreover, all those who have found Gramsci's
ideas and concepts useful would have to be written off as
confused.

Rather than either bemoan the unfinished nature of Gramsci's
notes or try to overcome it by fixing and polishing them, many
have argued that there is something to be gained from an active
use of conceptual categories without a set of fixed or static
definitions. This is the idea underlying the publication of the
critical edition of the *Prison Notebooks* and their translations.
Joseph Buttigieg, editor and translator of the English critical

edition, has emphasized the importance of 'attending carefully to the rhythms of Gramsci's thinking, ... his procedures and methods of analysis and composition ... and even to the fragmentariness itself of his whole effort'.[8] Others have emphasized the advantages of the more fluid and network-like nature of the *Prison Notebooks*, coupled with their heavy emphasis on historical examples rather than abstract definitions.[9]

While emphasizing such approaches to Gramsci, it is obviously necessary to introduce his concepts and theories in some accessible fashion. Many commentators have done so by relating the various themes of his arguments to what has been deemed his most important concept, hegemony. This chapter follows such an approach but does so by focusing on a linguistic understanding of hegemony. Using the context of the previous chapter, this chapter brings together fragmentary and seemingly disparate passages in the *Prison Notebooks* in which Gramsci addresses language, linguistics and grammar. Many of these sections appear within his discussions of philosophy, epistemology, Italian history, literature, culture and education; they are often difficult to understand due to their disjointed nature and the now arcane debates to which Gramsci continually refers. Yet piecing together these various perspectives involving language and linguistics will illuminate Gramsci's central themes of hegemony, the role of intellectuals, the importance of culture and folklore and his analysis of civil society.

Chapter 5 describes how this linguistic view of hegemony does more than just illuminate Gramsci's own writings; it allows us to see more clearly how his theory relates to positions, developed after his death, that use language as a central metaphor for social analysis, especially to current debates around postmodernism and globalized commodity production.

## Non-Linguistic understandings of hegemony

As noted above, Gramsci adds a number of dimensions to both the traditional notion of hegemony as leadership and the more specific ways it was used by the Russian Social Democrats, Plekhanov and Lenin, to signify the way the proletariat was to foster an alliance with the peasantry. It is this question of alliance building that has clear implications for contemporary politics, especially concerning the relations amongst the Left, women's movements, gay and lesbian movements, environmentalists, antiracist struggles, peace and antipoverty activists. In Gramsci's hands, the term hegemony became more analytic. He applied it to various types of leadership and rule, especially those of which he was critical. It was not only a theory of 'what is to be done?' as it had been for Lenin and Plekhanov. Gramsci also used it to analyse and criticize what one's adversaries have done. This facet has also led to some confusion about the extent to which Gramsci advocates hegemony. What is the difference between the bourgeois, semi-feudal or Fascist hegemonies that he criticizes and the hegemony that he advocates? Others have addressed this distinction by introducing the term 'counter-hegemony', but this is not a term Gramsci uses. It is sometimes unclear if Gramsci is using the term 'hegemony' as a critical term describing an almost watered-down form of domination or if he is using it more positively to describe how the working class or communists should proceed to gain power.

Joseph Femia provides a useful typology of three basic ways in which Gramsci uses hegemony; integral, decadent and minimal. *Integral hegemony* is the version or 'ideal type' that Gramsci advocated. Femia describes it as a situation of 'mass affiliation [that] would approach unqualified commitment' by all (or most) of society towards those that rule.[10] Such affiliation and commitment – what Gramsci will call the 'national–popular collective will' – is obtained because the ruling group is able to meet and surpass not only its own interests but also the needs and desires of all the major social groups. Many liberal, pluralist and postmodern thinkers find that even this most progressive version of Gramsci's hegemony resonates with a certain totalitarianism in that, as the above quotations indicate, what is hoped for is 'unqualified commitment'. Such approaches are suspicious of goals and ideals aimed at eliminating dissent or interpreting criticisms of the government as signs of systemic power imbalances. Liberal pluralists contend that it is impossible to reconcile competing values held by different members of a community. Thus, Gramsci's aim of even the most democratic, progressive and popular integral hegemony will squash certain individual's values and decrease pluralism. As we shall see, that Gramsci saw language structures as one model for hegemony provides a different understanding of this tension between Gramsci's advocacy for an *integral* hegemony and a respect for differences within such a hegemony. One can be a proponent of a single language without arguing that everyone should say the same thing or hold the same position within that language. Language is a fascinating metaphor since its very structure, that which constitutes it as a language, is what allows for the creation of different meanings within it. Moreover, Gramsci understood language as a human institution that should and will change with usage.

The crucial point about the *integral* hegemony that Gramsci was trying to create is that in it the relationship between leaders and led would not be contradictory or antagonistic, rather it would be 'organic'[11] and continuous; an educative and reciprocal relationship. Gramsci gives the historical example of post-revolutionary France, when the bourgeoisie forced economic, political and cultural changes that, he maintains, addressed the needs of France as a whole, not just the corporate interests of the middle and professional classes. He also clearly had the proletariat in mind as the potential leaders for such a hegemony in early twentieth-century Italy. As we shall in Chapter 5, scholars such as Ernesto Laclau and Chantal Mouffe maintain that this is an economically 'essentialist' theory that 'assumes' – that is, unjustifiably presupposes – that an economic class (the bourgeoisie or proletariat) is the leading element in a hegemony. It seems undeniable that Gramsci was concerned with the economy and production and, like us, might have difficulty imaging a world where our needs and desires did not involve production. Thus he did argue that social groups form, at least in part, due to people's role within the economy. But, as I will argue, Gramsci's notion of hegemony does not so much presuppose this to be universally the case as argues why, in early twentieth-century Italy, it was the industrial proletariat that had the greatest (and perhaps the only) potential to form an active hegemony that included the peasantry and could revolutionize society. Of course, Gramsci was all too aware as he sat in prison that this potentiality had not been met. In all his efforts to figure out the rise of Fascism, he never did find a reason to question the importance of the working class. The crucial point here is that Gramsci saw this notion of what Femia calls *integral hegemony* as a morally and politically justifiable and exemplary goal.

Femia's notion of *decadent hegemony* is that of an outmoded form of leadership that has lost its integral nature and decayed. That is, a ruling class – the feudal aristocracy and bourgeoisie are Gramsci's historical examples – is unable to maintain the ability to further everyone's interest and it loses the mass and active support and commitment of large portions of the population. Such a hegemonic class maintains its predominance mostly due to the lack of an effective alternative challenging it.

Femia labels *minimal hegemony* the type of hegemony that Gramsci is most critical of – one that applies only to portions of society, most commonly elites. They govern primarily to bolster their corporate interests and rule by *trasformismo*, that is by transforming or incorporating the leaders of antagonistic social groups into their elite networks. Here hegemony looks most like domination and requires a greater degree of coercion in order to maintain its power. It is best characterized by Gramsci's assessment of Italy's 'passive revolution', which we will examine in Chapter 4.

Femia's typology is a useful starting place because it raises several issues central to hegemony; the relationship between leaders and led, between coercion and consent and the degree to which it is active or passive. It shows that while hegemony in its integral sense can be seen as based on consent and opposed to coercion,[12] the other two forms of hegemony, decadent and minimal, include significant degrees of coercion. But Femia's typology does not specifically address our concerns, especially those concerning the relationship between linguistic and economic activity. Moreover, looking at Gramsci's writings on language as a metaphor for these different types, or differing degrees of hegemony, we will come to a more nuanced and detailed picture of Gramsci's concerns, a picture that has become more relevant with developments central to the twenty-first century, outlined in Chapter 1. We need to step back from Femia's three types of hegemony and reframe the question of hegemony in a manner that emphasizes its explanatory power and applicability to more contemporary debates on language, agency and power in relation to economic and class analysis.

### Two broad themes in hegemony

Gramsci's hegemony can be seen to incorporate two broad themes. The first is the expansion of the definition of politics from activities of government and operations of state power to questions of how people come to understand the world. That is, Gramsci's notion of hegemony is rich in large part due to its philosophical and epistemological elements that show how seemingly private or personal aspects of daily life are politically important aspects of the operation of power. This point, that capitalist hegemony includes structuring our everyday lives, feelings and ideas, has been best captured by the women's movements' slogan, 'the personal is political' and feminist scholarship on distinctions between public and private. In this context, Gramsci's focus on language is crucial to understanding how we interpret the world and create meaning. As with later 'linguistic turns' especially semiotic investigations of popular culture, Gramsci's attention to language provides insights into the daily and molecular operations of power.

The second, and equally important, broad theme of Gramsci's hegemony consists of institutional and social analysis of various classes and organizations in society, from actions of the state, to the realm of 'civil society' and institutions such as schools, churches, newspapers, book publishers and entertainment enterprises (as will be discussed in Chapter 5). Hegemony enables institutional analyses of ideology. Much of Gramsci's influence is attributable to his successful connections between the various elements in these two broad themes. Likewise, his insights on language are powerful in relating institutional analysis to philosophical and cultural questions of meaning.

Relating these two themes, Gramsci also addresses perhaps the most fundamental relationship of democratic political theory: namely, the relationship between coercion and consent. Since seventeenth century English liberalism and eighteenth century French Enlightenment, the idea that governments rule legitimately because of the consent of those governed has been central to political theory. Moreover, with the social contract and natural law theories of Hobbes and Locke, such consent was understood on an individual basis. It was not an abstract or generalized notion of society recognizing and accepting a monarch's rule. Hobbes' famous articulation of the formation of a Commonwealth is a covenant made by every individual to every individual.[13]

How is this consent formed? Does it involve the absence of coercion and violence?[14] How does this relate to Max Weber's observation that the state is defined by its monopoly in the legitimate use of coercion or violence within a territory?[15] All these questions central to political and social theory relate to one of Gramsci's consistent concerns, the relation between coercion and consent. His discussions of hegemony, his broadening of the realm of politics and his focus on institutions within society all address our understanding of this relationship. His writings on linguistics provide a suitable terrain on which to map his conceptualization of coercion, consent and hegemony. Language also illustrates a narrower version of these two broad themes of all of his writings – the expansion of the political and an organizational analysis.

## Gramsci's expansion of 'politics'

As illustrated in Chapter 2 with the example of Esperanto, Gramsci expands the very definition of what is political by using language as a metaphor for how we conceive of the world. It is central to his investigations into questions of knowledge and ideology. He makes philosophical and epistemological issues relevant to politics and the operations of power. In addition to language being a useful metaphor, Gramsci is also concerned with the literal role of languages and institutions such as schools, newspapers and popular novels. As we saw in the previous chapters, language in late nineteenth- and early twentieth-century Italy was generally understood as a political issue. Looking at these two broad aspects of Gramsci's writings on language provides a clearer picture of the complex theory of coercion and consent that constitutes his understanding of hegemony. Chapter 4 addresses how this notion of hegemony relates to his other major concepts and distinctions such as passive revolution, war of manoeuvre/position and state/civil society.

## Language, philosophy and intellectuals

Gramsci understands language as intricately connected to how we think about and make sense of the world. Thus, it is central to politics and hegemony. As we saw in the previous chapter, he argued against the tradition of the historical linguists especially in the extreme form of the Neogrammarians, who viewed language as a collection of words, sounds and phrases that change over time. He found such views too narrow and incapable of answering the important questions of how language and different languages function within society, politics and culture. He also rejected the Idealist approaches of Benedetto Croce and Karl Vossler, which saw language as the conglomeration of individual aesthetic expressions. Instead, language plays a central role in how Gramsci describes his influential ideas about intellectual activity, his distinction between 'organic' and 'traditional' intellectuals and his notions of philosophy and common sense.

In the *Prison Notebooks*, Gramsci expands his conception of language and how it relates to everyday life, politics, culture and philosophy. Language becomes integral to his redefining of the very idea of philosophy. It is worth quoting a long section from the *Prison Notebooks*:

> It is essential to destroy the widespread prejudice that philosophy is a strange and difficult thing just because it is the specific intellectual activity of a particular category of specialists or of professional and systematic philosophers. It must first be shown that all men are 'philosophers', by defining the limits and characteristics of 'spontaneous philosophy' which is proper to everyone. This philosophy is contained in: 1. *language itself*, which is a totality of determined notions and concepts and not just words grammatically devoid of content; 2. 'common sense' and 'good sense'; 3. popular religion and, therefore, also in the entire system of beliefs, superstitions, opinions, ways of seeing things and of acting which are collectively bundled together under the name of 'folklore'.
>
> Having first shown that everyone is a philosopher, though in his own way and unconsciously, since even in the slightest manifestation of any intellectual activity whatever, in 'language', there is contained a specific conception of the world, one then moves on to the second level, which is that of awareness and criticism ...[16]

There are many points in this passage that need to be unpacked.

Gramsci attacks the elitist idea that philosophy or intellectual activity is somehow beyond the ability of most people. Rather everyone performs intellectual activity or 'spontaneous philosophy' and the designation of some as professional philosophers or 'traditional' intellectuals has to do with how they organize ideas and understandings of the world in such a manner that makes them useful for the dominant social group. Gramsci explains:

> All men are intellectuals ... but not all men have in society the function of intellectuals. ... When one distinguishes between intellectuals and non-intellectuals, one is referring in reality only to the immediate social function of the professional category of the intellectuals. ... There is no human activity from which every form of intellectual participation can be excluded: *homo faber* cannot be separated from *homo sapiens*.[17]

Gramsci is rejecting the notion that 'philosophers' or intellectuals, in the traditional sense, are those who think or reason well, whereas the rest of us do not. For him, we cannot define 'intellectual activity' by its 'intrinsic nature' but must locate it in 'the ensemble of the system of relations in which these activities (and therefore the intellectual groups who personify them) have their place within the general complex of social relations'.[18]

Professional philosophers or traditional intellectuals are distinguished not by their intellectual activity per se, but because of how such activity functions within society, the effect it has on presenting a specific world-view. Thus everyone implicitly holds a philosophy, as seen in their general belief systems, opinions, and also their 'common sense' and 'good sense', that is their everyday sense of practical issues.

This is a classic example of Gramsci's method described above. He is taking the idea that everyone is a philosopher from Benedetto Croce and turning it on its head, so to speak. Croce's point is that philosophy has an impact on everyday understandings of the world, on common sense. Unlike English, the Italian notion of common sense (*senso comune*) does not so much mean good, sound, practical sense, rather it means normal or average understanding.[19] So in Italian, good sense (*buon senso*) is more distinct from 'common sense' than in English. For Croce, important philosophical ideas and systems find their way into popular and everyday beliefs and opinions.[20] Gramsci questions Croce on this: 'Croce often likes to feel that certain philosophical propositions are shared by common sense. But what can this mean concretely? Common sense is a chaotic aggregate of disparate conceptions, and one can find there anything that one likes.'[21] The issue then becomes one of organization, awareness and criticism. In other words, philosophers or intellectuals are a distinct group not because of the 'essence' of intellectual activity but because of how they are effective in organizing the elements of common sense. It is the function of intellectuals that defines them, not any privileged access to 'truth' or 'reason'. This is how Gramsci redefines the very idea of intellectuality:

> The most widespread error of method seems to me that of having looked for this criterion of distinction in the intrinsic nature of intellectual activities, rather than in the ensemble of the system of relations in which these activities (and therefore the intellectual groups who personify them) have their place within the general complex of social relations.[22]

Thus, it is not the activity itself that qualifies or fails to qualify as 'intellectual' or philosophical. Philosophers and intellectuals do not necessarily possess higher intelligence or profundity or even a greater ability to reason per se. Rather, professional philosophers and traditional intellectuals perform different functions from other people. This is not to say that Gramsci rejects the importance of sound reasoning or the difficult work required to think, study and analyse. Quite the contrary, he places great emphasis on the arduous *work* and training that scholarship and effective intellectual ability require.[23] But his point is that being an intellectual is a position within society and it has to do with the way you organize and disseminate ideas and the impact that they have. One's ideas are never free floating and totally individual but rather they are rooted in one's position within society. 'Philosophy in general does not in fact exist. Various philosophies or conceptions of the world exist, and one always makes a choice between them.'[24] And whether we are aware of it or not, that choice has to do with our position in society, especially our class position.

This is the root of his distinction between traditional and 'organic' intellectuals. A traditional intellectual is one who puts herself or himself forward as 'autonomous and independent of the dominant social group'[25] but who functions as an intellectual of the dominant social group. Sometimes, like the clergy, they pre-exist the dominant social group and are absorbed by them. At other times, they are formed 'organically' as the dominant social group rises to power. Industrial technicians and managers are 'organically' bound to capitalist entrepreneurs. The common characteristic of the various different kinds of intellectuals, whether they are professional intellectuals, like scientists, philosophers and writers who deal explicitly with ideas, or 'functionaries' like technicians, notaries, lawyers, teachers and even organizers of political parties, is that they all organize ideas and present ways of understanding the world that are adopted by others.

The 'organic' character of intellectuals comes from the degree to which they are bound to a specific social group. This binding is not solely a question of class origins or where they live and work. It is a question of the relationship between the ideas they put forth (the understanding of the world that they propagate) and their position within society. In other words, the 'organic' quality of intellectual activity is related to how people justify the way a given society is organized and their role in that organization. This is seen in a most pronounced way in the Church intellectuals, who, vowing celibacy, were unable to reproduce themselves, and depended upon recruits mostly from the peasantry. But the ecclesiastics from peasant backgrounds are not 'organic' in that their religious world-view, according to Gramsci, does not come from the life *activity* of being a peasant. To explain this we need to look at Gramsci's use of 'organic' and his distinction between thought and action.

Gramsci uses the term 'organic' in a complex manner. It has the overtones common in social theory of being non-mechanical and non-artificial. We have already seen Gramsci's emphasis on 'ensembles' and 'relations', which lends the term 'organic' a sense of being related to an organism or an organ, with all the parts functioning together and in relation. As is evident with his discussion of intellectuals and their role in society, organization seems to be a key factor. The other major distinction that Gramsci invokes with the term 'organic' is against 'conjunctural'. He discusses 'organic' movements and phenomena as more fundamental, relatively permanent and structural; whereas 'conjunctural' ones are ever-changing combinations that are immediate, ephemeral and almost accidental.[26] Once again, looking to the linguistic roots of Gramsci's vocabulary is helpful. The linguistic term 'organic' means related to the root or etymological structure of the word rather than being secondary, incidental or fortuitous, such as verb conjugations or endings indicating case or a plural.

In a sense, then, all intellectuals have an 'organic' quality unless they are totally idiosyncratic, in which case they will lack influence and be ineffective. Traditional intellectuals are those that obscure their organic connections, presenting themselves as independent and autonomous. They act as if they are presenting an 'objective world-view' that is not connected to the dominant class or most powerful social groups of the time.[27] Gramsci indicates that this occurs almost always because such intellectuals do function to help legitimate the status quo and thus the dominant social group. The pope may present himself as linked to Christ just as professional philosophers see themselves connected to Aristotle and Plato, but the ideas they propagate will be influential or not depending on the sociopolitical forces in society.[28]

Traditional intellectuals act as 'functionaries' of the complex mediation whereby 'social hegemony' is secured through attaining a seemingly ' "spontaneous" consent given by the great masses of the population to the general direction imposed on social life. ...'[29] We shall see below why Gramsci puts 'spontaneous' in quotation marks, since it is not simply 'spontaneous' but the result of the activity of intellectuals.

Language then is a central feature of how Gramsci thinks about intellectuals, philosophy and common sense. As he states in the above quotation, 'in "language", there is contained a specific conception of the world. ...' and that philosophy is contained in 'language itself, which is a totality of determined notions and concepts and not just words grammatically devoid of content'. Gramsci uses the metaphor of language to analyse different possibilities for organizing 'common sense' and philosophies which are central to the notion of hegemony and why people consent to the power of the dominant social group.

## Subalternity and fragmented 'common sense'

From these descriptions of language, we can see not only that Gramsci is tying language to culture, philosophy and ideology, but that in doing so, he uses language to describe one of the most important aspects of his political theory: the fact that phi-losophy cannot be divorced from politics and the operations of power.[30] It is of the greatest political consequence, he argues, that there are discrepancies between the thoughts and actions of people in subaltern social groups – people who accept the hege-mony of a ruling class that has very different interests from their own. Other Marxists understand ideology as a 'false conscious-ness' or deception based on ignorance, lack of fortitude and intellect. Gramsci suggests that this may explain why individu-als hold views that are at odds with their own experiences and lives, but it cannot explain why whole groups of people adopt such positions.

Gramsci maintains that subaltern social groups have their own conceptions of the world, although these conceptions may be embryonic and manifest themselves only in action, not in coherent and articulated thought or language. This is one of the key elements in Gramsci's development of the term 'subaltern'. Gramsci's elaboration of the concept of 'subalternity' is another example of his thinking through existing language, not invent-ing new terms, but applying concepts from one field to a wider one. As Marcus Green has shown, in Gramsci's initial prison writings he uses the term 'subaltern' literally, to mean lower ranks of military personnel who are subordinate to captains. He then expands it, referring at one point to Engels as subaltern to Marx,[31] and finally to refer to a variety of non-dominant social groups, including not only the working class, peasants and slaves but also religious groups, women, and various racial groups.[32] One of the central aspects that makes all these social groups subaltern is that they lack a coherent philosophy or world-view from which to understand and interpret the world. One could say, they lack their own language. Rather they work with a 'common sense' that is a fragmentary result of the sedi-mentation of ideas and beliefs elaborated by various traditional intellectuals who are organically related to other social groups with different experiences and places within society. Not only are their thought and belief systems fragmentary but they do not correspond sensibly to their own lives and experiences.

Again, a long passage is worth quoting:

In acquiring one's conception of the world one always belongs to a particular grouping which is that of all the social elements which share the same mode of thinking and acting. ... When one's conception of the world is not critical and coherent but disjointed and episodic, one belongs simultaneously to a multiplicity of mass human groups. The personality is strangely composite: it contains Stone Age elements and principles of a more advanced science, prejudices from all past phases of history at the local level and intuitions of a future philosophy which will be that of a human race united the world over. ... The starting-point of critical elaboration is the consciousness of what one really is, and is 'knowing thyself' as a product of the historical process to date which has deposited in you an infinity of traces, without leaving an inventory. It is necessary initially to make such an inventory.[33]

Here is one of Gramsci's most important contributions to the analysis of ideology and consciousness. Subalternity and domination are not only physical domination, power and control over the use of resources. They are constituted by the inability to develop a coherent world-view, a 'spontaneous' philosophy that actually relates to your own life and place in society. This is not only an integral aspect of domination; it is also a key factor that prevents subaltern groups from being able to effectively resist physical domination and the exercise of power against them.

Following Marx's discussion of alienation, Gramsci focuses on the gap between thought and action. As he states:

This contrast between thought and action, i.e. the co-existence of two conceptions of the world, one affirmed in words and the other displayed in effective action, is not simply a product of self-deception [*malafede*]. Self-deception can be an adequate explanation for a few individuals taken separately, or even for groups of a certain size, but it is not adequate when the contrast occurs in the life of great masses. In these cases the contrast between thought and action cannot but be the expression of profounder contrasts of a social historical order.[34]

Because these groups often do not have effective intellectuals of their own, they are subordinated and adopt conceptions which are not their own but borrowed from the hegemonic social group.[35] Such conceptions are necessarily 'passive'.[36] The members do not actively participate in creating or critically assessing the philosophies that guide their lives. They just accept them, but suffer the consequences of continual incoherence and contradiction between their actions and their thoughts.

Let us use a specific example to illustrate this point: the continual support of the working classes for property rights. It is obvious why property owners think that it is essential to have protection of private property and the ability to do with it what one pleases without worry about it losing value. But how do people who for generations have been unable to amass any substantial amount of property come to have such a respect for property rights? Why do people with little empirical experience of class mobility and achieving, for example, the 'American dream' of owning one's house, come to rely on it as a mainstay of their own understandings of 'freedom'? Or to raise another example, why did so many people, especially in the working classes, support the Fascists and Nazis in Italy and Germany? Gramsci rejects the simplistic answers that these people are tricked or duped by evil geniuses like Hitler and Mussolini. This is a common mainstream explanation that is used time and time again to explain why people in oppressive regimes do not rise up against totalitarian dictators, whether Joseph Stalin, Idi Amin or Saddam Hussein. Where liberals often focus on the individual attributes of the brutal dictators, Marxists have been more insistent that we explain in a plausible fashion how such ruthless individuals were able to come to power against challenges from other potential leaders. Of course, ignoring the masses' role in how dictators come to power suggests that the masses are either powerless or lack the intelligence or ability to have any effect. One of the few characteristics that all these different dictatorial regimes shared is that they were not good – by almost any definition of 'good' outside some Aryan or nationalist fantasy – for the majority of the people. So why did such large proportions of people support Hitler and Mussolini even when they had little to offer the average people in terms of their actual interests? Gramsci presents a much more complex method of analysis that takes into account not just these isolated ideas, property rights or authoritarian regimes, but the entire system of thought of which they are a part, the whole world-view that accompanies them.

Because values and ideas are not unconnected sets of interests but components of ideologies, they must be countered in a more holistic way. Gramsci adds to the discussion of ideologies that they are not just sets of ideas presented by intellectuals, but rather they derive from institutions, organizations and life activities that create and support them. Fundamental beliefs and values may not even be explicit or conscious. Because of this, it is not enough for Marxism to provide a critique of capitalism or Fascism. A group of traditional intellectuals who have never worked in a factory nor been exploited will have a very difficult time convincing workers that their view of the world is superior in any way to that of the capitalists whose ideas seem so much more congruent to how the world actually works. Such 'traditional' Marxist intellectuals have neither the institutional support nor the life activities to present an effective alternative. Gramsci understood that for many people, Marxist views seem demonstrably inferior to the hegemonic world-views since it is the capitalist world-view that shapes the world.

Gramsci's notion of hegemony raises a similar issue within Marxist theory: if capitalism is so detrimental to working people, why do working people continue to vote for parties that support capitalism? Moreover, as the Marxist reformist Eduard Bernstein argued in 1899, if Marx is correct that the working class is growing and destined to be a majority (or even the largest minority), why not just wait and vote in communism?[37] While Vladimir Lenin and Rosa Luxemburg revealed specific flaws in this reformism, the most crucial facet of this debate for most of the twentieth century was that of ideology.

Gramsci's approach is more sophisticated than that of 'false consciousness' for several reasons. Primarily, it enables us to analyse the complexity of how people determine their various and often conflicting ideas, values and actions. To argue that vast numbers of people have simply been duped and lack the intelligence to 'see the light' of Marxism drastically oversimplifies the situation. It hides precisely those elements that Gramsci argues are important to understanding why people consent to rule and how they adopt values and attitudes towards life and politics. These include religious ideas and religious institutions, school systems, folklore, family structures, tradition and what Gramsci generally labels 'common sense'. Moreover, as individuals, in an individualistic society, it becomes difficult to argue that it is in anyone's 'real' interest to resist the status quo and those values and rights that can be seen to improve their lives.

## Language, nation, collective popular will

In addition to stating that language is one of three locations of 'spontaneous philosophy', Gramsci explicitly relates the study of language to his concern with hegemony and its correlates, the role of intellectuals, culture and national–popular unity. He proposes to study the relation between intellectuals and the 'people–nation' in terms of language and specifically the tensions between Latin and the vernaculars in medieval Italy.[38] It is from differences between literary Latin and spoken Italian dialects that Gramsci deduces '... a split between the people and the intellectuals, between people and [high] culture'.[39] This split is at the root of his distinction between traditional and organic intellectuals and his development of hegemony. As he writes:

> I feel that if language is understood as an element of culture, and thus of general history, a key manifestation of the 'nationality' and 'popularity' of the intellectuals, this study [of the history of the Italian language] is not pointless and merely erudite.[40]

He repeats this point, specifically tying the investigation of language to the notion of hegemony:

> Every time that the question of language surfaces, in one way or another, it means that a series of other problems are coming to the fore: the formation and enlargement of the governing class, the need to establish more intimate and secure relationships between the governing groups and the national–popular mass, in other words to recognize the cultural hegemony.[41]

Thus, language is an important constituent element of hegemony. It is central to Femia's distinction between integral hegemony as consent and commitment of much of the population and decadent and minimal hegemony that applies to certain sections or social groups, but fails to have active popular commitment.

Gramsci continues in elaborating his notion of 'language' (often placing it in quotation marks); 'in language, there is contained a specific conception of the world. ...' Elsewhere he repeats this sentiment, emphasizing how closely language is tied to understanding and thinking, including how the lack of knowledge of specific languages is limiting:

> If it is true that every language contains elements of a con-
> ception of the world and of a culture, it could also be true that
> from anyone's language one can assess the greater or lesser
> complexity of his conception of the world. Someone who
> only speaks dialect, or understands the standard language
> incompletely, necessarily has an intuition of the world which
> is more or less limited and provincial, which is fossilised and
> anachronistic in relation to the major currents of thought
> which dominate world history.[42]

Gramsci is not only defining language in a technical sense, he is
using language as an analytical tool with which to investigate
different conceptions of the world, different philosophies. And,
like language, our 'spontaneous philosophies' are neither
absolutely consistent nor are they just an arbitrary set of unrelated
ideas. ' "[L]anguage" is in reality a multiplicity of facts more or
less organically coherent and co-ordinated.'[43] It is in this sense,
Gramsci argues, that we can even say language actually means
'culture and philosophy (if only at the level of common
sense)'.[44]

As we shall see in the next chapter, one of Gramsci's great
insights is that people's desires, values and actions are connected
to the institutional arrangement of society. Thus, Gramsci ties his
conception of hegemony to definitions of the state and civil society. The question is *where* this organization of consent or this
intellectual and moral leadership, broadly defined, is located
within society? Is hegemony created by the actions of the government, narrowly defined? Does it include operations of the
judicial system, police forces, agencies such as those for child and
family services, welfare, etc. ...? Does it include public schools,
private schools, churches and religious institutions, private clubs
and associations? Does it take place in our places of work, factory
floors and office buildings? Within the mass media?

Of course, the answers to such questions vary tremendously
from society to society and throughout different periods in
history. Gramsci's answers are mostly directed at early twentieth-
century Italy, with comparisons to the rest of Europe and Russia
and earlier periods in history. We might ask, how are Gramsci's

answers informative for us in the twenty-first century, especially outside Italy? The answer is that Gramsci provides a set of concepts and a framework for posing such questions. That is, he does not so much provide a theory or analysis himself that is particularly useful to us, but he shows us a very powerful method, a process of analysis.

For these reasons, language becomes a powerful element of Gramsci's argument that culture and everyday philosophies are essential to political analysis. The language situation in Italy (discussed in Chapter 2) was a useful metaphor for what Gramsci was saying about culture, world-views and hegemony. That is, people spoke different dialects from one another, they saw the world differently. Such linguistic differences were distributed along North–South lines in Italy, not unlike the economic, social and cultural differences. The industrialized regions of northern Italy had dialects which were comparatively similar to each other, but quite different from those of the South. But on top of these dialect differences, a national, standard language was being imposed. This standard Italian was based on the dialect from Florence in the North. While the dialects and national languages had some similarities in grammar and lexicon, there were vast differences between them, making them mutually unintelligible. But, as with ideologies, using 'standardized' Italian was not a matter of changing individual words. 'Standardization' is the process of adopting a whole new system of words along with a new grammar. It had the material benefit of enabling people to understand newspapers, books and, by the 1920s and 1930s, the radio, which brought ideas and information from outside one's region. But it also created confusions for older people who had not learned 'standard Italian', making it difficult for them to understand the young and maintain a sense of continuity and tradition within the community. Language became a powerful symbol of the modern unity of national Italy and the prestige or dominance accorded to the industrialized, city life of northern Italy.

## Language and metaphor

I have been contending that Gramsci uses language as a metaphor for social and political relations. As we shall see below, although he never states it explicitly, his twenty-ninth Notebook suggests that the structures of language, especially different types of grammar, are metaphors for hegemony. This reason alone would make an investigation of metaphor important. There is another related – but even more important – reason to raise the question of metaphor. Gramsci conceives of language as a metaphorical process. Like Saussure and Wittgenstein, discussed in Chapter 1, Gramsci rejects the nomenclature model of language. Instead, all three see language as a system or process of meaning production. And they all agree that meaning is not produced primarily through the relationship between individual words and non-linguistic objects or ideas. Instead, all three see that meaning is produced within language through the relationship among words and other elements of speech (units smaller than words such as sounds as well as units larger than words such as phrases, sentences, etc. ...).

To lay out this picture of Gramsci's understanding of language, we will begin with the following quotation:

> The whole of language is a continuous process of metaphor, and the history of semantics is an aspect of the history of culture; language is at the same time a living thing and a museum of fossils of life and civilisations.[45]

What does Gramsci mean by stating that language is metaphorical? Of course, there is a distinction between language being used as a metaphor, as a method of describing the more abstract workings of spontaneous philosophy, and language itself working through the process of metaphor – whereby words, phrases and idioms 'stand in for' or denote something else. To what extent, according to Gramsci, does this process rely on a similarity between the metaphor and its meaning? Moreover, what sort of things constitute this 'something else'? Are they material objects? Conceptual categories? Or even other words, phrases and idioms?

Using language as a metaphor for political analysis is about having it stand in for or represent how ideas and behaviours operate on a political terrain. Whether or not language itself operates using a process of metaphor, where words or linguistic structures stand in for objects, ideas or other words is a different, if related, question. Gramsci's unambiguous position is that language can be used as a metaphor for political analysis. But his response to the second question is more complex and qualified. In some important senses, he argues that all language operates metaphorically, but we must be careful what metaphor means. And as we shall see in Chapter 5, both are important in considering the 'linguistic turns' and the rise of postmodernism well after Gramsci's death.

Gramsci engages in such questions in his critique of Nikolai Bukharin, the prominent Soviet theoretician who in 1921 published *The Theory of Historical Materialism: A Manual of Popular Sociology*.[46] This book was aimed at popularizing Marxist theory. Bukharin takes up Marx and Engels' point that they are developing an 'immanent' philosophy. Bukharin is concerned that it would be too easy to misinterpret this notion as an endorsement of the religious notion of 'immanence' meaning that God exists within the physical or temporal world. Bukharin argues that Marx and Engels could not be accepting such a notion, even in the form described by Kant or Hegel. Clearly, according to Bukharin, this literal notion of immanence is one of Marxism's key criticisms of Idealist and bourgeois philosophy that imports mystical, religious, or metaphysical notions of God into our understandings of the world. To explain Marx and Engel's use of 'immanence', Bukharin contends that it was only a metaphor.[47]

Gramsci, not satisfied with the superficiality of Bukharin's position, asks why some terms remain in use 'metaphorically' while others are replaced with new words. Is it enough, Gramsci wonders, just to say, as Bukharin does, that these concepts are purely metaphorical? Does not this shut down discussion of how Marx and Engels were using but modifying Hegel and Kant's concepts? Gramsci is critical of Bukharin's determinism and undialectical thinking. Not only is Bukharin's Marxism not cognizant of what Marx learned, especially from Hegel, but in distancing Marxism even from Marx's criticism and working-through of Hegel's ideas, Bukharin creates an overly static and economistic version of Marxism. Gramsci demands a more thorough understanding of this new Marxist conception of 'immanence'. He describes how this process of developing the concept of 'immanence' is a 'translation from the speculative form, as put forward by classical German philosophy, into a historicist form with the aid of French politics and English classical economics'.[48] Thus, in Gramsci's well-known criticisms of Bukharin's overly deterministic Marxism, he uses both the linguistic concept of 'translation' and techniques that he was familiar with from studying linguistics in the realm of political philosophy. He pays particular attention to how concepts and terms develop, where they were borrowed from and how they have been changed. As we saw in Chapter 2, this is the approach of Bartoli's neolinguistics.

It is in the context of criticizing Bukharin that Gramsci makes the above-quoted point, that language is a continual process of metaphor. Meaning is produced by having words 'stand in for' or represent ideas that are usually expressed by different terms. Thus for Bukharin to note that Marx and Engels used certain terms 'metaphorically' needs further explanation. Gramsci uses the example of the word *disastro* (disaster) to drive home this point. Etymologically, *disastro* refers to a misalignment of the stars. But if I described an earthquake as a disaster, no one would accuse me of believing in astrology. The misalignment of the stars then becomes a metaphor for a calamity or devastating event. The literal term 'disaster' became a metaphor in that it shed its literal reference but retained a sense of its meaning. But to use the word 'disaster' and have it understood, neither the speaker nor the listener requires any knowledge of its history. Rather, disaster becomes almost synonymous with catastrophe or calamity. Nuances between 'catastrophe' and 'disaster' (whether one is seen as more extreme than the other or 'disaster' is commonly used for 'natural' events whereas 'catastrophe' is used for personal situations) have little connection to the initial origin of 'disaster' in astrology.

However, borrowing heavily from his linguistic studies with Bartoli, Gramsci argues that we should not ignore the roots of 'disaster' in astrology, paganism and folklore. This would be analogous to what Bukharin is doing with Marx's use of 'immanence'. Rather these roots are evidence of how modern civilization developed from earlier and antithetical ideas. This is why Gramsci states that 'present language is metaphorical with respect to the meanings and ideological content which the words used had in preceding periods of civilisation'.[49] However, and this is a key point to understand his general notion of language, he argues we should not think of language as metaphorical 'in respect of the thing or material and sensible object referred to (or the abstract concept). ...'[50] That is, language is not metaphorical in the sense that a word takes the place of (or creates meaning by relating to) a given object or idea. Language is not a nomenclature for non-linguistic entities, either objects or ideas.[51] 'Disaster' or 'rose' are not metaphors for, or simple references to, either the location of stars or the object or even idea of a type of flower. Language does not create meaning through a simple relationship between language and a non-linguistic world of objects or ideas. Gramsci rejects the notion that 'every proposition must correspond to the *true* and to *verisimilitude*'.[52] We shall see in Chapter 5 that this is a central feature of Gramsci's epistemology and rejection of what he calls 'the so-called existence of the external world'.

Where Gramsci differs from Saussure is in the role of history and the development of language through this process of metaphor. Saussure's linguistics seemed to deny the importance of history, bracketing historical linguistics as merely a branch of the discipline that should be dominated by synchronic linguistics. Foreshadowing poststructuralism and other critiques of structuralism, Gramsci argues that history and the historical residues within language are fundamental in operations of power, prestige and hegemony. Gramsci emphasizes that meaning is created by language in its metaphorical development with respect to previous meanings. New meanings replace previous ones in a continual process of development.

Gramsci's discussion of the concept of 'immanence' is conducted with the very ideas of language that we found in the previous chapter. He writes:

> The new 'metaphorical' meaning spreads with the spread of new culture, which furthermore also coins brand-new words or absorbs them from other languages as loan-words giving them a precise meaning and therefore depriving them of the extensive halo they possessed in the original language. Thus it is probable that for many people the term 'immanence' is known, understood and used for the first time only in the new 'metaphorical' sense given to it by the philosophy of praxis [i.e. Marxism].[53]

Through this discussion of 'immanence', Gramsci is describing the importance of his linguistic method to philosophy but especially hegemony. It is within this discussion that he writes:

Language is transformed with the transformation of the whole of civilisation, through the acquisition of culture by new classes and through the *hegemony* exercised by one national language over others, etc. ..., and what it does is precisely to absorb in metaphorical form the words of previous civilisations and cultures.[54]

Gramsci does not share with certain Marxist critics of Saussure, structuralism and poststructuralism a condemnation of deemphasizing the role of the physical objects or the ideas that language refers to (what in semiotics is termed the referent). On the contrary, Gramsci's Marxist notion of hegemony is fully compatible with this aspect of Saussure's conception of language. Chapters 4 and 5 build on this depiction of language, contributing to this point by providing a better picture of Gramsci's epistemology. But before proceeding in that direction, we must first investigate Gramsci's specific discussion of different types of grammars that provide a crucial insight into his notion of hegemony.

## The structures of language

Gramsci uses language as more than a general metaphor for discussing various issues from the importance of local culture, 'spontaneous philosophies' and how they relate to national culture and official philosophies or dominant world-views. In the last substantive notebook that Gramsci started in prison, he began mapping out more specific linguistic concepts that can be understood as metaphors for components of hegemony. As we shall see below, this linguistic version of hegemony is tied to Gramsci's other major concepts that also act as the constituent elements of his political theory of hegemony, namely, civil society, state and historical bloc.

The previous chapter illustrated Gramsci's attention to how language usage was affected by both state action and non-state activities in civil society. We saw that while Gramsci argued that Italy required a national standardized language, he rejected both the 'artificial' creation of such a language as Esperanto and the actual government policy of Manzoni's to adopt and spread Florentine to the rest of Italy. What then was Gramsci's solution? How did he think a national language could and should be created? How does his method differ from that of Manzoni's or Esperanto?

These questions are decisive not only because Gramsci saw language as a crucial element of politics. More important for our purposes is that in his alternative answer to the 'Language Question' he makes a distinction between the type of hegemony that he criticized in the way the bourgeoisie maintained rule (what Femia termed minimal or decadent hegemony), and the form of hegemony, or counterhegemony, that he advocated for the Italian Communist Party (integral hegemony). It is of the utmost importance in understanding Gramsci's political theory to realize not only that he used 'hegemony' to describe different contexts and arrangements, but most importantly that he advocated some of these arrangements and criticized others.

## Two grammars of hegemony

Gramsci develops two central concepts that help us understand hegemony: 'normative grammar' and what he calls interchangeably 'spontaneous grammar' or 'immanent grammar'. I will refer to the latter as 'spontaneous grammar' since its connections with spontaneous philosophy discussed above are paramount. However, we should not lose sight of other connections between this form of grammar and Gramsci's discussion of immanence, as touched on briefly above. His very equation of 'spontaneity' with 'immanence' is significant. The word 'spontaneous', introduced into English by none other than Thomas Hobbes, is derived from the Latin *sponte* ('of one's own free will'), which refers to voluntary acts as opposed to those that are coerced or induced by fear. The term 'immanence', discussed above, adds to the 'spontaneous' free will the notion of coming from within, not subject to external forces. Gramsci's employment of these concepts to specify a type of grammar – normally thought of as external rules that should be followed – is noteworthy. And as we shall see, his dialectical understanding of this spontaneous grammar with normative grammar reveals one of the fundamental dynamics of hegemony.

## Spontaneous grammar

By 'spontaneous grammar', Gramsci means those patterns we follow while speaking that are unconscious and *seem* natural: 'There is the grammar "immanent" in language itself, by which one speaks "according to grammar" without knowing it ...'[55] He rejects the idea that we could speak without grammar. Instead, for Gramsci, '... one is "always" studying grammar (by imitating the model one admires, etc.)'.[56] Unlike Croce's more narrow definition of grammar – the rules with which grammarians analyse language and impose proper ways of speaking – for Gramsci, the order and patterns of language, even when unconscious, are significant and labelled 'spontaneous grammar'. This is similar to what linguists now call 'descriptive grammar'. It may remind us of Chomsky's 'generative grammar', but Gramsci would reject the notion of 'hard-wired', 'universal' or biological aspects of grammar offered by Chomsky. Such patterns and structures are historically situated and vary not only among cultures but even among social groups and individuals within a society: 'The number of "immanent or spontaneous grammars" is incalculable and, theoretically, one can say that each person has a grammar of his own.'[57]

While discussing the relationship between spontaneity, sincerity, discipline and conformism, Gramsci clarifies the limit for one's degree of spontaneity:

> Sincerity (and spontaneity) means the maximum degree of individualism, even in the sense of idiosyncrasy (in this case originality is equal to idiom). An individual is historically original when he gives maximum prominence to social being, without which he would be an 'idiot' (in the etymological sense which is however not far from the common and vulgar sense).[58]

Gramsci is referring to the Greek root of the word 'idiot', *idios*, meaning 'private' or 'one's own'. So, he argues, individualism, spontaneity and sincerity have value and merit only if they are disciplined, only if they have a social connection that keeps them from becoming mere idiocy or idiosyncrasy. Thus we cannot simply think of individualism and spontaneity as being personal 'free choice', or what Isaiah Berlin famously articulated as negative freedom.[59] But what could Gramsci mean by 'social being' in this context? How can we understand 'disciplined spontaneity' as more than just a contradiction in terms?

The answer lies in the other form of grammar that Gramsci discusses, namely, 'normative grammar'. Normative grammar, for

Gramsci, is close to our common-sense understanding of 'grammar' as meaning the conscious rules that we follow in order to speak correctly. This is what Croce has in mind when he discusses grammar and how it is different from logic or aesthetics.[60] It is similar to what linguists now call 'prescriptive grammar'.

## Normative grammar

The label 'normative grammar' is rooted in the grammar book published in 1660 by the Jansenist Abbey of Port Royal des Champs near Paris. It was primarily a pedagogical tool aimed at making it easier to learn a language by explaining its structure. It used the idea of a 'universal grammar' shared by all languages to further its aim of teaching people not necessarily how language *is* used, but how it *should be* used.

Ferdinand de Saussure pointed to the Port Royal Grammar as the precursor to his insistence that linguistics must be studied from a 'synchronic perspective'.[61] As explained in Chapter 2, meaning, according to Saussure, is not produced by the history of words, or their relation to the non-linguistic realms of physical objects or conceptual ideas, rather meaning is produced through the synchronic structures of language and the place of individual words, phrases, sounds and patterns within those structures. Gramsci agrees with Saussure on both of these points. It is in this sense that Gramsci uses the image of a photograph to define grammar.[62] As in Saussure's synchronic approach, grammar, like photograph, is frozen in time.

This, then, is the third element of Saussure's linguistics with which Gramsci agrees. With the addition of this final point, we can list three basic points of agreement between Gramsci and Saussure:

- They both reject a purely historical approach to the study of language in which linguistic phenomena are analysed as individual units tracing them back to their history and development. Linguistics must address how speakers understand and construct meaning with language. That is, speakers need to be able to distinguish between words that sound similar but have different meanings and connect words that sound different but have similar meanings. Both Gramsci and Saussure noted that for speakers to do this, they do not need to know the historical lineage of word forms that had been the focus of the dominant approach to linguistics at the turn of the twentieth century.

- Both Gramsci and Saussure reject all versions of language as nomenclature, the theory that language is fundamentally a collection of words that stand for non-linguistic things, whether they are physical objects, qualities or ideas.
- They argue that meaning is produced in the relationship among the various elements of language operating synchronically. The history of words and language in general is often forgotten and unconscious.

Gramsci's development of 'normative grammar' has two unique attributes not found in the Port Royal or other traditional notions of normative grammar, nor in Saussure's synchronic linguistics. The first is his expansion of normative grammar to include how we use grammatical correctness or what is appropriate and proper in order to mark social distinction, and thus power differentials amongst different speakers. The second is his relation of it to history. Gramsci makes both points by relating normative grammar to spontaneous grammar.

Gramsci broadens the usual notion of normative or prescriptive grammar:

> Besides the 'immanent [spontaneous] grammar' in every language, there is also in reality (i.e. even if not written) a 'normative' grammar (or more than one). This is made up of the reciprocal monitoring, reciprocal teaching, reciprocal 'censorship' expressed in such questions as 'What did you mean to say?', 'What do you mean?', 'Make yourself clearer', etc., and in mimicry and teasing. This whole complex of actions and reactions come together to create a grammatical conformism, to establish 'norms' or judgements of correctness and incorrectness.[63]

Thus he includes within the very concept of normative grammar the social processes of how such grammars are formed. Where most linguists limit normative grammar to the rules that constitute it, he includes the more informal processes and by extension the less codified rules and how they are enforced in everyday speech. From the perspectives of Port Royal, traditional grammar and Saussure, it is impossible to have more than one normative grammar (or synchronic structure) within a given language. But for Gramsci, borrowing from his linguistic professor, Bartoli, conflict within language is one of its most fundamental features. Moreover, for traditional grammarians, the rules are defined by some logical or natural or traditional standard. Their social origins, including teaching and censorship, are not investigated. In describing this process as both 'censoring' and teaching, we should keep in mind that Gramsci is not necessarily condemning this process nor arguing against such power relationships.

Gramsci continues this passage by noting how such normative grammars occur spontaneously:

> But this 'spontaneous' expression of grammatical conformity is necessarily disconnected, discontinuous and limited to local social strata or local centres. (A peasant who moves to the city ends up conforming to urban speech through pressure of the city environment. In the country, people try to imitate urban speech; the subaltern classes try to speak like the dominant classes and the intellectuals, etc.)[64]

In this passage, Gramsci connects these concepts of spontaneous and normative grammar with Bartoli's concerns with points of language prestige and ultimately with the political questions of classes, intellectuals and hegemony.

The second unique aspect of Gramsci's conception of normative grammar is that it is not divorced from history; quite the contrary, it is predicated on it. But this connection with history need not be conscious for the speaker. So while Gramsci uses the image of a photograph to define grammar, he notes that such a photograph is 'of a given phase of a national (collective) language that has been formed historically and is continuously developing'. He asks the question on which he and Saussure disagree: 'what is the purpose of such a photograph? To record the history of an aspect of civilization or to modify an aspect of civilization?'[65] Saussure's answer is the former, the photograph is to record scientifically an aspect of civilization. He argues that a synchronic or frozen picture of the language – what he calls 'language as a structured system' – is the only way to provide scientific and objective (and essentially unpolitical) knowledge of language.[66] As an objective science, Saussurean linguistics could not address political and moral issues of how this frozen picture alters people's behaviour and contains within it social power structures. Gramsci's answer is the opposite. Such frozen pictures of language are always moral judgements with political effects. Not unlike Marx's Eleventh Thesis on Feuerbach that the point is not only to understand the world but to change it, Gramsci too argues that the point of such a linguistic photograph is to change the world. This might seem to contradict my earlier point that Gramsci and Saussure agree in rejecting the historical linguists' (and especially the Neogrammarians') approach. The agreement is that speakers can use language without knowing its history. Thus speakers produce meaning in a synchronic manner. Gramsci emphasizes that the historical traces within language are often forgotten, becoming unconscious and fragmented with the historical process of metaphor. But such processes are social and depend upon power differentials among different groups of speakers. Subaltern classes whose lives (and thoughts) tend to be dominated by ruling classes are most subject to this process of fragmentation and forgetting. Where Saussure uses this point to relegate such histories to a subfield of linguistics delimited by the overriding and organizational concern with synchronic linguistics, Gramsci argues that the power relations that operate through language, common sense philosophy, ideology and world-views are obscured by the purely synchronic approach to language – both in use and in studying language.

Thus, from Gramsci's perspective, traditional intellectuals, including Saussure, who just try to describe how language operates, or those that try to prescribe a normative grammar (in an objective and non-political way), deny that linguistics is a political act:

> But it is obvious that someone who writes a normative grammar cannot ignore the history of the language of which he wishes to propose an 'exemplary phase' as the 'only' one worthy to become, in an 'organic' and 'totalitarian' way, the 'common' language of a nation in competition and conflict with other 'phases' and types or schemes that already exist ... the linguistic fact, like any other historical fact, cannot have strictly defined national boundaries, but that history is always 'world history' ...[67]

Gramsci here presages many of the criticisms that were later lodged against structuralism and Saussure's attempt to divorce the synchronic scientific study of language from the actual practice of both speaking (or writing) and creating such linguistic structures.

In describing how someone writes a normative grammar by choosing a spontaneous grammar as the exemplary or normative one, Gramsci is both referring to Manzoni's method of standardizing Italian, and describing the relationship between heterogeneous, fragmented and unconscious disorganized patterns within language and homogeneous, codified, conscious grammar that defines how a language *should* be used. Normative grammar, according to Gramsci, does not come from some natural or logical process outside society and its tensions. Rather, normative grammars are produced through the organization, codification and legitimization of certain spontaneous grammars. Of course, this is a competitive process whereby many (if not most) spontaneous grammars are often delegitimized and suppressed.

In sum, Gramsci insists (against Saussure, Croce and others) that 'normative grammars' are not created through recourse to logic or nature or some apolitical tradition, but are created by political choices from 'spontaneous grammars'. Normative grammars are the conscious organization and codification of one or more spontaneous grammars. This is one half of the dialectical relationship between normative and spontaneous grammars. But where, according to Gramsci, do spontaneous grammars come from?

### Normative history in spontaneous grammar

Nowhere in the twenty-ninth Notebook does Gramsci directly answer this question about the origins of spontaneous grammar, although he intimates an answer and this corresponds to his description elsewhere of 'spontaneity'. In discussing the relationship between 'normative grammar' and the history of grammar he writes:

> We are dealing with two distinct and in part different things, like history and politics, but they cannot be considered independently, any more than politics and history. Besides,

since the study of languages as a cultural phenomenon grew out of political needs (more or less conscious and consciously expressed), the needs of normative grammar have exerted an influence on historical grammar and on its 'legislative conceptions' (or at least this traditional element has reinforced, during the last century, the application of the positivist–naturalist method to the study of the history of languages conceived as the 'science of language'.)[68]

In other words, where 'spontaneous grammar' seems to be those natural patterns that we use unconsciously as we speak or write, they are influenced by previous normative grammars. The positivist–naturalist study of language seems to reinforce this impression that these grammars – the results of a history of political acts and choices – are natural, spontaneous and independent of political needs and cultural phenomena.

When writing not about grammar, but 'spontaneity' in general, Gramsci argues:

The term 'spontaneity' can be variously defined, for the phenomenon to which it refers is many-sided. Meanwhile it must be stressed that 'pure' spontaneity does not exist in history ... In the 'most spontaneous' movement it is simply the case that the element of 'conscious leadership' cannot be checked, have left no reliable document. It may be said that spontaneity is therefore the characteristic of the 'history of the subaltern classes,' and indeed their most marginal and peripheral elements; these have not achieved any consciousness of the class 'for itself'; and consequently it never occurs to them that their history might have some possible importance, that there might be some value in leaving documentary evidence of it.[69]

Referring back to its etymology, spontaneity is redefined by Gramsci from being some unencumbered free will made with no influence or pressure from history, nor limited by external structures, to being the process whereby previous influences, leadership, and 'normative grammars' are forgotten and undocumented. That is, spontaneous grammars are not the opposite of normative grammars, they are not the individual or internal expression that is totally consented to as opposed to external imposition from the outside.

What Gramsci provides with his discussions of these two types of grammar is an elaboration of his already noted argument about how to approach popular philosophy from a Marxist perspective:

> The starting-point of critical elaboration in the consciousness of what one really is, and is 'knowing thyself' as a product of the historical process to date which has deposited in you an infinity of traces, without leaving an inventory. First it is necessary to create such an inventory.[70]

Using his linguistic terminology, previous normative grammars have exerted influences and left traces on how we organize our language, thoughts and impressions. Gramsci's argument is that we usually do ignore such traces (for example the etymology of 'disaster') and we still use language to communicate and create meaning. This is especially true for subaltern groups. But rather than take these spontaneous grammars as some sort of source of free will or sincerity or freedom, we need to uncover this history and compile an inventory. We need to become conscious of the normative traces within what seems and feels spontaneous.

In one sense, this completes a circle: normative grammars are produced from one or more spontaneous grammars which are themselves the historical result of an interaction of previous normative grammars that have been internalized. Thus Gramsci is not positing spontaneous grammars by definition as a source of free will or freedom that is being suppressed or repressed by normative grammars. However, this circle should not lead us to overly generalize this process. He sees all the difference between how 'regressive' normative grammars are formed and how a 'progressive' communist normative grammar (or hegemony) *should* be formed. As we investigate Gramsci's distinction here, we should keep in mind that while he never explicitly states it, it is fully complementary with the distinctions he makes between the types of hegemony that he criticizes, those practiced by the bourgeoisie (or proposed by communists such as Bordiga), and the hegemony he advocates for the Italian Communist Party.

## Normative grammar and progressive hegemony

From Gramsci's use of hegemony and normative grammar to criticize bourgeois rule and Manzoni's language policy, it may seem as if he is arguing against all hegemonic forces. But in fact it would be a misunderstanding to think he favours spontaneous grammar as if it is 'free' and 'non-alienated' against normative grammar that is a form of control and domination. In other words, there is a danger of a simplistic understanding that spontaneity is a metaphor for consent whereas normativity is perhaps a more benign and less forceful or violent form of coercion. As we have seen, Gramsci's complex arguments about spontaneity belie such simplistic oppositions with normative grammar. Moreover, he unequivocally favours creating a national Italian language including a normative grammar: 'it is rational to collaborate practically and willingly to welcome everything that may serve to create a common national language. ...'[71] Just as he criticizes the Italian bourgeoisie and its 'passive revolution' for being unable to galvanize the unity of the Italian people, so too he argues that the lack of a common national language, '... creates friction particularly in the popular masses among whom local particularisms and phenomena of a narrow and provincial mentality are more tenacious than is believed'.[72] This complements Gramsci's analysis of the Southern Question and folklore. As we have seen, Gramsci's criticisms of the parochial views of the peasantry are not aimed solely at trying to make them more rational and modern. His concerns are to show how such world-views allow the southern peasants to be so easily pitted against the northern proletariat. That is, the northern industrialists allied with the southern landowners can maintain a regressive hegemony by using the 'friction' created amongst subaltern groups, especially the peasantry and proletariat.[73]

So what makes the type of hegemony or normative grammar that Gramsci advocates different from that of the bourgeoisie that he criticizes? We can address this question by focusing on language and grammar, keeping in mind that they are metaphors for hegemony in the social and political realm. Gramsci's criticism of Manzoni and what I will call the regressive method for making a normative grammar and national language is that it chooses just one spontaneous grammar as normative. For all the speakers who have spontaneous grammars significantly different from the Florentine (specifically middle-class Florentine) dialect, this normative grammar is imposed from outside their previous language, life and experience. As one moves away from Tuscany, the dialects generally become increasingly different from this 'national standard', and this sense of the imposition of a foreign language increases, especially for those outside the intellectual and cultural elite that has knowledge of the literary Italian of written texts.

Gramsci suggests an alternative, preferable process for creating a normative grammar or a national, common language. It would involve combining the existing spontaneous grammars into a single, normative grammar. As he states, 'What this [unified national language] will be, one cannot foresee or establish: in any case if the intervention is "rational", it will be organically tied to tradition, which is of no small importance in the economy of culture.'[74] One could foresee such a unified language only if, like Esperanto or a currently spoken Florentine dialect, it was an already existing language that was imposed, and all the other existing spontaneous grammars were suppressed. But, if, as Gramsci proposes, the normative grammar was the result of the interactions of all the spontaneous grammars occurring 'through a whole complex of molecular processes ...',[75] it would be a more truly democratic normative language that would still be unified, national and popular.

This process resonates with much of Gramsci's general discussion of hegemony and how the form that he advocates would be the result of organic intellectuals working from within 'common sense' to create culture, a world-view and institutions that integrate and organize diverse ways of understanding the world. Although Gramsci never explicitly states it, normative grammar seems to be a powerful metaphor for hegemony. As with hegemony, Gramsci uses normative grammar in many different ways, both positively and negatively. He goes beyond just accepting or rejecting particular normative grammars. As with hegemony, he uses normative grammar in a more analytic manner. For example, one of his significant concerns with Manzoni's 'solution' to the language question is that it would not be effective. As we saw in the previous chapter, the 'linguistic pressures' that are exerted from what Ascoli had called the 'linguistic substratum' that varied throughout Italy would alter the 'standard' imposed language to the extent that it would no longer be standard. Thus, the standard language and normative grammar would not have the active effect that was intended.[76]

## Conclusion

Hegemony is obviously a very complex concept for Gramsci and in the *Prison Notebooks* he uses it to connect a wide range of ideas and analyses. As by far the most influential of Gramsci's many terms, different readers have found quite diverse aspects to it. This chapter is not arguing that the lens of language alleviates the controversy surrounding diverse interpretations or uses of 'hegemony'. Instead, by looking at the linguistic aspects of hegemony, I hope to have shown that for Gramsci language is both an element in the exercise of power and a metaphor for how power operates. This allows us to connect it to some of the central dynamics and points described by Gramsci with the term 'hegemony'. It also emphasizes the role of force and power in the very creation of consent without sacrificing an emphasis on agency and possibilities of radical political change. Moreover, language has hopefully served as a useful nexus through which to introduce and relate his other influential terms, subalternity, 'common sense', and organic versus traditional intellectuals. Chapter 4 continues this process by addressing the other terms that have come to be known as 'Gramscian', which serve to constitute a more complete theory of hegemony.

# 4

# Gramsci's Key Concepts, with Linguistic Enrichment

This chapter continues the previous chapters' exploration of Gramsci's use of linguistic concepts and language in the service of political and social analysis. His attention to language in the *Prison Notebooks* is an integral element in his understanding of power dynamics within society. Chapter 3 dealt with several concepts that Gramscian scholarship has shown as central to hegemony: philosophy, intellectuals, culture and subalternity. As we saw, language – as both a metaphor and a topic – is inseparable from how Gramsci understands these concepts.

Chapter 4 extends this exploration by focusing on the major concepts of Gramsci's legacy: 'passive revolution', war of manoeuvre/position, national–popular collective will, civil society and state. It introduces these terms, illustrating important parallels and dynamics, especially surrounding the relation between coercion and consent. Thus, this chapter furnishes a linguistically enriched overview of some of Gramsci's most fundamental concepts, making them more applicable to contemporary debates in social theory influenced by the various 'linguistic turns' of the twentieth century. The concluding chapter turns more explicitly to such theories, showing Gramsci's continued relevance.

## Passive revolution and ineffective national language

Gramsci's discussion of normative and spontaneous grammars (see Chapter 3) has strong resonance with his discussion of 'passive revolution'. Gramsci borrows this term from the historian Vincenzo Cuoco. But in Gramsci's hands, Cuoco's conception of 'passive revolution' is totally transformed. Cuoco used it in analysing the short-lived Republic of Naples of 1799. Revolutionaries, especially from the educated middle classes, successfully drove Ferdinand IV and the Hapsburg dynasty out of Naples to Sicily, with relatively little violence and a high level of popular support. They hoped to create a republic based on the ideals of the French Revolution. Cuoco argued that their revolution devolved into violence, terror and parochial counter-revolution because the revolutionaries tried, unsuccessfully, to bridge the wide gap between Enlightenment political ideals and the wants and desires of the plebeian masses. Cuoco insisted that they should not have tried to involve the masses so actively. The failure was in part due to the difficulties of teaching the masses such foreign ideas. Thus, Cuoco favoured a more 'passive revolution' led by the bourgeoisie, that did not attempt to change the world-view of the people. Gramsci reverses the implications of Cuoco's point (or as he notes, ironically, he uses 'an expression of Cuoco's in a slightly different sense from that which Cuoco intended') highlighting the problems created when such a revolution fails to engage a majority of the population.[1]

Gramsci understands the 'passive revolution' as one of the possible strategies for the relatively small and powerless bourgeoisie in the face of the Vatican's opposition to national unity. Rather than making an alliance with the peasantry, workers or other social classes in order to further unification, the Moderate Party, the major ruling bourgeois party in late nineteenth-century Italy, succeeded in forming alliances with traditional ruling groups, especially the Piedmont leaders and their armies, but also the northern industrialists and southern landowners. In the process known in Italian as *trasformismo* (literally, transformism), the Moderates deflated the power of their main adversaries, the Action Party, by incorporating its leaders – political, cultural and economic – into its own governing networks. This strategy, in effect, allowed the Moderates to lead without engaging the masses precisely by absorbing leaders most closely connected to the masses. Gramsci argues that such a strategy 'decapitated' the popular masses, creating a 'passive' citizenry.[2] This dynamic of ruling through co-optation was a standard practice of colonial powers and thus Gramsci's critique of it has been useful to colonial and postcolonial theorists.[3]

According to Gramsci, the leaders of the unification movement did not 'lead' (*dirigente*) but instead wished to 'dominate' (*dominante*) the nation.[4] In other words, they did not create an active relationship whereby the masses decided to follow their leadership. Instead, it was a 'revolution from above', to which the great majority of newly defined Italians acquiesced. Gramsci describes this 'passive revolution' as a ' "revolution" without a "revolution" '.⁵ Changes occur and often they are reactions to problems and tensions of previous political and economic arrangements, but they rarely resolve such problems and are not really democratic in the true sense of the term – they do not come from the people. Rather leaders propose policies that the people do not reject.

This description of a passive revolution is parallel to his discussion of how Manzoni's solution can create a 'standard language' without standardizing the various dialects or languages spoken in Italy. In both cases (or more accurately, the two dimensions of the same process)⁶ a nominal revolution in political form or national language exists, but it has not 'led' the people to change their language, culture or lives, except in that it has 'dominated' them by 'imposing' the interests and language of the northern ruling class. This further increases the gap between action and thought that was investigated in Chapter 3. Those who tend to produce opinion within the masses, who have the ability to develop, expand and improve the languages of the peasants, the working class and other subaltern groups – those that Gramsci calls organic intellectuals – are absorbed by the dominant group, taught a new national language and become traditional intellectuals. The average people's previous languages remain unchanged as do their world-views and economic situations. Likewise, Gramsci's major critique of 'passive revolution' is that it fails to eliminate the old semi-feudal power bases that the active French Revolution destroyed, clearing the ground for bourgeois capitalism. In Italy, these feudal remnants remain, as does the linguistic substratum (see Chapter 3).⁷ On top of them, a new language or set of political institutions, goals and projects is imposed.⁸

Thus, Gramsci is criticizing the failure to actually produce an effective revolution in Italian society, a hegemony that is integral as opposed to minimal, a normative grammar that is constituted from the diversity of spontaneous grammars rather than by imposing one single grammar on everyone. As we saw with the question of a national language, passive revolution and minimal hegemony may be effective at one level, but they will continually face pressures from the underlying grammars, economic situations and world-views that they failed to engage.

Gramsci is interested both in the achievements of a passive revolution and, more importantly, in its weaknesses, which a proletarian hegemony can overcome through an active revolution, integral hegemony and a truly popular national language. He argues that the Moderate Party was able to create a hegemony over only a small portion of the Italian nation – the upper classes and the intellectuals.[9] It is this lack of success due to the passive nature of the Italian *Risorgimento* that laid the groundwork for the rise of Fascism. With the crisis of the First World War, universal suffrage and the rapid expansion of heavy industry in the North, the tensions underlying the 'passive revolution' came back to the surface. The resentment of the petit bourgeoisie combined with the northern agrarian forces formed a basis for Fascism to become a broad mass movement.[10]

Like Marx, Gramsci understands both the positive and negative aspects of the bourgeoisie or ruling class's ability to secure an effective integral hegemony over an entire population. For Marx, the rise of the bourgeois class is progressive in that it eradicates feudalism, creating many formal freedoms for citizens, and is able to enact an incredibly productive and efficient capitalist system. Gramsci emphasizes Marx's position that often such movements transcend their narrow mostly economic interests, what he calls their corporate interests. In the struggle to achieve these goals, they effectively embrace the needs of the entire people or nation at that given moment in history. This is a dimension of political struggle very important to Gramsci. He calls it the 'national–popular collective will'.[11] Gramsci cites the Jacobins early in the French Revolution as an example. He argues that the Jacobins represented the 'future needs' not only of the French bourgeoisie, but of the entire nation. In the Jacobins, Gramsci argues, '[t]he revolution had found its widest class limits'.[12] While they represented the bourgeois class's interests, given the historical conditions, they were revolutionary for the peasantry too. The 'revolutionaries of yesterday – today become reactionaries'. Gramsci holds such successful hegemony on the part of the bourgeoisie to be much superior to Garibaldi and Italy's Action Party, who were unable to garner even 'intellectual and moral leadership' of the masses.

Gramsci describes the hegemony that the Moderate Party was able to maintain successfully. But theirs was not a hegemony over the masses but purely over the intellectuals. It lacked the national–popular element. The Moderates' hegemony consisted of satisfying the intellectuals' needs and it 'welcomed the exiled intellectuals, and provided a model of what a future unified State would do'.[13] In this way, the Moderates' hegemony can be distinguished from 'old ideologies which dominated by coercion'. Gramsci applies 'hegemony' to the Moderates because they offered a sense of 'dignity' and inclusion to those who were potentially adversaries representing opposing forces in society. Thus, while 'hegemony' here signifies a degree of consent as opposed to coercion, it does not lead to Gramsci's total adoration, nor rule out the threat and use of coercion altogether. The Moderates attained a relatively minimal hegemony although they were able to overcome the Vatican's opposition to national unification and the bourgeois' own weakness in economic and physical strength. For these reasons Gramsci characterizes them as hegemonic and not dominant. He clearly admires this hegemonic aspect in the Moderates and views it as central to their success and their ability to use the Action Party for their own advantage. But this admiration of Gramsci's for their hegemonic success (although limited) does not blind him from a scathing critique of their programme to create a delicate alliance among the rural landowning elite, the southern urban forces and the northern urban forces, that is a bloc of the important right-wing forces.[14]

Gramsci's criticisms of normative grammar have clear parallels in his discussion of 'passive revolution', national–popular collective will and hegemony. As with normative grammar, hegemony can be more or less inclusive of various social groups and it can be more or less effective or active in really garnering the deep support of people and their world-views. Like a Manzonian national language, the hegemony created by a 'passive revolution' can still be effective in filling the lacunae of no national language, or no national political force. Even minimal hegemony (which may rest on a degree of domination and coercion, or its threat) is based on a greater degree of consent, or one filled purely by methods of domination and coercion. Nevertheless, it will remain tenuous and have particularly damaging consequences as it increases the alienation of the subaltern groups by imposing thoughts and ways of understanding the world that are at odds with their own lived experiences.

## War of manoeuvre and war of position

Gramsci connects his discussion of 'passive revolution' to one of his other central distinctions, that between the war of manoeuvre and war of position. Like subalternity, these are military metaphors.[15] A war of manoeuvre is a frontal attack on one's enemies, in this case on state power. It characterizes any attempt to gain actual control of the government, whether through armed combat, democratic election or other means. 'War of position' refers to a host of other processes related to the struggle. It includes preparations for the war of manoeuvre, positioning one's troops on the battlefield, working out where, or on what terrain, a battle might be staged.[16] The metaphor extends the general idea that setting the agenda is half the battle. It enriches this idea both institutionally and philosophically.

Gramsci derives his emphasis on 'war of position' from the experiences of trench warfare in the First World War. With the new technologies, especially rapid-firing small arms, defensive trenches acquired greater importance than in previous wars. Strategic questions about where and how trenches should be constructed became more decisive for success. Gramsci also stresses the larger implications of the prolongation of war due to the trenches, which required greater civilian, economic and social support. As he describes, 'A war of position is not, in reality, constituted simply by the actual trenches, but by the whole organizational and industrial system of the territory which lies to the rear of the army in the field.'[17] Lines of supply and the entire mobilization of national economies and public morale took on new importance. The First World War introduced the phenomenon of total and mass war requiring mass production and fantastic degrees of social mobilization.[18]

Gramsci uses this as a metaphor for the type of struggle that he thinks the Italian working class and communists will have to wage against Fascism and capitalism.[19] One reason for employing these metaphors was to make a distinction between the successful methods that Lenin and the Bolsheviks used in 1917 and the strategy that Gramsci thought was required in the significantly different circumstances of Italy and other western European countries. While Lenin took great interest in cultural and social matters, he argued that in Russia they could only be dealt with *after* the seizure of state power. Lenin may have agreed with Gramsci on the need to attain power not only over the military and state, but more importantly over the hearts and minds of the masses. However, Gramsci's point was that given even the minimal degree of democracy and social conditions of Italy, and western Europe in general, the cultural struggle to gain active consent of the masses required that a 'war of position' preceded any outright 'war of manoeuvre'. Thus, Gramsci uses the trenches of military battle to represent large popular organizations of a modern type.[20] He argues that the October Revolution was successful because 'the general-economic-cultural-social conditions ... ' and 'structures of national life are embryonic and loose, and incapable of becoming "trench or fortress" '.[21] But in Italy, national cultural life and the institutions outside the state will become like trenches of resistance to any communist war of manoeuvre. Thus, while the war of manoeuvre should not be ignored completely, the war of position is, for Gramsci, the more important focus. Just as in actual war, the war of position will ultimately determine the success or failure of the war of manoeuvre. This of course fits the more general theme from Chapter 3 about expanding the very concept of politics, and the integral role played by language in that project makes it also central in comprehending just what Gramsci meant with his focus on the war of position.

From our linguistic perspective, we can understand the distinction like this: there is the war of manoeuvre that is the overtly political and governmental power, including government policy on language, funding for books and dictionaries, and educational policy from curriculum to teacher training. But the popular support and potential success of such policies will depend on the previously waged struggle over what actually constitutes standard Italian. The war of position is akin to the struggle over how the national language will be constituted. Will it be the adoption of one particular dialect (as Manzoni proposed) or created by combining (standardizing) a wide number of dialects spoken in many regions and by various classes? In this latter case, how will this synthesis take place? Such questions of what constitutes the possible languages that will vie for usage are the precursors to the war of manoeuvre, the actual struggle and interaction amongst these languages. For Gramsci, that no real contender against Florentine existed meant that the linguistic battle would be lost. Florentine had the prestige of being close to literary Italian, partially due to the fact that Dante was Florentine. With Manzoni's success, described in the previous chapter, it had the political and economic support of the government. Gramsci understood that it would be absurd (and useless) to present some other dialect as a contender, whether Sardinian, Calabrese or Esperanto. In this way, the outcome of the war of manoeuvre is presaged by the results of the war of position.

Gramsci was not against the creation of a national language per se. As already noted, he wrote in Notebook the twenty-ninth:

> ... it is rational to collaborate practically and willingly to welcome everything that may serve to create a common national language, the non-existence of which creates friction particularly in the popular masses among whom local particularisms and phenomena of a narrow and provincial mentality are more tenacious than is believed.[22]

His suggestion was that a new language and normative grammar be created from the interaction of the subaltern spontaneous grammars. That is, rather than speakers passively accepting a language from above, he argued for what might be called an active, linguistic revolution. But the possibility that such an alternative solution could win out over Manzoni's solution – that is the war of manoeuvre between these two responses to the language question – is predetermined by the war of position, the defining of the problem, lack of a national language, and the goals of its solution. If the Language Question is defined as the immediate need for one national language, and Florentine has prestige through its relatively close relation with literary Italian and the cultural and economic status of Florence and Tuscany, then any other single contender faces a steep uphill battle. This situation is created through the narrowing of possibilities, especially the longer term prospects of creating a new language by synthesizing various elements of many Italian dialects.

## War of position as passive revolution

Gramsci makes a potentially confusing equation of 'war of position' with 'passive revolution'. He asks, under what conditions is a 'war of position' the same as a passive revolution?[23] At first glance, one may suppose the answer is none, since he seems to be critical of passive revolutions and in favour of the war of position. Yet Gramsci argues that in given historical periods they can become the same. He even uses a slash to equate these terms and distinguish them from the war of manoeuvre as popular initiative: '… Cavour [leader of the Moderate Party] is the exponent of the passive revolution/war of position and Mazzini [and the Action Party] of popular initiative/war of manoeuvre.'[24] This seems to be unclear at best and possibly incoherent.[25]

If we look at it from our linguistic perspective, we take the war of position to be the struggle over what constitutes the languages involved. Is national Italian an evolving conglomeration of the dialects, perhaps Tuscan (or written) basic grammar including vocabulary and expressions from Calabrese, Sardinian (or Sardu), Friulian and the like? Is such a national language supposed truly to be a language for all Italians to use and feel comfortable with in expressing themselves and their political desires and creating their own meaning and interpretations of the world? Or, is it to be just a codified version of bourgeois Florentine with little or no inclusion of other dialects (i.e. Manzoni's plan)? Is its function to facilitate the governing elite and enable its subjects to understand the laws and accept their new role as Italians, but a role not as active participants but rather as passive receivers of ideas, informaion and values? This latter option is in fact a 'passive revolution'. Little is changed in terms of the make-up of the language, and the battle shifts into a war of manoeuvre as the question becomes, is this language going to be successfully imposed, what resistance will it face and what will be the outcome? If the other alternative wins out, a passive revolution is replaced by an active process of linguistic transformation (and, given the metaphor discussed in Chapter 3, changes in 'common sense', everyday philosophy and world-views) during which the terrain is prepared so that when the war of manoeuvre, the overt contest for power, is ignited, there is the chance of an active, democratic and revolutionary change in society.

## National–popular collective will

Gramsci's argument here is related to another one of his key concepts that was raised in Chapter 3; his discussion of the national–popular collective will. Put simply, a revolution is passive when it is not connected to developing such a popular will. These four terms, 'national', 'popular', 'collective', 'will', often appear in the *Prison Notebooks* in different combinations. He uses 'national–popular' as an adjective describing, for example, the character of French culture,[26] or the national–popular masses.[27] He combines this general concern about the national–popular with the notion of a 'collective will' in his famous use of Machiavelli's *The Prince* to present the Communist Party as a modern prince.[28] In perhaps the most quoted of the letters that Gramsci wrote while in prison, a letter where he lays out the plan for his research project that would become the *Prison Notebooks*, he outlines four major topics: (1) nineteenth-century history of Italian intellectuals; (2) comparative linguistics; (3) Pirandello's theatre and Italian theatrical taste; and (4) serial novels and popular taste in literature. He then notes that 'if you look closely at these four arguments, a common thread runs through them: the popular creative spirit, in its diverse phases of development, is equally present in each'.[29] As Renate Holub has argued, his development of the 'popular creative spirit' is the leitmotiv running throughout his *Prison Notebooks* that ties them all together.[30] In a sense, the national–popular collective will is what characterizes the differing types and degrees of hegemony.

Many commentaries have noted that this is one of the key ways in which Gramsci contributes a cultural dimension to Marxist political theory. Gramsci's exploration of the collective and cultural dimensions of will formation or consciousness, what we now understand as subjectivity, means that the very constitution of identities is altered through the process of politics. Challenging capitalism, for Gramsci, is not a matter of examining how preconstituted class positions, or predefined identities, can be organized into a coalition led by the vanguard elements of the working class. He is concerned with creating a movement that would include FIAT workers in Turin, peasants in Sardinia, peasants in central Italy's Po Valley, small shop owners, women married to workers in Naples, etc. But for him, the hegemonic process, the actual creation of such a movement, would be much more than an alliance of such distinct identities, or an organization of their diverse interests, to determine possible common goals. Gramsci would call such concerns questions of these classes' corporate interests. But for Gramsci, the hege-monic process must go beyond such corporate interests and become universal, altering these people's very identities through the creation of a 'collective will'.

Previous Marxists were clear that the non-economic dimen-sions of such people's lives, such as religion or ethnic identity, served as impediments to their understanding the benefits of communism and becoming class-conscious. But Gramsci relocates the struggle to the cultural realm, whereby the very identity of Catholic woman, southern peasant and urban worker are related to hegemonic processes. He has moved far beyond any notion of politics as the accommodation or clash of various interests, determined by either one's economic position or one's individual choice or will. He has also moved beyond a simplistic model where the economic base determines the superstructural elements of culture. Rather, he uses the term 'historic bloc' to describe how from various possible alliances and relations among classes and social groups, one arrangement is solidified.[31] This is neither predetermined nor inevitable. Nor are historic blocs ever totally stable. Rather, they are in continual need of reproduction. Because of this, the war of position is never totally decisive even after a clearly victorious war of manoeuvre, as Mussolini's rise to power seemed to have been.

## War of position and new social movement alliances

Roger Simon goes so far as to define Gramsci's war of position as a strategy of 'building up a broad bloc of varied social forces, uni-fied by a common conception of the world. ... '[32] He points out how such social forces might include what we now call 'new social movements', including feminism, the student and peace movements, other minority movements and struggles for national liberation. This is one way in which Gramsci's influence has been taken up in discussions of new social movements and identity politics, which will be discussed in the next chapter.

However, this raises obvious questions about how this war of position is to be waged, how such different movements are to be unified by a conception of the world, a collective will. Defenders and detractors of Gramsci alike take his focus on the proletariat as the hegemonic force as an assumption that its world-view (and interests) will be the core that is expanded to include other groups in an alliance, but never compromised. Critiques from feminist or anti-racist perspectives should, on this reading of Gramsci, be addressed and incorporated, but not at the expense of the working class.[33] Gramsci's very language of forging a 'collective will' through a myth akin to Machiavelli's *Prince* has been taken as a dogmatic, even totalitarian argument, not unlike Rousseau's notion of the 'general will' that, some argue, inevitably subordinates individual wills.

But as we saw in Chapter 3 (pp. 98–101), Gramsci's use of language as a metaphor suggests that he is not proposing the creation of a monolithic world-view or ideology in which there is no room for dissent and differing opinions. Nor is he even suggesting a monolingual nation. Rather he is proposing a hegemony that is like a national language. In this language, dissent, alternative views and critical ideas can and should be raised. This national language does not even rule out the continued and frequent use of other languages and dialects. Rather, it demands that this hegemony is created democratically through the active participation of the many people who constitute it. This national language as opposed to class position or identity becomes the core of hegemony.

## Language as a model for the national–popular collective will

Conceiving of a 'unified conception of the world', a 'national–popular collective will', as a language, as opposed to a homogenous and static perspective or position, makes Simon's contention (and the attraction of Gramsci) much more persuasive. One could not expect a women's movement premised on showing the centrality of gender categories in policy making to adopt the same entire conception of the world as environmentalists or workers whose very identities and livelihoods are based precisely on different concerns and interests. Within a theory of hegemony, the war of position, or alliance-building realm, is clearly of great importance to anyone engaged in political movements or social activism. If Gramsci's point is that this phase should produce one singular and unified conception of the world, one may doubt his applicability to twenty-first century activism. Such a contention is certainly related to Laclau and Mouffe's reading of Gramsci as 'essentialist' and too much rooted in economism, which we shall explore in the next chapter. But thinking about this unified conception of the world, or national–popular collective will, as a language certainly opens up numerous possibilities. First, and most importantly, it makes such a hegemonic movement that includes a diversity of social groups seem more practical and probable. Hegemony becomes a process including negotiations and critical alterations of one's world-view. The goal is to achieve a common language, not a singular dominant interpretation of everything that happens in the world and all human activity. Various and opposing perspectives can be expressed in such a language. However, this hegemonic (or counterhegemonic) language must be unified enough, coherent enough, to yield effective resistence to capitalist hegemony (and its language).[34] This is what separates counterhegemonic projects from loose alliances of different movements with unrelated goals. This is an important antidote to liberal defences of capitalism and criticisms of socialism and Gramsci.

A second advantage of Gramsci's focus on language as a model for his idea of national–popular collective will is that it is fully congruent with his discussions of language and conceptions of the world, the connections between politics and language issues, and his continual references to linguistics. It connects his philosophical perspective discussed in Chapter 3 to his political theory expressed in the concepts described in this chapter: passive revolution, war of manoeuvre, war of position, state and civil society.

## Hegemony, political alliances and the united front against Fascism

Some background to the types of alliances that Gramsci would have been thinking about will assist in determining the extent to which his concepts, such as hegemony and passive revolution, are useful on the very different political terrain of the twenty-first century. Because Gramsci has been accused of being too mired in presupposing that class should be a privileged category, such an inquiry will reveal the extent to which it makes sense to use his concepts in very different historical circumstances and to think about substantially different types of terrain on which the war of position has to be fought.

During Gramsci's most politically active years, from 1919 to 1926, he seems to have had a complex position about who to work and enter into alliances with. On one hand, his experiences in the *Biennio Roso* led him to extreme frustration with the Socialist Party and its leaders, persuading him to join forces with Amadeo Bordiga to form a separate Communist party. As the representative of this new party to the Communist International (the Comintern) in Moscow, Gramsci resisted pressure to reunite the Communist and Socialist Parties of Italy. From these issues, he may seem to be a staunch separatist, wary of making alliances that are too broad. However, Gramsci was more open than other communists and socialists to alliances with anti-Fascist liberals and other bourgeois forces. At the time, the other contender for leadership of the Communist Party, Amadeo Bordiga, rejected such alliances, claiming that Fascism was a product of bourgeois liberalism and essentially no different from it. The specific details of these positions have been the subject of considerable scholarly research, which we will leave aside. But we can think about his general approach in not putting individuals, parties and groups of people in a simple Right–Left spectrum. Rather, Gramsci seems to be considering a more complex set of issues about how a counterhegemonic force can be created to provide the greatest resistence to Fascism. Or, put in the metaphors of language, how a language and grammar, a discourse, can be created to counter the popular attraction of Fascism. While the Socialist Party may share more values and ideals in the abstract with the communists than do many liberals or Catholics, they create portions of a grammar that make it more difficult to speak to the wider, national popular concerns. Specifically, Gramsci argued, the Socialist leaders discouraged active political protest and involvement by its general membership, refused to face Mussolini and Fascism head-on, and did not incorporate the southern peasantry into its movement. Perhaps the Socialist Party was at some abstract level closer to the ideology of Gramsci and the communists in their critique of capitalism and focus on the northern proletariat in opposing capitalism, but the Socialist Party position created other values – grammatical forms if you will – that were more inimical to the creation of an effective progressive movement – or language – than the values of liberals, especially of those like Gramsci's friend, Piero Gobetti.[35]

How does Gramsci assess whether or not a particular alliance will help construct an effective national–popular grammar? That is, how is his distinction between spontaneous and normative grammar related to the 'passive revolution' and war of position? Before coming to this, we need to sketch out Gramsci's related distinction between 'civil society' and the 'state'. This is a crucial distinction because the war of position is often thought of as taking place within civil society, whereas the war of manoeuvre is seen as a struggle over the state.

## State and civil society

Gramsci explains his metaphor of 'war of position' with recourse to the concept of 'civil society'. This term has a long history but has gained new mainstream prominence since 1989 and the fall of the Soviet Union. Liberals and neo-liberals understand civil society as that realm of society separate from the government and its control. This includes everything from individual businesses, business associations, lobby groups and trade unions to charities, community groups like the YM-YWCA or Rotary Club and churches and religious groups. In other words, institutions that either did not exist in the Soviet Union, or existed only under the ambit of the state. The concept of civil society became a convenient term to emphasize the supposed freedom of capitalist democracy and how it should be exported or encouraged in post-Soviet societies. As we shall see, Gramsci uses civil society in a more sophisticated manner to investigate how the state and the various institutions of civil society are often intertwined or related.[36] For Gramsci, civil society is the terrain in Western societies upon which a 'war of position' is fought. It is also inherently connected to the state (its various institutions and influences) to varying degrees in different societies.

We shall explore the nuances below, but civil society is central to Gramsci as a location of hegemony and political power in modern democracies. In discussing how the image of trench warfare, raised previously in relation to the war of position, is pertinent to political struggle, Gramsci states:

> The superstructures of civil society are like the trench-systems of modern warfare. In war it would sometimes happen that a

fierce military attack seemed to have destroyed the enemy's entire defensive system, whereas in fact it had only destroyed the outer perimeter; and at the moment of their advance and attack the assailants would find themselves confronted by a line of defenders which was still effective. The same thing happens in politics, during economic crises.[37]

Gramsci argues that because of this situation – the importance of civil society in western Europe – communists could not just wait for a crisis, nor mount an all-out war of manoeuvre. Instead, the strategy should be one of creating a trench system, fighting to win over the superstructures of civil society, attempting to create a coherent world-view that could unify a wide variety of different groups amongst the popular masses. When a crisis did occur, a war of manoeuvre could actually be successful, rather than just a revolutionary moment that would give way to a restoration of the old regime when the economic crisis subsided. The argument is that as long as a pro-capitalist government held adequate prestige and legitimacy in civil society, any momentary conquest of the state or government would be viewed as illegitimate and undemocratic. Civil society would still be able to effectively defend the legitimacy of the overthrown capitalist forces that could make a comeback similar to counter-revolution and restoration successes in England, France and Germany from the seventeenth to the nineteenth centuries. In sum, Gramsci understands civil society as the terrain of struggle.[38] But what exactly constitutes civil society for Gramsci, his predecessors and for us today?

### The history of state and civil society

While the terms 'state' and 'civil society' both have long histories and were used by Aristotle, Locke and Rousseau, amongst others, for Gramsci, the crucial points of reference are Marx and Hegel. Hegel divided society up into three spheres, the family, civil society (*bürgerliche Gesellschaft*) and the state. He emphasized civil society as the realm of individuals, outside of family units, who enter into interactions that are competitive, especially those involving economic activity. Civil society, for Hegel, is the distinctively modern realm that is neither public nor private strictly speaking, but is the social world where individuals attempt to meet their particular needs. For Hegel, this includes the legal system and police, which guarantee the security of one's person and property.[39]

In his famous Preface to *A Contribution to the Critique of Political Economy*, Marx argued that the anatomy of civil society was to be found in the economy. While he did not deny that civil society was more extensive than purely economic organizations and activities, he focused his attention on the narrower or more fundamental aspect of civil society, the economy. Through an analysis of the capitalist economy, Marx argued that the state, far from being separate from civil society or neutral and 'universal' (Hegel's argument), contained the particularities of the ruling class, favoured capitalists over workers and fostered class divisions.

There is a substantial debate about whether Gramsci derived his notion of 'civil society' primarily from Hegel and in opposition to Marx, or whether he was developing Marx's insights in a more detailed manner with respect to state theory, a project of Marx's that he left incomplete.[40] Indeed, Gramsci refers to Hegel's conception of civil society as the way it is 'often used in these notes (i.e. in the sense of political and cultural hegemony of a social group over an entire society, as the ethical content of the state)'.[41]

There is, however, relative agreement that Gramsci's major point is that in 'the West' – that is, the relatively democratic, liberal and industrialized countries such as England, France, Germany and to a lesser extent Italy – hegemony is created through the institutions of civil society. In describing civil society, Gramsci presents if not a different definition from Marx's, at the very least, a different focus on the important elements of civil society.[42] The Church, the trade unions, the Rotary Club, the Freemasons and a wide variety of other institutions that exist outside direct state control are central elements of civil society as Gramsci uses the term.[43] But he also follows Hegel in including the public education system, the justice system and even the police: institutions often thought of as part of the state.[44] This is where the confusions and complexity lie, since institutions like these and the Church can be seen as belonging to both Gramsci's state and civil society. This potential confusion will be addressed below with a discussion of the state. But for now we can say that Gramsci's conception of 'civil society' creates a different emphasis than Marx's focus on the economy as the anatomy of civil society.[45] That is, Gramsci agrees with Marx that schools, churches and such institutions cannot be analysed separately from the economy, but if by 'anatomy' Marx meant the most fundamental or determining part of civil society, then Gramsci disagrees.

Indeed, Gramsci criticizes Marx's use of this metaphor, noting that its roots in the natural sciences are perhaps not applicable to social science. He then links Marx's 'anatomy' metaphor to the notion that 'superstructures' are merely appearances, which, he argues, is a deviation from the philosophy of praxis. He compares such ideas to a pubescent boy thinking about love for a woman in relation to her skeletal structure and the width of her pelvic girdle. Noting how such an attitude is inherently pessimistic and superficial, Gramsci severely undermines any such reduction of civil society to the economy.[46] This is not to say he veers at all from Marx's critique of the capitalist economy as the central dynamic of exploitation and power in industrialized bourgeois society. His point is to look in greater detail at how the exploitation of capitalism is maintained through bourgeois ideology and garners considerable acquiescence and consent (even if this is passive and created through veiled coercive threats).

## The state

We now turn to Gramsci's writings about the state. This is the most complex and disputed of the debates within Gramscian scholarship. Where there are disagreements over his notions of hegemony and civil society and his other concepts, there is substantial agreement on what these concepts add to political and social theory. But when it comes to discussions of the state, there seems to be less consensus. This is partially due to the fact that in dealing with the state, one confronts Gramsci's clearly different and possibly irreconcilable formulas for relating hegemony, civil society, the state (including what he describes by more specific terms, such as 'integral state' and 'ethical state'), political society, coercion and consent. Some argue that these differences constitute relatively distinct 'models' and either bemoan their inconsistency or provide complex systems for reconciling them.[47] The most attentive scholars have placed these equations of Gramsci's within differing historical contexts, expanding on the types of distinction that we saw with Femia in relation to integral, minimal and decadent hegemony. The argument is clearly that different societies contain different relations between civil society and the state. This is indeed the major point of Gramsci's most famous passage concerning the state and civil society:

> In Russia [before 1917] the state was everything, civil society was primordial and gelatinous; in the West, there was a proper relation between state and civil society, and when the state trembled a sturdy structure of civil society was at once revealed. The state was only an outer ditch, behind which there stood a powerful system of fortresses and earthworks. ... [48]

In addition to highlighting the importance in the West of the struggle for civil society, this passage presents the state and civil society as elements of the enemy camp that require overcoming. In other words, in contrast to current liberal and mainstream uses of the term, for Gramsci civil society is far from a neutral terrain with respect to the state. The structures and institutions of bourgeois civil society prop up and reinforce the state. As we saw earlier, civil society seems to be able to maintain bourgeois rule even if the trembling state actually crumbles.

But the question of how Gramsci understood the specific relationship between civil society and the state is less clear. He is certainly broadening earlier Marxist and Leninist definitions of the state as just a tool of the ruling class to cope with class antagonism through the use of coercion. Lenin used Engel's writings to argue that the state is by definition the product of class antagonisms. As such, it uses military and police capacity to control such antagonisms within a territorial boundary.[49] Gramsci accepts an aspect of Lenin's point: 'It is true that the state is seen as the organ of one particular group, destined to create favourable conditions for the latter's maximum expansion.' But he adds to this a much greater sense of the state being a balance of forces including subordinate classes such as workers and peasants:

> ... the dominant group is coordinated concretely with the general interests of the subordinate groups, and the life of the

State is conceived as a continuous process of formation and superseding of unstable equilibria (on the juridical plane) between the interests of the fundamental group and those of the subordinate groups – equilibria in which the interests of the dominant group prevail, but only up to a certain point ...[50]

His emphasis on the balance of forces within the state is comparable to the stream of political theory from Machiavelli and Montesquieu to Charles Taylor and other non-Marxist analyses of 'balance of power'.[51] Here, Gramsci's discussion of the state as a balance of forces is in the context of two other aspects of how social forces are assessed: material forces of production (how human needs are met) and military force (including the police). So Gramsci is not necessarily departing from Lenin's argument, except by paying greater attention to the types of concession the ruling class must make in order to govern without having to use extensive coercion and violence. Once again, we need to keep in mind that Gramsci was comparing the different conditions of western Europe to those of Russia, where the Czarist regime used greater degrees of coercion.

Gramsci repeats and expands this idea that it is crucial to investigate how the state rules without resorting to brute force. He writes,

If political science means science of the State, and the State is the entire complex of practical and theoretical activities with which the ruling class not only justifies and maintains its dominance, but manages to win the active consent of those over whom it rules, then it is obvious that the essential questions of sociology are nothing other than the questions of political science.[52]

In these instances, Gramsci is using the term 'state' in its broadest sense, or what he labels its 'integral meaning', as in his oft-quoted equation, the state in its integral meaning is 'dictatorship + hegemony'.[53] In another of the most quoted parts of the *Prison Notebooks*, he writes, 'one might say that State = political society + civil society, in other words hegemony protected by the armour of coercion'.[54] These and other passages have led Perry Anderson to argue that Gramsci has three different, incompatible models of how hegemony, civil society and the state are related.

In the first model, according to Anderson, Gramsci's major distinction is that between civil society and state, which is roughly synonymous to the distinction between coercion and consent; or hegemony and dictatorship; or, as in the above equation, civil society and political society; or hegemony and the armour of coercion. The second model rests on a similar opposition between coercion and consent, but hegemony (and/or the integral state) is now a balance of the two terms, civil society (consent) and political society (coercion). In the third model, hegemony fuses the very notions of civil society and state.[55] According to Anderson, this model is at odds with Gramsci's idea that hegemony is the consensual authority located in civil society as distinct from the coercive power of the state.

Other scholars are less disturbed by the variations of scope and reference in Gramsci's terms. Anne Showstack Sassoon, for example, notes that Gramsci uses two different definitions of the state, one limited and the other enlarged. The latter includes civil society, the former is distinct from it. She attributes what Anderson sees as a confusion in Gramsci's understanding to his awareness 'of the problem of delineating the differences or boundaries between civil and political society'. In other words, Gramsci's ambiguities are due to the complexities of the relations he is describing, not his own shortcomings. Sassoon argues that these are differences of emphasis, not essentially different notions of the state.[56]

Roger Simon offers still another way of reconciling Gramsci's seemingly ambiguous and different ways of relating hegemony, state and civil society. He argues that civil society and the state do not for Gramsci describe categories of institutions or physical (or metaphorical) spaces or spheres, but rather different sets of relations. Thus any organization, such as the school system, can embody relations belonging to both civil society and the state. The teacher–student relation that is supposed to be non-coercive is embedded in the compulsion of truancy laws and school rules and discipline.[57]

Others have taken similar approaches, but noted that Gramsci's key distinction between civil society and the state is that the activity of subaltern groups exists solely within civil society, whereas ruling groups act within both civil society and the state, and thus there is an overlap. Joseph Buttigieg explains that 'civil society is the arena wherein the ruling class extends and reinforces its power by nonviolent means. ...' and thus the space that the proletariat must struggle to occupy. Buttigieg emphasizes that for Gramsci, the proletariat power in civil society cannot and should not rely on the coercive power of the state.[58]

While I do not contend that a recourse to the analogy of language solves these complexities, it does seem that it provides some insight. Some of the potential confusions about how Gramsci defines the state in relationship to civil society and hegemony are reminiscent of his distinctions between normative and spontaneous grammars. Though he makes a distinction between the two, as we saw in Chapter 3, he does not separate them. With the argument that state and civil society are distinct concepts but not separated we enter into a potentially fuzzy arena about the difference, as emphasized by Anderson. The lack of clarity is exacerbated because of the centrality of the coercion/consent distinction. If Gramsci's whole point is that hegemony is substantially supported by the consent of those governed, it is essential that his concepts do not confuse us with respect to where and how this consent is formed, and how it is related to coercion.

In distinguishing (but not separating) normative and spontaneous types of grammar, Gramsci provides a specific model for these relations. Normative grammars are formed (made normative) by codifying one spontaneous grammar and excluding others, or through a process of engaging and transforming a multitude of spontaneous grammars. This process can include both coercion and consent. More than that, this process combines – to different degrees – consent and coercion. You alter your language when those you are speaking to continually ask 'What do you mean?' 'Explain yourself', as discussed in Chapter 3. In many instances, no explicit coercion is necessarily involved here. You consent to change your language. However, depending on the context, there is considerable coercion at play.[59] If you do not make yourself understood, you are the one who suffers the consequences, not your listener. This is clearly a power relationship. A student, worker or job applicant, for example, is more apt to alter their language in order to be judged favourably than a teacher, employer or interviewer. But this latter group still may try hard to be understood, and they may even suffer grave consequences if they fail, such as an unwieldy class resulting in a bad reputation for the teacher; or an unproductive workforce; or the inability to fill crucial job postings. In such circumstances, it may be difficult to demarcate clearly the distinction between consent and coercion. Such situations also illustrate how resistance is possible even in subtle ways. Those who are the recipients of force can react in various ways.

As we saw in the last chapter, one is tempted to think of spontaneous grammar as the location of consent and normative grammar as the process whereby varying degrees of coercion come into play. This is not unlike Anderson's first model of hegemony, civil society and the state. Civil society and hegemony are the realm of consent and the state is coercive. But Gramsci gives us a more sophisticated theory of coercion and consent by considering where spontaneous grammars come from. Just as he rejects the liberal assumption that civil society is the realm of consent and the state the realm of coercion, he similarly rejects the simplistic equations of spontaneous grammar with consent and normative grammar with coercion. Spontaneous grammars are the result of historical loss of consciousness and fragmentation from previous normative grammars. Thus, neither spontaneous grammar nor civil society are defined as realms of consent (or free will). Nor is either coercive in essence. Rather coercion and consent operate through both normative grammars and spontaneous grammars, in both active and passive forms. We shall see in Chapter 5 how this complex notion of power has brought about comparisons of Gramsci with Michel Foucault. Partially because of this, it is important to note that Gramsci differs from Foucault in arguing that the war of position is never an end in itself, but is always the preparation for a war of manoeuvre.

Gramsci argues that at some point a war of manoeuvre, or an attempt to topple the bourgeois state, is necessary. A normative national language must be the goal of linguistic change for communists and any progressive movement. But, as with his argument that a war of manoeuvre without a sufficient war of position (at least in the West) will result in defeat from civil society, so too, the adoption of Esperanto or some already created language will be short-lived due to pressures from the language practices that have not been altered. That is, a passive revolution, in language or government, will leave a residue from the pre-revolutionary period, which will continue to frustrate and trouble any new institutions or practices. This can be fought against, but only through recourse to ever more brute force, as in the case of the rise of Fascism. But this is neither practical nor ethical from Gramsci's position, even for the short-term goals of the proletariat.

On both the linguistic front and the political front, what is required is a more thorough process of reciprocal change throughout civil society, an interaction among various ways of understanding the world, institutions and languages of different subaltern groups. It is only from this process that a normative grammar (or national–popular collective will) can be formed that will be able to launch a truly effective war of manoeuvre and topple the bourgeois state and capitalist society.

## Conclusion

Chapter 3 noted how Gramsci's hegemony is attractive in part because it combines a sense of institutional and economic analysis with less tangible questions of ideology and belief systems. Where that chapter focused more on the latter and raised philosophical issues through a focus on language, this chapter has concentrated on several of Gramsci's concrete historical investigations, especially the failures of Italy's liberal past and the consequences of the lingering tensions surrounding unification. Where political scientists often focus on his conceptions of the state and civil society, those involved with cultural studies tend to be more attuned to his notions of 'common sense', the roles of intellectuals and the shaping of ideas, beliefs and commitments. Of course, any introduction that attempts to provide a more complete overview must give weight to all such aspects. Language is a fortuitous topic with which to link these aspects of Gramsci's hegemony precisely because it too can be concrete and empirical but also rich with philosophical complexity. But now it is time to engage in a different reason to focus on language. Chapter 5 does not only address Gramsci's ideas and analyses, it compounds this project with a theme that has been an undercurrent in this book until now: that is, how does Gramsci's cultural and political theory relate to current theoretical debates; and perhaps most pressingly, how does it help us to understand the world in which we live today?

# 5
# Postmodernism, New Social Movements and Globalization: Implications for Social and Political Theory

This chapter expands the opening chapter's discussions of Gramsci's focus on language, which puts him in line with some of the major themes in social and political theory emerging from the twentieth century that predominate our concerns today. The intervening chapters have introduced Gramsci's political theory through this concern with language, showing how for him linguistics was an important source of the metaphors and concepts that he used in cultural and political analysis. Chapter 2 in particular, but also Chapters 3 and 4, demonstrated the importance that Gramsci attributed to language politics in Italian history and the molecular operations of political power, and the potential for revolutionary organization of resistance against capitalism. This final chapter ties together these themes with those addressed in the Introduction and Chapter 1 by examining three of the most central developments in political and social theory in the latter half of the twentieth century: postmodernism, new social movements and globalization. These major developments – each of which alone could be the basis of a book on Gramsci – all relate to language in important ways.

Gramsci holds an interesting role within debates between Marxism and postmodernism. Although it is difficult to demonstrate conclusively, his unique position seems in part due to the complexities surrounding the ways in which language, ideas and beliefs relate to the more tangible domains of economic production and the control of wealth and resources. In this way, the questions raised by debates around postmodernism continue to be important for understanding and utilizing theories about new social movements and globalization.

Marxist critics of postmodernism often focus on the opposition between the materialist perspective of Marx, especially his focus on the economy, and oppose it to postmodernism, which often focuses on language, text, discourse and culture. Likewise, critics of 'orthodox' Marxism, whether postmodernist, post-Marxist or something else, often argue that Marx's and Marxism's obsession with the economy and production is too narrow and outdated for addressing current political and social dynamics. Gramsci has been used to play both sides of the field. Some see him as a Marxist who pays adequate attention to culture and the non-economic aspects of power relations.[1] Others see him as still too mired in Marxism, production and the economy, so much so that he is not useful for understanding 'new social movements' since he presupposes that any revolutionary change must be led by an industrial working class.[2] Many of these debates are premised on a basic distinction between language as a non-material entity and the economy, production and commodities as non-linguistic, 'material' entities. Culture is such an interesting concept because it travels on both sides of this distinction. My contention is that among other attractive features of Gramsci's writings is his refusal to accept the assumed opposition between the materiality of the economy and commodities versus the non-materiality of language, signification and communication.

By providing tools for us to investigate the various factors involved, Gramsci does a great service, especially when looking at the current world economy, in which more and more commodities have both material or physical components, and also non-material components, whether the prestige of a brand name or a patented design or a computer program. More precisely, Gramsci provides a Marxist framework that does not impose an unworkable separation of the 'material' versus the 'non-material'. As Gramsci argues:

> ... 'matter' should be understood neither in the meaning that it has acquired in natural science (physics, chemistry, mechanics, etc. – meanings to be noted and studied in terms of the historical development), nor in any of the meanings that one finds in the various materialistic metaphysics. The various physical (chemical, mechanical, etc.) properties of

matter which together constitute matter itself ... should be
considered, but only to the extent that they become a
productive 'economic element.' Matter as such therefore is
not our subject but how it is socially and historically organised
for production. ...[3]

This passage does not mention language or the non-material.
Nor does it present a relativist epistemology. Indeed, it is preoccupied with the 'economic', the question of production. But
Gramsci here rejects a crude materialist perspective in favour of
a social and historical perspective. It is this perspective that
opens up the crucial questions relating to the organization of
meaning, value and communication when looking at production.
From our historical vantage point, given the technological developments begun in Gramsci's time and discussed in Chapter 1,
it is easy to see that the 'economic' characteristics of many
increasingly important commodities – television shows, computer programs and brand names themselves – are difficult to
conceptualize as 'material' in the sense of physical properties as
studied by the natural sciences outside human relations of
meaning.

Gramsci's use of the label 'historical materialism' to describe
Marxism places a heavy emphasis on the 'historical' adjective,
allowing us to go beyond an overly simplistic opposition
between 'materialism' and 'idealism'. It is this approach, including his theorization of language, that makes Gramsci especially
relevant in a world of debates about postmodernism, new social
movements and globalization.

## Postmodernism, language and relativism: is all the world a text?

It is almost impossible to adequately define the term 'postmodernism', and such a project may be of questionable value given
the myriad debates surrounding the term and the trends that it
is supposed to describe. Nevertheless, in the diverse theories and
phenomena that have been associated with postmodernism,
some notion of language consistently takes centre stage.
Moreover, Gramsci is often compared to other theorists associated
with postmodernism, especially Foucault, and plays an important role in debates around postmodernism and post-Marxism.

This makes postmodernism important when assessing Gramsci's influence, continued relevance and future importance.

Among those who are often labelled 'postmodernist' – although many of them, such as the French theorists Jacques Derrida and Michel Foucault, reject the label – language and discourse are central objects of study. Not unlike what we have seen with Gramsci, linguistics and the philosophy of language are sources of central concepts, ideas and metaphors. For example, Jean-Francois Lyotard, one of the most prominent figures in developing the term 'postmodern', relies heavily on Wittgenstein's notion of 'language games' in order to describe how what he calls postmodern knowledge is legitimated by the users of language, not by some appeal to a non-linguistic, eternal truth.[4] Perhaps the other most notable theorist who accepts the label 'postmodernist', Jean Baudrillard, argues that our society has entered a postmodern era that can no longer be described or understood using concepts of material commodities, economies and production but looks to the semiotics of symbolic exchange and its dynamics. Once again, as a major example of symbolic exchange, language is an underlying focus.[5]

Others, such as Fredric Jameson and David Harvey, who are critical of positions or methods that could be labelled 'postmodern theory', argue that 'postmodern' is a useful description of our contemporary historical circumstances and its cultural products. Such theorists emphasize that the 'post' of postmodern does not constitute a break from or fundamental change in the exploitative dynamics of capitalism. Rather, postmodernism is a new or advanced stage and development of processes integral to modern capitalism.[6] (As will be discussed below, such questions lead to our other themes, new social movements and globalization.)

In addition to such basic disagreements about whether 'postmodern' should be used to describe a historical era or a political and philosophical position, there is the fundamental question of what notion of 'modern' or 'modernism' it is that the 'post' relates to. 'Postmodernism' is used differently in contexts such as architecture, art or literature from the way it is used in political theory, sociology and philosophy. For example, in political philosophy, the 'post' of postmodernism implies a rejection of, or moving beyond, modern European theory, especially that rooted in the seventeenth and eighteenth centuries. Postmodernism is often associated with what are called 'anti-foundationalist' critiques of the Enlightenment, especially its commitment to progress, truth and reason as transcendental values located outside of history and culture.[7] In literature and art, the modernism that 'postmodernism' is beyond refers to movements of the late nineteenth and early twentieth centuries. Where modern political philosophy includes the Enlightenment and a relatively positive assessment of industrialization and advances in science, literary and artistic modern*ism* includes more critical reactions to modern, that is industrialized, urbanized and rationalized, society.[8]

Adding to such complexities is another question about the implications of postmodern theory. Steven Best and Douglas Kellner note the difference between what they call 'extreme postmodern theory' and a more moderate position. The extreme pole sees the 'post' of postmodernism as a total and complete critique and rejection of modern positions – both as a theoretical position and as a description of a historical epoch; whereas thinkers such as Foucault, Harvey and Richard Rorty, whatever their differences, pay great attention to the continuities between modernity or modern theory and postmodernity or postmodern theory.[9]

These are just a few of the reason why discussions of postmodernism are riddled with complexities, polemics and confusions. It is no wonder that postmodernism is often dismissed as merely a fad. Nevertheless, it is useful, especially for our purposes here, to note that many of the trends often associated with the term 'postmodern' are related to language and the semiotic methodology that developed out of the study of language as a system of signs. While the debates about postmodernism seem to have waned since the 1980s and early 1990s, many of the issues central to those debates are also related to theories of new social movements and have resurfaced in the burgeoning literature on globalization. Language is a case in point, especially as it addresses questions of epistemology, agency and political change, social consciousness and technological and economic developments of the so-called 'information age'.

Friedrich Nietzsche (1844–1900), while clearly only anachronistically associated with postmodernism, captured nicely one central feature of postmodernist attacks on Enlightenment notions of truth, reason and progress.

> Every concept originates through our equating what is unequal. No leaf ever wholly equals another, and the concept 'leaf'; is formed through an arbitrary abstraction from these individual differences, through forgetting the distinctions; ... What, then, is truth? A mobile army of metaphors, metonyms, and anthropomorphisms – in short, a sum of human relations, which have been enhanced, transposed, and embellished poetically and rhetorically, and which after long use seem firm, canonical, and obligatory to a people: truths are illusions about which one has forgotten that this is what they are; metaphors which are worn out ...[10]

Nietzsche connected his critique of modern philosophy and society with the cardinal theme of postmodernism; the centrality of language to perception, an emphasis on difference and a scepticism about our ability to derive truth by anchoring words into some non-linguistic, unmediated 'truth' that is outside human history and culture. These themes became central points of criticisms of postmodernism by Marxists and others.

### Nietzsche, Saussure and Derrida on language

Nietzsche argued that language does not refer to any ultimate non-linguistic truth on which to gauge the truth of language. In the terms of Chapters 2 and 3, language is not a nomenclature for the labelling of non-linguistic objects of the 'real' world. Moreover, not unlike Gramsci (see pages 84–9), Nietzsche argues that we often forget the extent to which language is based on metaphor. Many of these themes were extended by Martin Heidegger (1889–1976) and became the basis for what was labelled postmodernism.

While Ferdinand de Saussure, as we saw in Chapter 1, had a very different approach to truth and did not accept Nietzsche's criticisms of positivist science, his notion of language has important parallels. Specifically, as detailed in Chapter 1, Saussure argued that language is a system of signs that creates meaning through the differences between those signs (specifically the differences between different signifiers and, on another axis, the differences between different signifieds). Thus Saussure's notion that 'in language there is only difference' concurs with Nietzsche's contention that language cannot be anchored in some external, non-linguistic truth (although it is important to note that Saussure nowhere rejects the notion of a non-linguistic referent of a sign; he just does not give it a place within his science of language).

Jacques Derrida's philosophy of 'deconstruction' is based on the idea that language is unstable. He argues, as Saussure and many structuralists do, that the way we make meaning in language is through differences, specifically series of binary distinctions such as presence/absence, male/female, black/white, up/down. But against structuralism, Derrida argues that such systems of differences can always be 'deconstructed' since they are inherently unstable. In many of his texts, Derrida illustrates this instability of binaries by showing how one term is often privileged over the other, is used as if it does not need the other term – which Derrida most often calls the 'supplement' since it is supposedly merely supplementary. But this initial term's very identity is dependent on how it differs from the supplement. Thus the 'supplement' is not really just supplemental or secondary, but is central to the primary supposedly independent term.

In one of his earlier and most famous works, *Of Grammatology*, Derrida connects his criticisms of Western philosophy with a critical reading of Saussure's theory of language, which is so central to structuralism. Derrida's broad argument is that Western thought and society have elevated the idea of speech because it is associated with reason and rationality (the Greek word *logos* means both speech and reason), but also because it is the voice of an individual subject who, if present, can articulate 'truth'. In so doing, Derrida argues, the history of Western philosophy from Plato onwards has denigrated writing as being a secondary technique that necessarily comes after speech in order to preserve it, or to overcome the unfortunate situation of people who are unable to be present and to speak for themselves. In such cases, their words can be written and then read. Writing, according to Derrida, is often depicted as that which is artificial, secondary, and a mere reflection. And yet, he contends, writing is necessary because of the inadequacy of speech on its own. Speech requires writing to make up for what it cannot enact by itself, most notably codification, demarcation and presentation of a speaker's voice, even when the speaker is present. Derrida uses the texts of Rousseau, Saussure and Lévi-Strauss to illustrate this dynamic.

For Derrida, the relationship between speech and writing becomes a vehicle for one of his most important presentations of 'deconstruction'. He takes apart this supposed distinction and argues that the notion of speech, including reason, truth, authenticity and presence, actually depends upon the ideas of irrationality, falsity, artificiality and absence, and thus, conceptually, speech cannot exist before or without writing. They are a binary in which each term depends on the other term, and yet, that binary is constituted by the claim that speech is independent of and prior to writing, and, especially, that it is merely represented or inadequately copied in writing.[11]

Derrida uses an extended reading and criticism of Saussure's *Course in General Linguistics* (which we looked at in Chapter 1) to present much of this argument. Not unlike Gramsci's criticism of the Neogrammarians and the naturalization of 'normative grammar', Derrida criticizes Saussure for assuming that language could be a stable system of signs.[12] Gramsci also rejects notions of 'normative grammar' that present it as a stable or 'natural' system. But where Gramsci does this through the concept of 'spontaneous' or 'immanent' grammar, Derrida takes this basic point about the instability of language in a very different direction, mobilizing it to criticize Western philosophy and the general stability of 'meaning'. Gramsci is more concerned with the political ramifications of competing systems of meaning, with alternative 'grammars' and how they are incorporated into or resisted by normative grammars.

Derrida contends that the differences in language that create meaning are always unstable (and presumably they are equally unstable, since their degree of instability and its ramifications play no role in Derrida's deconstructions). They are binaries such as signifier/signified, or writing/speech, or female/male, that are not just distinctions. However, they are asymmetrical distinctions whereby one is defined as secondary to the other. Signifiers are those elements that signify the signified. Writing is described by Saussure (and accepted by common sense) as representing speech. Therefore, the common-sense assumption goes, writing is necessary only when speakers are absent and require to communicate. But, Derrida argues, the meaning of speech is derived from its distinction from writing, and thus it is necessary for us to understand what speech is.

Derrida does not equate deconstruction with rejection or even criticism in a simplistic way. Just because he unravels the supplementary dynamic of speech/writing, for example, he does not argue that we should not use these terms or distinctions. Rather, he wants to uncover the process of these binaries and make us aware of them. The process has similarities with the artistic notion of 'defamiliarizing' or 'making strange', whereby we are made more aware of something in our everyday world as our attention is drawn to it but we see it from a different perspective, in a new, less familiar, strange light.[13] Derrida and his deconstructive method have been criticized for undermining clear political objectives and the distinctions upon which they rest, because he indiscriminately 'deconstructs' all binaries, including just/unjust, legitimate/illegitimate, exploitation/freedom, friend/enemy. This could lead to nihilism or political apathy.

One of the crucial questions concerning Gramsci, Derrida and language is the degree to which Gramsci's critique of 'normative grammar' is comparable to Derrida's critique of the presumed stability of sign systems. For numerous reasons, many of the objections lodged against Derrida, especially around the political significance of 'deconstruction', are inapplicable to Gramsci. The question is, to what extent do Gramsci's notions of 'spontaneous grammar' and 'normative grammar' help those who have found Derrida's ideas politically useful? Are Gramsci's concepts preferable in illustrating the potential political effects of showing the instability of hegemonic conceptual categories, grammars, 'common sense' and world-views? This is a question I will leave open for the reader.

Without conflating the positions of Nietzsche, Saussure and Derrida, we can see that all of them understand language as a system of signs (stable for Saussure, unstable for Derrida) that does not create meaning through its external relations to some world outside of language. It is precisely this point with which many Marxist critics of postmodernism take issue. They argue that this notion of language based on metaphor, this

Postmodernism, New Social Movements and Globalization   135

'mobile army' that is not rooted in a non-linguistic so-called external reality, necessarily leads to apolitical positions that have no normative foundations from which to criticize capitalism.

## Language and relativism in Gramsci

There is a debate within Gramsci scholarship about his epistemology. Some offer a 'realist' interpretation. While they admit that some of Gramsci's writings seem to suggest a suspicion of the empiricist notion of an 'objective reality' that humans interpret, the realist interpreters argue that he never rejects such ideas.[14] However, his writings on language reinforce the opposite interpretation and square quite closely with Nietzsche's notion that language is a 'mobile army of metaphors'. This brings Gramsci much closer to the anti-foundationalism often characteristic of postmodernism, although Gramsci's approach does not emphasize that no objective notion of reality is possible, nor that such a perspective on language leads to relativism in the moral or epistemological sense. 'Relativism' is another tricky term that has numerous different definitions. They range from the more extreme notion that every belief is as valid as any other to the more moderate position that there are different (and contradicting) methods for determining what is 'true'.

Gramsci's argument is that the very question about the connection between the human subjective world and the 'natural' objective world external to humanity is based on an abstract and ultimately (or originally) religious foundation. Gramsci argues that the bugaboo question of relativism, or what he calls the 'so-called existence of the external world', presupposes a separation between the world of humans and a world without humans, which is a hypothetical abstraction. It is based on the idea that the world was created before humans (by God for example) and then humans were placed in that world; whereas the Marxist perspective of historical materialism understands humanity as developing from within the natural world and only becoming alienated from it due to the human development of the division of labour, and especially the division of human society into classes and the expropriation of the labour of some by others. Gramsci's source for this argument is Marx's writings.

It helps to start from a famous passage in *Capital* where Marx distinguishes between humans and animals (i.e. elements of nature). Marx notes that

> [a] spider conducts operations that resemble those of a weaver, and a bee puts to shame many an architect in the construction of her cells. But what distinguishes the worst architect from the best of bees is this, that the architect raises his structure in imagination before he erects it in reality ... he realises a purpose of his own that gives the law to his modus operandi, and to which he must subordinate his will.[15]

Gramsci never explicitly addresses this passage or this distinction although he too is highly concerned with human intellectual labour and its role in production. But we can presume that he does not conceive of the exceptional qualities of human consciousness and intellect in terms akin to religious separations between soul and matter, sacred and profane. Gramsci raises this issue in a discussion of the Hungarian Marxist philosopher, Georg Lukács:

> It would appear that Lukács maintains that one can speak of the dialectic only for the history of men and not for nature. He might be right and he might be wrong. If his assertion presupposes a dualism between nature and man he is wrong because he is falling into a conception of nature proper to religion and to Graeco-Christian philosophy and also to idealism which does not in reality succeed in unifying and relating man and nature to each other except verbally.[16]

While he never addresses whether or not it makes sense to call animal communication language, this quotation shows that he cannot hold that humans use language to communicate about a non-human, natural and non-linguistic world. His writings on language, as we saw in Chapters 2 and 3, make it very clear that he rejects the idea of language as nomenclature, but instead sees language as central to the production of meaning and creating the world. His discussion of the metaphoric nature of language, coupled with the argument against a 'so-called objective external world' yields an epistemology and perspective that rules out any notion that language is separate from some 'real' non-subjective world, and yet anchored or secured in that world through reference to it.

So Gramsci agrees with some of the major themes around language that many scholars (both detractors and advocates) attribute to postmodernism; although we should make clear that for him this does not lead to some free-floating world in which meaning is somehow ephemeral or infinitely sliding. Rather, his emphasis is on the historical production of meaning and the interconnectedness of human history and 'objective' knowledge. For Gramsci, it is the abstractions of traditional philosophy, which are impossible to sustain in our daily experiences, that lead to debates about objectivity.[17] Most people do not raise such questions in their everyday lives.

But when questions of 'objectivity' and 'reality' are raised, Gramsci notes that 'common sense' often provides a deficient answer. 'Common sense', as noted in Chapter 3, is fragmentary and includes the residue from religious and mystical world-views. This is particularly true, according to Gramsci, with questions of the 'objective world'. Gramsci argues that the very question is framed by the idea that God created the world and then created humans, his chosen creatures, and put them into an already created world. This is the root of what Gramsci calls 'the "fearsome" question of the "objective reality of the external world"', which he argues 'is badly framed and conducted worse and is to a great degree futile and useless'. He continues:

> The popular public does not think that a problem such as whether the external world exists objectively can even be asked. One just has to enunciate the problem in these terms to provoke an irresistible and gargantuan outburst of laughter. The public 'believes' that the external world is objectively real, but it is precisely here that the question arises: what is the origin of the 'belief' and what critical values does it 'objectively' have? In fact the belief is of religious origin, even if the man who shares it is indifferent to religion. Since all religions have taught and do teach that the world, nature, the universe were created by God before the creation of man, and therefore man found the world all ready made, catalogued and defined once and for all, this belief has become an iron fact of 'common sense' ...[18]

Once we truly secularize 'science' and rational thought, according to Gramsci, we realize that we cannot separate human knowledge from some other foundation of truth. To do so is to create philosophical abstractions. This does not make Gramsci a relativist in terms of holding that all beliefs and positions are equally legitimate. Nor is he saying that there is no 'reality'. Nor is Gramsci an environmentalist or animal rights activist. He focuses on human experiences as more important than any other and presumes that morality is about acting towards humans and not necessarily the environment. But, not unlike many who are labelled postmodernists, Gramsci is suspicious of abstract distinctions that have important political ramifications, such as those between humans and nature, science and religion or language and physical reality. What distances him from some postmodernists, such as Baudrillard, is his disdain for any theoretical perspective that leads to passivity or fatalism. He does not share the apocalyptic nature that is often associated with postmodernism. Lastly, he is much more careful than those like Baudrillard in addressing questions about whether we can think of society as having moved into a new phase or general characterization such as postmodernity.[19]

## Foucault, language and power

In a manner quite different from Derrida, Foucault also is renowned for his conceptualization of language and specifically what he calls 'discourse'. While he has made several important incursions into the history of the study of language,[20] his greatest influence has been his approach in his studies on psychiatry and madness (*Madness and Civilization*), medicine and illness (*The Birth of the Clinic*), the human sciences of economics, biology and linguistics (*The Order of Things*), criminality (*Discipline and Punish*) and sexuality (*The History of Sexuality*).

Foucault is ultimately concerned with how our conceptualizations of issues like madness or illness or criminal activity shape our societies. He investigates how such issues, which he calls 'discourses', intersect and include the institutions such as asylums, hospitals and prisons. So, like Gramsci's, his understanding of power has a philosophical and institutional aspect. Where modern political philosophy tends to celebrate the freedoms associated with reason and the rational organization of society, Foucault's investigations into madness reveal the underside of such developments that serve to dominate, control and regulate human behaviour based on new discourses or disciplines like psychiatry, medicine and criminology. In this way, Foucault's work raises many criticisms of modernity, or at the very least exposes many of the less positive sides of modern 'progress' that are often overlooked.

Foucault's methods and especially his notions of 'discourse' and 'discursive formation' have been particularly important to his legacy. Thus, it is not just his investigations into the history of fields of study like biology or economics that account for his wide influence. Nor is it just his analysis of the rise of institutions like clinics and prisons that makes Foucault stand out. It is the way he investigates such topics and the general picture of the development of modern society that has garnered so much attention, positive and negative. What he means by 'discourse' and 'discursive formations' is not always clear nor agreed upon by scholars.

'Discourse' is derived from the Latin *discursus*, 'running to and fro'. It can mean the process of reasoning, most narrowly from premise to consequence, but also a discussion or conversation. Today, in common language it is most often used to mean a treatise or systematic written document about a given topic, such as Descartes' *Discourse on Method*. Foucault uses it to describe objects like biology, or medicine, or sexuality. They are specific groups of concepts and ways of thinking about some domain, but are larger than a single book or the works of any one author. For example, in his work *Madness and Civilization*, he traces how 'madness' comes to be seen as a threat to human reason, so that the insane must be confined and separated from the 'sane' population. Foucault argues that this development was due to the advent of science and medicine. However, he does not depict it as arising simply from increased knowledge about human mentality. Rather, the discourse of sanity and insanity has to do with a wider set of ideas, institutions and practices.

This notion of discourse and its inclusion of ways of thinking with institutions is illustrated by his opening section of *The Order of Things* (*Les Mots et les choses*). He recounts Louis Borges' short story about a Chinese encyclopaedia in which animals are classified according to whether they (a) belong to the Emperor,

(b) are embalmed, (c) are tame, (d) are sucking pigs, etc. ...
(h) are included in the present classification, or (n) from a long
way off look like flies.[21] This passage induced a shattering laugh-
ter for Foucault, but was also the starting point for a book that
attempts to analyse the relationships between our unspoken
ways of ordering our world and perceptions and reflections on
the codes and systems of order. He traces the developments in
the study of language from grammar and philology to linguistics, from natural history to biology, and the development of
political economy and economics.

Many have noted this similarity between Gramsci and
Foucault.[22] Both emphasize the institutional connections in
how we perceive the world – questions of ideology, culture and
world-view.[23] Such comparisons are fleshed out by considering
how 'discourse' relates to Gramsci's discussions of language,
especially grammar.

Manfred Frank describes Foucault's use of 'discourse' as being
'situated more or less halfway between a norm-following linguistic system and a purely individual use of language'.[24] That is,
Foucault's analyses place great emphasis on those systems of
knowledge, ordering and perception that are more specific than
what can be described in any given language like English, but
more broad than a given argument or perspective on a given
topic by one or a handful of individuals. The English language
can be used to describe religious creation theory as well as
biology or physics. Thus, discourse is not synonymous with
language. 'Biology' as a specific method for studying 'life' is, like
creation theory, more than one coherent and unified perspective on living organisms. Biology as a discourse extends well
beyond its initial formulations by Carolus Linnaeus (1707–78),
Georges Cuvier (1769–1832) or Charles Darwin (1809–82).

This is similar to Gramsci's criticism of Benedetto Croce's narrow and formalistic definition of 'grammar', which we investigated in Chapter 2. To respond to Croce, Gramsci developed the
distinction between normative and spontaneous grammars both
of which, like Foucault's 'discourse', are broader than specific
arguments but more constrained than an entire language – such
as English. Both Foucault's 'discourse' and Gramsci's 'grammars'
are connected with how one views the world and organizes its
contents. Croce, according to Gramsci, places too much emphasis
on individual expression and ignores the way that expressions

are structured through relatively explicit normative grammars, but especially through less explicit spontaneous grammars. This implies a distinction between 'grammar' and language that Gramsci never explicitly makes. Gramsci's discussion of these two types of grammar may provide a clearer framework than Foucault's 'discourse', especially around the question of agency and the operations of power. But before we address such criticisms of Foucault, a point about epistemology is necessary.

The epistemological implications of Foucault's work are that there is more than one way to order things. In other words, he rejects any notion that science progresses simply as it accumulates knowledge or approaches the 'truth'. That biology, criminology or medicine are discourses, specific ways of ordering objects, concepts, institutions, etc. means that different cultures and time periods utilize different such orders and it is impossible to determine in a simple way which is right or wrong, positive or negative. Foucault never states that the progress of human reason since the sixteenth century has been negative, but he calls our attention to some of the darker developments that go hand in hand with European society's embrace of reason, rationality and science. For Foucault, such 'modernization' is not innocent of domination and coercion. Indeed, one of Foucault's most famous images is that of the panopticon in *Discipline and Punish*, taken from his discussion of the Enlightenment philosopher Jeremy Bentham's prison, designed so that guards in a central position can see all the prisoners at once. The prisoners, however, cannot see whether or not the guards are observing them at any given moment. This means that the prisoners imagine that they are being watched even when they are not – a phenomenon replicated by the prevalence of security video cameras today that most often never record images that will be watched. The prisoner of the rationally designed prison of the eighteenth century is a model for the modern citizen who internalizes authority and regulation, and regulates themselves.

## Power in Gramsci and Foucault

Foucault and Gramsci are often compared, due to similarities in their notions of power and its operations.[25] Both see power as operating in complex ways in venues often not understood as political, strictly speaking. For them, politics as the operation of power is not just about governments, elections, or even the police and the army. Rather, politics occurs daily in everybody's lives, whether one is going to school, reading a novel or visiting the doctor. Some of the most crucial operations of power occur at the micro or molecular level.

Moreover, both Foucault and Gramsci see that power rarely operates in a simple unidirectional manner, with one person or group of people holding power and using it against another who is totally powerless. More often, those in dominant positions need to jockey and compete in order to exert their force and influence. And, more importantly, relatively powerless people acquiesce, consent to, enthusiastically encourage, or resist the use of such power. As we have seen, Gramsci makes this point in his concrete analyses of the *Risorgimento*, the Italian peasantry and working class and his concepts of the passive revolution, historic bloc and hegemony. Foucault makes related points in his analyses but critics question whether his analyses of power actually obscure the possibilities of political activism and progressive change. Feminists such as Nancy Hartsock argue that Foucault's concept of power is so molecular and multidirectional that 'systematically unequal relations of power ultimately vanish from Foucault's account of power'.[26] Moreover, she contends that Foucault's critical stance of undermining dominant institutions and those who hold power is muted by his ambiguity with regard to powerless people gaining some degree of subjectivity, agency and power with which not only to resist power, but, more importantly, to change its dynamics and operations. It is worth noting that Hartsock sees Gramsci as a positive alternative to Foucault as a source of theories of power for women.

Gramsci is often invoked for an activist perspective that provides not just a ruthless criticism or deconstruction of dominant hegemonies, but also an alternative 'counterhegemony', a concrete alternative to oppression. Such sentiments are borne out in his theory of language specifically because he distinguishes spontaneous from normative grammar. But, as we saw in Chapter 2, he does not make this distinction in a simplistic manner favouring spontaneous grammar as non-oppressive and criticizing normative grammar. On the contrary, in a way that is closer to Foucault's analysis of power, Gramsci's notion of spontaneous grammar shows how political influence works at the micro level and how even those who seem to have little power, working-class children for example, exert their dominance over peasant or immigrant children by making fun of the way they speak. Even the benign form of correcting someone's grammar or asking for clarification is not free of power relations or politics. This does not lead Gramsci to condemn people who correct grammar. In other words, Gramsci, like Foucault, is not trying to create some space free of power, free of such grammatical corrections. Rather both see the most significant political problems deriving from the denial that power is operating. Gramsci is not arguing that I should not correct your grammar. He is insisting that I cannot justify such correcting based on the notion that my grammar is 'better' than yours from an 'objective', ahistorical, natural perspective. That is, correcting grammar is an apolitical exercise. He leaves open the important case where teaching you the 'dominant' grammar in some circumstances can be empowering.

Similarly, Foucault is not against confining any mentally unstable individual. He wishes to show how the justification for such treatments cannot be reduced purely to objective, non-political, ahistorical, scientific knowledge. For both Gramsci and Foucault, we need to admit that power is operating in such cases. My grammar is correct because it is defined by the dominant social groups. For this very reason, it may be very important for members of 'subaltern' social groups to learn the dominant grammar.

The most significant difference between Foucault and Gramsci is that Foucault does not concentrate on the mechanisms by which people could consciously mobilize to change a given 'discourse' in a progressive direction. In a sense, 'discourse' fills too much space between a language – in which any perspective or world-view can be expressed – and individual expression. This may be connected to Foucault's more radical rejection of the notion that power operates vertically and unidirectionally from the dominant leaders to the dominated. While Gramsci analyses the complexity of power and its imbrication with consent, Foucault's notion of power as 'capillary' has been criticized for obscuring power differentials.[27]

Gramsci is very concerned with the complex contradictions within discourses, as is Foucault. But by mapping out how

spontaneous grammars can be combined and synthesized into a
progressive normative grammar, a unified common language,
Gramsci places much greater emphasis on agency and how collective political action can topple, or at least alter, systematic
inequality and oppression and lead to more equal power relations. Where Gramsci suggests better ways of forming normative
grammar than those of the dominant groups in Italy, Foucault is
vocal about positive alternative 'discourses'. The implication is
that all 'discourses' mobilize power and it is impossible to compare or judge the justice or equality of them.

### New social movements and discourse: Laclau and Mouffe

Postmodern theory is related to new social movements in a
number of ways. In the 1980s, theorists and activists used the
term 'new social movements' to relate the similarities among a
number of different political forces that were predominantly
progressive, non-parliamentary and that fitted neither the mainstream pluralist paradigm nor other analyses of labour, capital
and the state as proposed by Left and Marxist perspectives. The
African-American civil rights movement of the 1950s and 1960s,
Second Wave Feminism of the 1960s and 1970s, lesbian and gay
activism, student movements, anti-war, anti-nuclear, ecological
movements and many others have diverse historical roots and
demand political as well as social change. However, new social
movement literature emerging in the 1980s argues that the
advent of such movements constitute a general shift in politics
that did not result from any one of these movements alone.

These various groups and movements have diverse goals and
differing analyses of society, whether implicit or explicit. This can
create tensions, for example between environmentalists, who see
development and the consumption of natural resources as a primary harm, and workers concerned with low wages, exploitation
and dangerous working conditions, who may see development
and consumption as ameliorations of exploitative jobs. Should an
endangered animal species be protected if that means the clo-
sure of saw mills or other well-paying union jobs? Likewise,
working-class activists experiencing sexism often face a tension
between 'gender' and 'class' as important axes along which
power is unequally distributed.

Such obstacles and tensions can make the postmodernism rejection of 'grand narratives' particularly attractive. As we shall see, not requiring such overarching explanatory frameworks – whether gender, race or class are the fundamental or most significant axes of inequality and oppression in society – has been seen as a pragmatic way forward. It is much easier to create alliance or coalition politics across many groups of people who have grievances, experiences and goals that do not coincide, if you have rejected the notions of an absolute truth, of correct versus incorrect knowledge and unidirectional 'progress'. However, it may also open problems if these alliances break apart whenever their short-term, immediate goals cease to coincide. While on specific issues such differences within any given alliance may be inconsequential, if these movements wish to alter society substantially, such tensions are bound to cause problems.

Gramsci addresses this type of situation in noting that to gain and maintain hegemony requires more than an instrumental alliance. As Chapter 3 described, it involves going beyond mere 'corporate' interests of a given social group to embrace broader, more 'universal' needs of society at large, or at least, large sections of those groups in society that are subordinated. It is an open question how such postmodern ideas help build alliances to include such diverse goals as protecting the environment and the livelihood of workers, promoting women to prestigious and well-paying positions while struggling against capitalist exploitation. Whether postmodernism leaves very important questions unresolved and serves to obscure important questions about how power operates is a potential drawback that will be considered below.

New social movements are often defined negatively against the singular, old, political movements of the working classes. With the shrinking working class of post-industrial countries and declining union membership (if not earlier deradicalizations of labour movements), various radicals, Left activists and academics bid adieu, as André Gorz phrased it, to the proletariat as the potential leader of progressive change.

The most influential 'new social movements' theorists come from Left and Marxist backgrounds and retain much of their earlier 'radical' and 'progressive' goals. But they reject what they understand to be central tenets of Marxism: that the working class would play *the* primary role in progressive change; that such change was synonymous with the struggle against capitalism; that capitalism as a system based on the exploitation of surplus labour was the fundamental and overarching cause of oppression; and that history was somehow on the side of Marxism and its success was 'inevitable'. In 1985, with their book *Hegemony and Socialist Strategy*, Ernesto Laclau and Chantal Mouffe were some of the first theorists to explicitly present such a post-Marxist perspective through an appropriation of many postmodernist and post-structuralist ideas. As Alan Keenan has recently remarked, 'The importance of new social movements for Laclau and Mouffe's overall argument, and for their conception of radical and plural democracy, can hardly be overstated.'[28]

Laclau and Mouffe's work is an important focus since it has been among the most influential theoretically and draws significantly from Derrida, Foucault and the linguistically oriented poststructuralism discussed above. Gramsci plays a prominent role in their trajectory out of Marxism into post-Marxism and their 'radical democratic' theory of new social movements. As I will discuss at greater length below, theories of language play a perplexing role in Laclau and Mouffe's work, since they ignore Gramsci's writings on language, but present their move 'beyond' Marxism as a shift from economic essentialism (as will be explained below) to non-essentialist discourse theory. My particular position is that this picture is partial and one-sided to such an extent that it unravels their project to a significant degree, or at the very least their reading of Gramsci. Nevertheless, in this book I will try to present the issues in as fair a light as possible in order to introduce readers to the debates. One of the most influential criticisms of Laclau and Mouffe is that this shift from a Marxist critique of capitalism to 'radical democracy' that emphasizes pluralism, indeterminacy and contingency in effect leaves little room for analysis of, and struggle against, capitalism.[29] Gramsci's writings on language shed new light on both sides of this debate, putting into perspective the significance of Laclau and Mouffe's contributions. To engage such issues will require a fairly detailed overview of Laclau and Mouffe's work.

Prior to writing *Hegemony and Socialist Strategy*, both Ernesto Laclau and Chantal Mouffe were Marxists heavily influenced by

Louis Althusser and Gramsci.[30] Laclau had focused on the role of ideology in his home country of Argentina.[31] Mouffe, born in Belgium, also had formative experiences in Latin American politics, specifically the politics of Colombia.[32] *Hegemony and Socialist Strategy* describes a trajectory that parallels both authors' intellectual development with a description of the historical roots of hegemony that prepares the way for their reinterpretation. For them, 'hegemony' is the central concept leading them from specific traditions within Marxism that pay great heed to questions of ideology and culture and are critical of economic and class reductionism, to a rejection of what they themselves see as the fundamental tenets of Marxism. These are, according to them, the idea that history is 'inevitably' progressing towards the fall of capitalism and a communist revolution, that the working class will necessarily play the primary role in bringing about such a revolution and that such historical movement is irreversible. Gramsci plays a key role in this passage from the Marxism of Karl Kautsky and Georg Plekhanov through Rosa Luxemburg and Vladimir Lenin into their 'post-Marxism', which incorporates ideas of Jacques Lacan, Foucault and Derrida. In their words:

> Our principal conclusion is that behind the concept of 'hegemony' lies something more than a type of political relations *complementary* to the basic categories of Marxist theory. In fact, it introduces a *logic of the social* which is incompatible with those categories.[33]

They argue that the concept of hegemony within twentieth century Marxism has always been developed in response to a crisis of the central ideas of Marxism. Put simply, they focus on the difficulties surrounding the relationships between, on the one hand, class as an economic category, one's position within the economy, and, on the other hand, class consciousness, the collective identity and action of the working class. They argue that some early twentieth-century Marxists, especially Gramsci, become increasingly concerned with the latter term, class consciousness, as a political impulse but are unable to sever its connection with the former term, objective economic analysis. As we shall see, more or less explicitly, Laclau and Mouffe use language and concepts derived from linguistics to describe this notion of political consciousness and oppose it to economy as an objective, non-political realm.[34]

One of Laclau and Mouffe's prominent examples is the position of Rosa Luxemburg (1871–1917), a Jewish, Polish revolutionary who was also very influential in German and Russian socialism. Luxemburg was critical of the German Social Democrats' economic reductionism, which assumed that the economic conditions of capitalism would inevitably lead to a class consciousness that would transform capitalism into socialism. Luxemburg argues that mass strikes, often seen as a tactic of anarchists and 'backward' countries like Russia, are actually central and important tools for creating revolutionary consciousness driven by the spontaneous political will of the workers, and are necessary for a revolution against capitalism. She contends that the economic conditions of capitalism alone often, as in the German case, lead to a fragmentation of workers into different categories with diverse interests, demands and identities. Thus Luxemburg argues that the general strike and failed Russian Revolution of 1905 indicate that in terms of working-class consciousness Russia is more 'advanced' in its journey to revolution than Germany, though Germany may be more developed economically. Luxemburg presents this as a major challenge to German Socialism, which portrayed Russia as 'backward' both economically and politically and considered that the German working class was the more advanced along the path to socialism, characterized by a strong parliamentary party, the SPD (Germany's Social Democratic Party) and powerful trade unions.

Laclau and Mouffe favour Luxemburg's criticisms of the economistic Marxism. They also reject the notion that advanced capitalism's tensions, which give rise to large trade unions and voter resentment against industry, will create a revolutionary consciousness capable of ushering in a new economic system and society. Thus Laclau and Mouffe emphasize Luxemburg's insistence that revolutionary consciousness is not an automatic result of economic conditions, or even of the institutions that are formed to ameliorate such conditions. Luxemburg has thus separated, to some degree, the economic critique of capitalism from the formation of political consciousness. However, Laclau and Mouffe contend that Luxemburg retains the Marxist 'assumptions' that the proletarian revolution – caused by this unified class consciousness – is 'inevitable' and ultimately dictated by the 'laws of capitalist development'. This is why they insist that the revolutionary consciousness emphasized by Luxemburg must be constructed solely as what they call a 'symbolic' (that is non-economic) unity. Nevertheless, they fault her for assuming that 'both political and economic struggle would be symmetrical expressions of a class subject constituted prior to the struggles themselves'.[35] In other words, she poses a central question about the complex relationship between the capitalist economy and political action, although, according to Laclau and Mouffe, she never fully comprehends it nor takes it to the logical conclusion that there may not be an 'overlap', as they call it, between class positions defined by capitalism and the political subjectivity (or consciousness) needed for the revolution.

Laclau and Mouffe use Louis Althusser's concept of 'overdetermination' to highlight their reading of Luxemburg and others in the Marxist tradition.[36] Althusser borrowed the term 'overdetermination' from Sigmund Freud to reject Marx's notion of 'contradiction' especially the notion that a contradiction between the relations of production (embodied in the power of the bourgeoisie) and the forces of production (embodied in the power of the working class) would lead to a communist revolution. Althusser argued that this motif in Marx's thought was due to the undue influence of Hegel. Whereas, as Lenin understood, revolution was as likely to occur in a situation such as that of Russia prior to 1917, which was 'pregnant with two revolutions' – the bourgeois revolution against feudal or Czarist hierarchy and the proletarian revolution against capitalism.[37] Russia became 'the weakest link' in imperialist capitalism, *the most backward and the most advanced nation*' at the same time. It is this complex overdetermination that Althusser, Laclau and Mouffe all use to reject any model of Marxism that focuses so much on the economic conditions and class positions but does not take into account the non-economic dimensions of ideology, consciousness, and especially for Laclau and Mouffe, the 'autonomy' of the political dimensions.

Laclau and Mouffe turn to Eduard Bernstein, one of Luxemburg's major opponents within German Social Democracy, to further their depiction of the 'crisis' in twentieth-century Marxism that is recognized by Gramsci's concept of hegemony, ultimately introducing what they call a 'new political logic'. Bernstein was quite influential in presenting a 'revisionist' version of Marxism that claimed to update Marx's economic analysis, arguing that the polarization between the proletariat and the bourgeoisie had ceased to increase and create more extreme crises and that the middle class was actually growing. Bernstein argues that such developments require a strategy whereby the working class would use the state, and the parliamentary government, to forge an alliance with liberal and bourgeois forces to gradually transform capitalism into socialism by 'democratic', parliamentary means. Where critics of Bernstein (Luxemburg, Karl Kautsky and recent critics) note the empirical and non-theoretical character of Bernstein's analysis, Laclau and Mouffe emphasize his focus on political (non-economic) intervention in democratic values. They are at pains to distance Bernstein from the 'reformist' sections of German socialism that reject revolution in favour of political quietism, such as trade union leaders whose goals do not go beyond better wages and working conditions. Laclau and Mouffe see Bernstein's contribution as a rejection of the notion that '*the fragmentation and division characteristic of the new stage of capitalism would be overcome through changes in the infrastructure*'. They consider that Bernstein's revisionism '*held that this was to be achieved through autonomous political intervention*'.[38] Far from the crude economism that Bernstein is often charged with, Laclau and Mouffe find in his writings another recognition of the difficult nexus between economic conditions and political consciousness. And he looks to the Social Democratic Party as the organism that can create this link *within* the democratic parliamentary system, as opposed to overthrowing it. Bernstein, according to Laclau and Mouffe, tries to solve the crisis in Marxism by looking in the right direction, the 'autonomy' of the political from the economy. However, Laclau and Mouffe disagree with his insistence on the need for singular unity created by the Party.

These readings of twentieth-century Marxism, including discussions of Kautsky, Plekhanov, Lenin and Trotsky, all lead Laclau and Mouffe to Gramsci's conception of hegemony. It is the culmination of the position that the economy does not determine the 'superstructure' but superstructural political impulses are 'autonomous'. Trotsky and Lenin are important for

Laclau and Mouffe's trajectory because they suggest that in the situation of Russia, which had not been through a bourgeois revolution, the proletariat can take on the political role that Marx had assigned to the bourgeoisie – overthrowing absolutism in favour of democracy. This broadens the scope of the struggle that is led by the proletariat through its hegemonic alliance with the peasantry. But because, as they put it, 'Leninism evidently makes no attempt to construct, through struggle, a mass identity not predetermined by any necessary law of history', Lenin's hegemony 'inevitably' turns into antidemocratic authoritarianism.[39] In other words, for Lenin the vanguard has objective knowledge of laws that dictate history, and thus the alliance it constructs is tactical and not open to democratic exchanges that participate in constructing the vanguard's ultimate goals.

Laclau and Mouffe find Gramsci pivotal in going beyond Lenin's notion of hegemony as 'class alliance' between the Russian peasantry and the small urban working class. This 'Gramscian watershed' is his notion that hegemony is the *creation* of a 'collective will' – not merely an economic class coming into its own or becoming aware of itself – but the construction of a social–cultural unity. They applaud Gramsci's replacement of the notion of ideology as a system of ideas, especially the suspect system of 'false consciousness', with the idea of 'an organic and relational whole, embodied in institutions and apparatuses, which welds together a historic bloc around a number of basic articulatory principles'.[40] The linguistic concept of 'articulation' is central for Laclau and Mouffe in replacing the idea of representation. Where representation suggests the presentation of class interests defined economically and then re-presented on the political or subjective terrain of consciousness, articulation suggests, as they write, that

> [u]nity between these agents is then not the expression of a common underlying essence but the result of political construction and struggle. If the working class, as a hegemonic agent, manages to articulate around itself a number of democratic demands and struggles, this is due not to any a priori structural privileges ...[41]

That is, it is not due to its specific role within the capitalist economy.

'Articulate' can mean express in words (especially in a clear and distinct manner) but it also means joining together and bending by flexible joints. Laclau and Mouffe combine these resonances to emphasize that the creation of a hegemonic formation involves creating something new, not just presenting something that already exists. Such constructions or creations are more than the sum of the different elements involved. We might use the example from Gramsci's discussion, that the Italian Communist Party would articulate a hegemonic formation of the industrial workers and the peasantry that would actually change the consciousness of both groups, how they think about themselves and their role in society.

However much Gramsci fits Laclau and Mouffe's requirements of freeing the political project of Marxism from its economic essentialism, they find him unable to 'fully overcome the dualism of classical Marxism' because he retains the 'inner essentialist core' that privileges the working class due to its defining place within the capitalist economy. That is, according to them, Gramsci presupposes that it is the working class that can form a hegemonic force, not because of what it *does* on the political level, but because of what it *is* on the economic level. In their words:

> Yet even for Gramsci, the ultimate core of the hegemonic subject's identity is constituted at a point external to the space it articulates: the logic of hegemony does not unfold all of its deconstructive effects on the theoretical terrain of classical Marxism.[42]

Its consciousness and role are then 'predetermined' by the objective economic conditions, not articulated autonomously in the political realm. So for Laclau and Mouffe, Gramsci is ambiguous and inconsistent in making a radical break with Marxism's reliance on the economy.

In addition to this criticism of Gramsci's retention of the working class as the hegemonic agent, Laclau and Mouffe also reject the notion that hegemony, as they read Gramsci, is a singular or unitary formation, as opposed to being plural or uncentred:

> For Gramsci, even though the diverse social elements have a merely relational identity – achieved through articulatory

practices – there must always be a *single* unifying principle in every hegemonic formation. ... [A] failure in the hegemony of the working class can only be followed by a reconstitution of bourgeois hegemony, so that in the end, political struggle is still a zero-sum game among classes.[43]

Thus, it is the dual sins of economic reductionism and unity that prevent Gramsci from overcoming Marxism's crisis and advancing to post-Marxism.

How adequate is Laclau and Mouffe's reading of Gramsci? As we have seen, Gramsci argued that in his time in Italy, a progressive hegemony could only be led by the industrial working class, but he stressed that it would have to include the peasantry. He insisted that this inclusion had to be integral and organic, not merely mechanical. Moreover, his notion of 'subalternity' suggests less of a 'predetermined' 'single unifying principle' than the need for a historical analysis that may call for one social group to take the lead – as Gramsci thought was needed in Italy in the 1920s. Of course, the economic attributes of such a social group were very important to Gramsci. But if by 'single unifying principle' Laclau and Mouffe mean the struggle to overthrow capitalism, then this seems to be an adequate reading of Gramsci. To reject the unifying principle of overthrowing capitalism (which is, after all, an economic system) poses serious questions for any 'radical political theory' that does not embrace capitalism.[44] If by 'single unifying principle' they mean an economically determined class position, they seem to offer an overly superficial reading of Gramsci (at odds with both of their earlier interpretations of Gramsci). A closer look at Laclau and Mouffe's redefinition of 'hegemony' will help explicate these issues.

## Laclau and Mouffe's linguistically informed 'Hegemony'

As indicated above, Laclau and Mouffe take this step into post-Marxism by revising Gramsci's conception of hegemony, cleansing it of what they see as its economic essentialism. This process of de-essentialising Gramsci relies heavily on linguistic concepts and metaphors and various theories in which language takes centrestage. They invoke Foucault's notion of discourse,[45]

Derrida's dynamic of deconstruction, borrow from Wittgenstein the concept of 'language game' and modify Saussure's notion of linguistic value as purely relational and negative (although they reject Saussure's depiction of a 'closed' system of signs). Chantal Mouffe has summarized this post-Marxist, post-Gramscian notion of hegemony as follows: '... we should not conceptualize power as an *external* relation taking place between two pre-constituted identities, but rather as constituting the identities themselves. This point of confluence between objectivity and power is what we have called "hegemony" '.[46]

Before explaining this redefinition of 'hegemony' and Mouffe's emphasis on 'external' relations and objectivity, it is necessary to define a few more of their terms; moments, elements, discourse, the 'impossibility of society', antagonism, suture and chains of equivalences/differences. We saw above how they favour the notion of 'articulation' over the classical notion of 'representation' since it emphasizes the creation of a new collective will, altering the identities and consciousnesses of those involved. This notion of articulation is related to their terms 'elements' and 'moments'. They state, 'The differential positions, insofar as they appear articulated within a discourse, we will call *moments*. By contrast, we will call *element* any difference that is not discursively articulated.'[47]

An example that Laclau and Mouffe do not use may help to clarify. If someone's blindness is understood by them as their personal flaw or defect, it is merely a difference from the sighted majority and is an 'element'. A group of blind people may act together to make being blind easier (for example by lobbying for the installation of street lights with audio-indicators). But if they begin to create their own community and culture for which lack of sight is not just a negative or deficiency, their blindness becomes a 'moment'. Blindness is often accompanied by an increase in other senses (touch, hearing, smell). This 'moment' of blindness becomes part of a larger 'discourse' that is the culture oriented around such positive practices as using braille, relationships with guide dogs and the skills of navigating the world through hearing, touch and smell. Outside of the articulation of a discourse of blindness, these other senses remain merely 'elements'. They are not as central when 'articulated' in a society oriented around vision.

Blindness can also be connected to larger discourses of what gets defined as an 'able body', including ramps and elevators for people in wheelchairs, etc. Laclau and Mouffe would call this a chain of equivalence in that being blind is not the same as being confined to a wheelchair; but the two can be articulated as equivalent in that they require a different discourse about our physical abilities and how public decisions should be made with respect to them. Thus, Laclau and Mouffe define 'discourse' as 'a structured totality resulting from articulatory practice ... '[48] But as we shall see, discourses are never fully successful at creating such structured totalities.

I have to refine my initial example since blindness can be an 'element' when not articulated into discursive formations of 'disability rights' but, at the same time, be a 'moment' within the larger general discourse of health and functioning bodies in mainstream society. Mainstream discourse of blindness articulates it as a problem, a flaw, a disability. In common language, blindness is also a metaphor for being aimless, ignorant, lacking reflection or critical perspective, for example, 'the blind leading the blind'. It is a discursively constructed position – in some societies it matters more than others. We can imagine a society in which it is more of a problem for women to be blind than men, or for poor people to be blind than wealthy, or vice versa. This indicates that the physical ability of sight can have different 'articulations', none of which can be claimed to be superior, based on some universal, non-contextual standard.

It may seem that 'elements' – differential positions not articulated into discourse – can hardly be said to exist. Most differences amongst people fit into some discourse. This is why Laclau and Mouffe state, 'the transition from "elements" to "moments" can never be complete'[49] and indeed, that hegemony is only possible because ' "elements" have not crystallized into "moments" '.[50] Thus, hegemony is about constructing a discursive system that re-articulates differences.

Laclau and Mouffe adopt a crucial point from Foucault: discourses are not unified by logical coherence of all their constituent elements. Articulation cannot be judged as the correct way of transforming 'elements' into 'moments' based on some criterion outside the articulatory process itself – such as 'truth', 'reality' or even 'justice'. There is no point in trying to find an objective point from which to 'articulate' the equivalence among the blind and those in wheelchairs. Alliances created to change society are based on particular and contingent circumstances including how the dominant discourse articulates these differences. Laclau and Mouffe defend this position with recourse to Wittgenstein's notion that words are defined not prior to use but in their actual usage or practice. Linguistic rules are not created independently of speaking, but are created through their application.

Laclau and Mouffe try not to engage in debates between realism and idealism about the existence of a world external to thought. They explain:

> An earthquake or the falling brick is an event that certainly exists, in the sense that it occurs here and now, independently of my will. But whether their specificity as objects is constructed in terms of 'natural phenomena' or 'expressions of the wrath of God', depends upon the structuring discursive field.[51]

Critics have argued that this does not sidestep the realism/idealism debate, but lands clearly on the side of idealist relativism. Norman Geras, for example, describes Laclau and Mouffe's 'relativist gloom, in which opposed discourses or paradigms are left with no common reference point, uselessly trading blows'.[52]

Not only are discourses not guaranteed or secured by some extra-discursive reality that they represent (accurately or not), but they are inevitably open and unstable systems that do not have absolute fixity. Borrowing from Derrida, Laclau and Mouffe argue that discursive formations cannot close or stabilize their meanings. There can only be *nodal points* of partial fixation, around which hegemonies can be formed.

Their argument becomes more complex here due to their reliance on Jacques Lacan's psychoanalysis and its notion of the 'Real' and lack.[53] Put overly simplistically, in theorizing the development of the ego, Lacan posits a 'Real' prior to any separation between the ego and the world. This 'Real' is not physical or ontological reality, rather it is pure plenitude and fullness in which nothing is wanting or missing. Lacan call this 'the lack of a lack' where there is no identity because there is no differentiation among things in the world, or the ego and the world.

In order for the ego to develop, to become itself, to experience anything, it must leave this 'Real' and thus lack is introduced.[54] Laclau and Mouffe apply this notion that at the centre of all subjectivity is this lack, this empty space, to the question of social identity. All social identity for Laclau and Mouffe is defined by excluding some other possible articulations of the differential elements. Social identity, not unlike Lacan's notion of the individual ego, is constituted by the exclusion of other possible meanings, the excess of meaning. They call this the 'constitutive outside'. In order to constitute an identity an 'outside' or an 'other' is required.

Lacan's notion of lack is also central to one of Laclau and Mouffe's most enigmatic positions: society is impossible.[55] By this, they mean to 'renounce the conception of "society" as founding totality of its partial processes' or the idea that there is a social order and commonality underlying the differences and patterns that we call society. 'Society' is distinct from other terms that attempt to describe human groups, because it is often used as a generality in an attempt to describe humans in association together with all other humans. Even when used in the plural, 'societies', the assumption is that those belonging to each society are bound together by some commonality that underlies any differences amongst them. Laclau and Mouffe suggest that this denies the notion of an outside. However, according to Laclau and Mouffe, society is an impossible object of discourse. As they say, 'There is no single underlying principle fixing – and hence constituting – the whole field of differences.'[56] Thus the idea of society rests on what, again borrowing from psychoanalysis, they call a 'suture', implying that which fills in or ties together the lack of totality.[57]

The other key term in their argument is 'social antagonism'. They define antagonism as a situation when 'the presence of the "Other" prevents me from being totally myself. The relation arises not from full totalities, but from the impossibility of their constitution.'[58] In other words, antagonism is not just a situation in which different people have different interests, goals, needs or desires. To use their example, it is not just the fact that peasants have different political interests from landowners that leads to antagonism between them, 'it is because a peasant *cannot be* a peasant that an antagonism exists with the landowner expelling him from his land'.[59] We can define a peasant as someone who works the land but does not own it and a landowner as one who owns it but does not work it. But these identities could possibly be at odds with one another and in conflict without forming a social antagonism. Only when there is a conflict between two or more identities that involves the very definition of the identities involved do Laclau and Mouffe call such a conflict an antagonism. It is more than a battle over access to resources or a zero-sum game.

Again raising the model of language, they write, 'If language is a system of differences, antagonism is the failure of difference.'[60] In other words, if the differences (such as those amongst identity groups) were successful, and each identity could define itself against the others in a stable, systematic whole, society would not contain antagonisms. But most identities, according to Laclau and Mouffe's scheme, are defined only in relation to other identities, and more importantly, they are defined negatively, as lacking a characteristic that is identified with other identities.

This notion of antagonism is related to a central framework borrowed from linguistics that Laclau and Mouffe variously call 'chains of equivalence' and 'chains of difference', 'logics of equivalence' and 'logics of difference' or 'relations of equivalence' and 'relations of difference'. Here they utilize a basic distinction of Saussure's between syntagmatic and associative (or paradigmatic) relations, which both create linguistic value. Syntagmatic relations, like the notion of syntax, mean that an element in a series, or a word in a sentence, creates meaning through its relations of difference with other terms. For example, 'Jane threw John an apple' has a different meaning from 'John threw Jane an apple' because their word order, their syntax, is different. It is the syntagmatic differences that create meaning. Whereas 'Jane threw John a fruit' or a 'Granny Smith' has an equivalent (although not the same) meaning as 'Jane threw John an apple' since 'apple', 'fruit' and 'Granny Smith' are all related through a paradigm or pattern. Saussure notes that these different systems of similarity and difference in language take place on different axes. They cannot be related to one another. But both are crucial for the system of language to create meaning.

In Laclau and Mouffe's application of these ideas to politics, identities and subject positions are also defined both syntagmatically and paradigmatically, that is, based on chains of differences and chains of equivalences. Their notion of hegemonic formations are then about the ways that chains of equivalences and differences are articulated in the field of politics. In one sense, this theory shares a great deal with Gramsci's application of much earlier linguistic concepts to political and social analysis, especially spontaneous and normative grammar. This distinction of Gramsci's is not directly comparable to Laclau and Mouffe's chains of equivalences and differences, but nor are they necessarily incompatible. While both sets of distinctions are used to analyse the structured nature of different political identities and allow a degree of agency (individual and collective), Gramsci's is more clearly aimed at theorizing the creation of an alternative 'normative grammar' that can challenge the status quo and effectively address capitalism. This is precisely because of his focus on the need for a 'unifying' hegemonic core, even if understood not as a static ideology but as something more like a language.[61]

Gramsci seems to be in agreement with Laclau and Mouffe's major contention that unlike pluralist or interest group models of politics in which 'preconstituted' groups come into the political arena to vie for their own interests (including creating alliances), 'radical democratic theory' involves the organization of the very identities that form such movements. Such agreement wanes with Laclau and Mouffe's stark rejection of any 'privileged' aspect of society, such as the economy, around which identities can be formed. However, it seems from Gramsci's view of language and his use of it as a metaphor, his interest in 'subaltern social groups' (including those defined by non-economic categories, as discussed in Chapter 3), and his insistence on the complex relation amongst culture, politics and economics, he is not arguing that there is such a place as the economy, which is 'prior' to politics and culture and in which identities are defined or articulated. From this perspective, the role that Gramsci wanted the Italian proletariat to play within a hegemony including the southern peasantry was not 'predetermined' or assumed, but was 'determined' within the historical contexts that Gramsci writes about. Feminists, postcolonial critics and many other progressives not concerned primarily with class seem to understand this aspect of Gramsci's approach. With that said, his analysis obviously 'privileges' the economy if by that we mean that people's place within the economy in capitalist societies is tremendously important. This does not however mean that because the economy is the realm of 'matter' it is more important than the symbolic realm where other identities are constituted.

## Globalization

Increasingly since the end of the cold war, discussions and debates over 'globalization' have eclipsed those over postmodernism and new social movements. However, many of the issues overlap and were taken up in new ways – especially the issue of how or if capitalism can be resisted or overthrown. Just as there are with postmodernism, there are numerous definitions of globalization and a host of different contentions have been made about it. What is it? When did it start? Is it positive or negative? Can it be resisted? If so, how? These are all complex questions around which large academic literatures, public debates and activists' discussions have developed. This is clearly not the place to try to summarize these debates or provide any substantial Gramscian analysis. Moreover, it is unclear what lasting effect the events of 11 September 2001 and the wars in Afghanistan and Iraq will have on 'globalization' and how it is understood. Certainly, a Gramscian framework would highlight the heightened levels of coercion in the global hegemony of the United States and of market liberalism.

There is an important literature on Gramscian and 'neo-Gramscian' approaches to issues pertaining to globalization from the perspective of international relations.[62] Gramsci provides many elements for such approaches, from epistemological and methodological frameworks to the concepts of hegemony, civil society and historic bloc in the analysis of complex relations of forces. He is useful for helping integrate political concerns of the power and influence of states with questions both of cultural prestige and of economic production and commerce, matters which have also been a primary concern of this work.

The focus here must be restricted to questions of language and the analysis of capitalism. Laclau and Mouffe's movement away from economic considerations, coupled with similar trends within postmodernism, has the unfortunate impact (whether intended or not) of reinforcing apologies for capitalism, implying (often unwittingly) that capitalism is somehow 'natural' and that there is no alternative. As noted above, such criticisms are sometimes directed at social, political and cultural theory that takes language seriously and finds linguistic metaphors useful. I hope that this work has illustrated numerous ways in which Gramsci's thoughts on language strengthened his political analysis in the direction away from fatalism and passivity and towards revolutionary struggle against capitalism.

However one defines globalization, it clearly labels a series of phenomena that blur the line between the 'non-linguistic' or 'material' world of production and the realm of language, ideology and culture. Where postmodernists like Baudrillard collapse concerns of production back into 'symbolic economies', Gramsci's approach provides a distinct alternative whereby the economic and material impact of language and symbolic action are of paramount importance. The advent of the so-called 'war on terrorism' has certainly reinforced this need.

It is true that there is little in his writings that connect his own concerns with production processes to questions of language. But his writings on 'Americanism and Fordism', have been very influential. His analysis of the combination of Frederick Taylor's scientific management, Henry Ford's assembly line and innovations in production economies complement this book's general emphasis on Gramsci's non-reductionist approach to the interactions between the economy, culture and politics. When Gramsci looks at 'Fordism' he is as concerned with the purely economic factors as he is with the psychological impact on workers who must more radically adapt to machines. But, perhaps even more unique, is Gramsci's focus on the cultural issues of prohibition, sexuality and morality.[63]

Gramsci's perspective certainly has blind spots and requires further development, questioning, criticism and elaboration if it is to be useful for analysing the new situations that we find ourselves in, whether or not 'globalization' is an adequate term to describe them. Nowhere does Gramsci undertake an analysis of the commodification of cultural products in the manner of that provided by Max Horkheimer and Theodor Adorno.[64] Of course, during Gramsci's lifetime, such dynamics were in their infancy.

I have pointed out the various ways in which Gramsci illustrates the importance of culture to politics; as Dombroski notes, for Gramsci, 'Culture, indeed, is the stuff of which power is made and by which it is maintained.'[65] However, Gramsci never applies this insight to changes in commodity production, advertising and consumption.[66] But his approach to 'Americanism and Fordism' shows his keen awareness of the need to take such developments into account. He was unsure of the great significance of 'Americanism and Fordism', asking whether it constituted a new 'mode of production'. So, on one hand, Gramsci does not hold insight into many of the dynamics that distinguish twenty-first century global capitalism from earlier forms. However, as this work has repeatedly illustrated, the very fact that for him Marxist political economy is fully complementary with linguistics (and the rejection of the language-as-nomenclature view) provides a framework that is very useful when addressing our current so-called globalizing world.

When discussing 'globalization', the question of the nation, or nation-state, is clearly paramount. This raises his conception of the national–popular collective will, discussed in Chapter 4. There I left aside the question of why popular wills should be, as Gramsci implies, constructed on a national basis. From the standpoint of an 'internationalist' Marxist, one could easily argue that Gramsci 'presupposed' the nation as the crucial unit of analysis – his internationalism was inter-nationalism.[67] Perhaps this was not so much a presupposition, as a conclusion based on historical analysis. Gramsci's position was that in the 1920s the organization of culture, language and politics was required first on the Italian level (and that of other nations), then on the European level (with Soviet and other national communist parties) and finally on the world level. Gramsci explains this as perhaps being just a response to historical development:

> Even if one admits that other cultures have had an importance and a significance in the process of 'hierarchical' unification of world civilisation (and this should certainly be admitted without question), they have had a universal value only in so far as they have become constituent elements of European culture – in so far as they have contributed to the process of European thought and been assimilated by it.[68]

Whether a nationally rooted and Eurocentric strategy was appropriate or not to his historical circumstances is one question. Regardless of how this question is answered, current debates about the demise of the nation-state and its changing role call for a more detailed approach to the relationship between national identity, the state and internationality.

As noted in Chapter 2's discussion of Esperanto, Gramsci made a distinction that could be very important in thinking about current debates on the nation-state. That distinction is between bourgeois cosmopolitanism and proletariat internationalism (see page 56). Nevertheless, his discussions of internationalism follow Marx's tendency to conceive of it as different national formations coming together. Gramsci does not show great concern with the role of international migration or other developments that have led to our current situation of globally mobile capital and commodities with a tightening of restrictions on the movement of labour. As significant recent work has shown, the confluence of national identification, nationalism and migrant labour forces requires further analysis.[69] Language is central here, since Gramsci argued that Italy required a national language, and by extension, understood hegemony primarily as a national formation that could then interact on the international scene. It would take a significant, but not unimaginable modification to see how 'spontaneous grammars' formed across national lines could be worked into a 'normative grammar', or international hegemonic formation, that could address the antiglobalization struggles developing today.

Some of the most promising – and least studied – sections of Gramsci's writings are those where he uses 'translation' as a metaphor for cross-cultural analysis and an important element of the revolution against capitalism. In these sections, Gramsci conceives of translation as much more than just the transference of ideas or expression from one language to another. More like Walter Benjamin and current feminist translation theory, Gramsci argues that translation requires a change in both the original language and that into which translations are made.[70] This is central to Gramsci's use of 'translation' as a metaphor for cross-cultural analysis and revolution.

The term 'civil society' is a common feature of debates on globalization especially with reference to global or international

civil society. If electronic communications and global transportation are making our world a so-called 'global village', 'public opinion' and debate is often portrayed as developing
increasingly beyond the boundaries of nation-states. Moreover,
international non-governmental organizations such as Oxfam,
Greenpeace, Amnesty International, Médecins sans Frontières
and smaller NGOs are growing in their importance to global
politics. In these terms, Gramsci's discussion of 'civil society' can
provide a useful criticism of market liberalism, especially the use
of the term 'civil society' in ways that legitimate capitalism, as
was common especially after the fall of the Soviet Union.[71] But
it is not immediately obvious how such arguments can be
extended to current questions about anti-globalization struggles
and movements. Some find conceptions of international civil
society, or the transnational public sphere, to be potentially progressive in describing a new world order,[72] but others fear that
these approaches undermine progressive potential within the
nation-state.[73] I do not see any obvious way that Gramsci
provides the conceptual resources needed for anti-globalization
struggles to determine how to organize – along national lines
with international alliances or on a more global level. Keeping
these drawbacks and lacunae in mind is important, but does not
discount nor lessen Gramsci's substantial contributions to our
understanding of our current capitalist world and what must be
done to confront it.

On the terrain of actual language and language policy, the
Language Question is perhaps being posed at a more global level
than ever before. David Crystal has argued that since the 1950s
English has become what he labels a 'global' language, noting its
pervasiveness as the language of power and resources.[74] But he
does not highlight its role in the growing gap between
the world's wealthy, often those who speak English or have the
resources to learn it, and the poor. A Gramscian approach would
clearly show great concern with the growth and organization of
the burgeoning English-teaching industry around the world.
The language politics of the European Union are a specific
example close to Gramsci's home of the unresolved Language
Problem.[75] Gramsci's writings clearly point to the need to connect such language issues to political questions of democracy,
growing inequalities in wealth and neo-imperialism.

The argument of this book is not that Gramsci provides any answers to such questions. He does not supply a ready-made set of concepts or tools that we can simply apply to our current situation, our lives and our experiences. Rather, Gramsci provides an example of engagement. His particular concepts, hegemony, passive revolution, subalternity, normative and spontaneous grammars, can be very useful and thought-provoking. But just as for him they were not static models or rigid classifications, we too must engage with our worlds in a dynamic fashion if we are to try not only to understand them, but to change them.

# Notes

## Introduction

1. I am not aware of any explicit rejection of this perspective, but in the vast scholarship in English on Gramsci there is little attention paid to language. The notable exceptions are Craig Brandist, 'Gramsci, Bakhtin and the Semiotics of Hegemony', *New Left Review* 216 (March/April, 1996), pp. 94–109; and 'The Official and the Popular in Gramsci and Bakhtin', *Theory, Culture and Society* 13(2) (1996), pp. 59–74; Renate Holub, *Antonio Gramsci: Beyond Marxism and Postmodernism* (London: Routledge, 1992); Leonardo Salamini, *The Sociology of Political Praxis: An Introduction to Gramsci's Theory* (London: Routledge, 1981), especially pp. 181–96; and Niels Helsloot, 'Linguists Of All Countries ...! On Gramsci's Premise of Coherence', *Journal of Pragmatics* 13 (1989), pp. 547–66. I have also dealt with this in *Gramsci's Politics of Language: Engaging the Bakhtin Circle and the Frankfurt School* (Toronto: University of Toronto Press, 2004) and 'The Grammar of Hegemony', *Left History* 5(1) (Spring 1997), pp. 85–104 (reprinted in James Martin (ed.) *Antonio Gramsci: Critical Assessments* (vol. 2) (London: Routledge, 2001), pp. 319–36). The Italian literature will be discussed in Chapter 2.
2. There is a voluminous literature on this topic. A good starting place is Benedict Anderson, *Imagined Communities* (revised edition) (London: Verso, 1991) and Gopal Balakrishnan (ed.) *Mapping the Nation* (London: Verso, 1996).
3. The International Gramsci Society web site lists recent publications from Gramscian perspectives consistently ranging from, for example, city planning to African literature to global political economy. <www.italnet.nd.edu/gramsci>.
4. Rush Limbaugh, *See, I Told You So* (New York: Pocket Star Books, 1993), pp. 97–99. It may not be too surprising that the rendition of these lessons is superficial and flaccid.
5. For a good overview of other reasons why Gramsci's work remains pertinent see Benedetto Fontana, 'Politics, Philosophy, and Modernity in Gramsci', *Philosophical Forum* 29(3–4) (Spring–Summer 1998), pp. 104–18.
6. As this book investigates in detail, there is considerable complexity over how to determine what counts as people's interests. This is one of the central issues that divides many post-Marxists and liberal pluralists from Marxists and other radicals. Are interests 'subjective' so that whatever I think is in my best interest is in my best interest, by definition? Or, are interests 'objective' and capable of being determined apart from my desires? That is, can I be wrong about what is in my best interest?
7. Of course, this does not mean the military or police are not involved in language politics or using linguistic differences in order to help them govern or terrorize populations.

8. Franco Lo Piparo, *Lingua intellettuali egemonia in Gramsci* (Bari: Laterza, 1979) and 'Studio del linguaggio e teoria gramsciana', *Critica Marxista* 2(3) (1987), pp. 167–75.
9. Karl Marx, *The Eighteenth Brumaire of Louis Bonaparte* (Moscow: Progress, 1934), p. 10.

## Chapter 1   Language and Social Theory: The Many Linguistic Turns

1. As we shall show in Chapter 3 when considering 'organic intellectuals', Gramsci understood the dangers, in the 1930s, of separating mental from manual labour too starkly.
2. There is a large literature on production in the twentieth century including many debates over the role of technology. Some of the classics are Michael Burawoy, *The Politics of Production: Factory Regimes under Capitalism and Socialism* (London: Verso, 1985); and Harry Braverman, *Labor and Monopoly Capital: The Degradation of Work in the Twentieth Century* (New York: Monthly Review Press, 1975). Gramsci's writings on 'Americanism and Fordism' have been quite influential in some of this literature. Taking such changes seriously does not necessarily mean accepting the often hyperbolic and superficial analyses of our 'electronic age', in which ideas of products, work and property are seen as being replaced by information, entertainment and access. For example, see Jeremy Rifkin, *The Age of Access: The New Culture of Hypercapitalism, Where All Life is a Paid Experience* (New York: Putnam, 2000).
3. See, for example, Ester Reiter, *Making Fast Food: From the Frying Pan into the Fryer* (Montreal: McGill-Queen's University Press, 1991).
4. See, for example, Dale Spender, *Man Made Language* (London: Routledge & Kegan Paul, 1980), pp. 28–32 and 147–90; Julia Kristeva, *The Kristeva Reader*, edited by Toril Moi (New York: Columbia University Press, 1986); Luce Irigaray, *Speculum of the Other Woman*, translated by Gillian G. Gill (Ithaca: Cornell University Press, 1985); and Deborah Cameron (ed.), *The Feminist Critique of Language: A Reader* (second edition) (London: Routledge, 1998).
5. The label 'linguistic turn' is itself a little misleading in that it suggests a turn towards language, as if language did not play an important role in these disciplines before. In the social sciences for instance, the 'linguistic turn' was not a turn towards language per se, but the adoption of a particular method of studying language, namely structuralism.
6. While at times Saussure seems just to be making a distinction between two branches of linguistics, static and evolutionary or synchronic and diachronic, at other places he is very critical of all diachronic approaches to linguistics and argues that synchronic linguistics must be the primary focus of the discipline. Ferdinand de Saussure, *Course in General Linguistics*, translated by Roy Harris (La Salle, Illinois: Open Court, 1983), especially pp. 3 [16], 9 [25], 79–98 [114–140].
7. It has been argued that Saussure's *langue/parole* division has been overemphasized, and it is true that in the *Course in General Linguistics* he provides space for a more sophisticated relationship between language

as a system of signs and speakers' uses of those signs in utterances. But the 'linguistic turn' that Saussure's approach launched is very much dependent on the *langue/parole* division.

8.  Philology is the scientific study primarily of texts and literature, but in the nineteenth century the term was also used for the study of language more generally.
9.  Saussure distinguishes this from the actual sound itself which is a physical entity (presumably to be studied by physics), whereas the signifier as sound pattern is the 'hearer's psychological impression of the sound', p. [98].
10. *Hund*, for example, may actually be used to refer to breeds of dogs prevalent in Germany, Austria and Switzerland and *chien* to those in France.
11. Chapter 5 raises Saussure's related distinction between syntagmatic relations and associative or paradigmatic relations. These are two axes on which meaning is produced through difference. Syntagmatic relations have to do with word order, syntax; in other words, meaning is produced by differences between contiguous words. Associative or paradigmatic relations involve words that are not the ones being used but are associated within the language system. Saussure gives the example of the Doric column in architecture that conjures up the whole system of Greek architectural design (different from Ionic and Corinthian, but similar to other features of Doric architecture) signifying strength and simplicity. Saussure, *Course*, pp. 121–25 [170–75].
12. This example is taken from Jonathon Culler, *Saussure* (sixth edition) (London: Fontana Press, 1988), pp. 21–22.
13. Saussure, *Course*, p. [151].
14. Jacques Lacan, *Écrits: A Selection*, translated by Alan Sheridan (New York: W.W. Norton, 1977) and Elizabeth Grosz, *Jacques Lacan: A Feminist Introduction* (London: Routledge, 1990), especially pp. 82–114.
15. Grosz, *Lacan*, p. 81.
16. Louis Althusser, "A Ideological State Apparatuses", reprinted in Slavoj Žižek, ed., *Mapping Ideology* (London: Verso, 1994), pp. 100–140.
17. Humanism is the Renaissance movement based on the revival of Greek and Roman culture and ideas. It places humans at the centre of concern but is fully consistent with Christianity.
18. See, for example, Richard Rorty's 1967 collection, *The Linguistic Turn: Recent Essays in Philosophical Method* (Chicago: University of Chicago Press, 1967).
19. Ludwig Wittgenstein, *Tractatus Logico-Philosophicus*, translated by D.F. Pears and B.F. McGuinness (London: Routledge, 1974), p. 74.
20. Ludwig Wittgenstein, *Philosophical Investigations*, translated by G.E.M. Anscombe (second edition) (Oxford: Basil Blackwell, 1958), p. 20. Wittgenstein actually notes that this is true only for a large class of cases, not for all.
21. Wittgenstein, *Philosophical Investigations,* p. 8.
22. Wittgenstein, *Philosophical Investigations,* pp. 31–4.
23. Wittgenstein, *Philosophical Investigations,* p. x$^e$.
24. See Nerio Naldi, 'The friendship between Piero Sraffa and Antonio Gramsci in the years 1919–1927', *European Journal of the History of Economic Thought*, 7(1) (March 2000), pp. 79–114; and John B. Davis,

'Gramsci, Sraffa, Wittgenstein: Philosophical Linkages', *European Journal of the History of Economic Thought*, 9(3) (Autumn 2002), pp. 384–401.

25. Raymond Williams, *Marxism and Literature* (Oxford: Oxford University Press, 1977), p. 21.

26. Perry Anderson, *In the Tracks of Historical Materialism* (London: Verso, 1983); Ellen Meiksins Wood, *Retreat from Class* (London: Verso, 1986), pp. 5, 77–8; and 'Modernity, Postmodernity, or Capitalism', *Monthly Review* (July–August 1996), pp. 21–39.

27. For example, Centre for Contemporary Cultural Studies, *On Ideology* (London: Hutchinson, 1978); Stuart Hall et al., *Culture, Media and Language* (London: Hutchinson, 1980).

28. See David Harris, *From Class Struggle to the Politics of Pleasure* (London: Routledge, 1992). For Hall's uncomfortable relationship to postmodernism, see his interview by Lawrence Grossberg, 'On Postmodernism and Articulation', in *Stuart Hall: Critical Dialogues in Cultural Studies*, edited by David Morley and Kuan-Hsing Chen (London: Routledge, 1996), pp. 131–50.

# Chapter 2   Linguistics and Politics in Gramsci's Italy

1. It would be overly cumbersome to summarize all the specific contributions of the considerable Italian literature related to Gramsci and language. The most systematic exploration is Franco Lo Piparo, *Lingua intellettuali egemonia in Gramsci* (Bari: Laterza, 1979). He summarizes his analysis in 'Studio del linguaggio e teoria gramsciana', *Critica Marxista* 2(3) (1987), pp. 167–75. Other contributions include Maurizio Lichtner, 'Traduzione e Metafore in Gramsci', *Critica Marxista* 39(1) (January/ February 1991), pp. 107–31; Luigi Rosiello, 'Linguistica e marxismo nel pensiero di Antonio Gramsci', in Paolo Ramat, Hans-J. Niederehe and Konrad Koerner (eds), *The History of Linguistics in Italy* (Amsterdam: John Benjamins, 1986), pp. 237–58; and 'Problemi linguistici negli scritti di Gramsci', in Pietro Rossi (ed.), *Gramsci e la cultura contemporanea* (vol. 2) (Rome: Editori Riuniti, 1970), pp. 347–67; M. Emilia Passaponti, 'Gramsci e le questioni linguistiche', *Lingua, Linguaggi, e Società: Proposta per un aggiornamento* (second edition), edited by Stefano Gensini and Massimo Vedovelli (Florence: Tipolitografia F.lli Linari, 1981), pp. 119–28; Stefano Gensini, 'Linguistica e questione politica della lingua', *Critica Marxista* 1 (1980), pp. 151–65; Antonio Carrannante, 'Antonio Gramsci e i problemi della lingua italiana', *Belfagor* 28 (1973), pp. 544–56; Renzo De Felice, 'Un corso di glottologia di Matteo Bartoli negli appunti di Antonio Gramsci', *Rivista Storica del Socialismo* 7 (1964), pp. 219–21; and Luigi Ambrosoli, 'Nuovi contributi agli "Scritti giovanile" di Gramsci', *Rivista Storica del Socialismo* 3 (1960), pp. 545–50.

2. Antonio Gramsci, *Selections from the Prison Notebooks*, edited and translated by Quintin Hoare and Geoffrey Nowell Smith (New York: International Publishers, 1971), pp. 90–102. Hereafter cited as SPN. For a list of abbreviations see page xiii. In Gramsci's note on p. 100, he defines Sardinia as part of the South, whereas geographically this is not the case. See also 'Some Aspects of the Southern Question', where Gramsci makes

numerous distinctions among Sardinia, Sicily and southern Italy. Antonio Gramsci, *Selections from Political Writings (1921–1926)*, edited and translated by Quintin Hoare (Minneapolis: University of Minnesota Press, 1990), pp. 441–62. Hereafter cited as SPWII.

3. Antonio Gramsci, *Selections from Political Writings (1910–1920)*, edited by Quintin Hoare, translated by John Matthews (Minneapolis: University of Minnesota Press, 1990), p. 375. Hereafter cited as SPWI.

4. For example, Benedict Anderson, *Imagined Communities: Reflections on the Origin and Spread of Nationalism* (revised edition), (London: Verso, 1991); Anthony D. Smith, *The Ethnic Origins of Nations* (Oxford: Oxford University Press, 1986); Charles Tilly, *Coercion, Capital and European State, AD 990–1990* (Oxford: Basil Blackwell, 1990); and Eugen Weber, *Peasants into Frenchmen: the Modernization of Rural France, 1870–1914* (Stanford: University of California Press, 1976). For an interesting recent focus on the role of migration in the formation of national identity see Donna Gabaccia, *Italy's Many Diasporas* (Seattle: University of Washington Press, 2000). See also Chapter 5, pp. 162–4.

5. SPWII, p. 444.

6. Since the 1980s, there has been a growing Italian literature that is critical of earlier depictions of the Southern Question which, according to this literature, tended to ignore the diversities especially economic within the so-called South, and also the degree of economic change that did occur in southern Italy, Sicily and Sardinia. Chapter 4 addresses the relationship of Gramsci to this literature. For an overview in English see Robert Lumley and Jonathan Morris (eds), *The New History of the Italian South: The Mezzogiorno Revisited* (Exeter: University of Exeter Press, 1997). See also Jane Schneider (ed.), *Italy's "Southern Question": Orientalism in One Country* (Oxford: Berg, 1998). In this volume, see especially, Nadia Urbinati, 'The Souths of Antonio Gramsci and the Concept of Hegemony', pp. 135–56.

7. The two and a half per cent estimation is from Tullio De Mauro, *Storia Linguistica Dell'Italia Unita* (Rome: Editori Laterza, 1986), p. 43; for a brief discussion of the other estimates see Howard Moss, 'Language and Italian National Identity', in Bruce Haddock and Gino Bedani (eds), *Politics of Italian National Identity* (Cardiff: University of Wales Press, 2000), pp. 98–123, here p. 100.

8. For a general overview see Lori Repetti's editor's introduction to *Phonological Theory and the Dialects of Italy* (Amsterdam/Philadelphia: John Benjamins, 2000), pp. 1–5. Most intellectuals took Italian to be the language of great Italian literature from Dante onwards. The Language Question certainly pre-dates Italian unification, but historically it had been an erudite discussion and not a political issue about unifying the entire population.

9. De Mauro, *Storia*, p. 95.

10. Weber, *Peasants*, pp. 67–94.

11. Giacomo Devoto, *The Languages of Italy*, translated by V. Louise Katainen (Chicago: University of Chicago Press, 1978).

12. Bruce Haddock points out that in Italy, Romanticism was not associated with conservative or reactionary views as it was in Germany, France and England. Instead, it was often championed by the avant-garde, who

rejected Classicism's inability to adapt to changing times and different cultures. Bruce Haddock, 'State, Nation and Risorgimento', in Haddock and Bedani (eds), *Politics*, pp. 11–49, here p. 23.

13. Dante himself initiated this line of thinking in *De Vulgari Eloquentia*, although Reynolds notes that Manzoni had specific rejections of Dante's position. Barbara Reynolds, *The Linguistic Writings of Alessandro Manzoni* (Cambridge: W. Heffer & Sons, 1950), p. 127.

14. Reynolds provides a detailed argument that Manzoni's position was that the Tuscan language had already been chosen by history and the Italian people as the national language; that is the cause of its similarity to the literary language and why so many Tuscan words are found in other dialects. He specifically challenged other Tuscan advocates such as Niccolo Tommaseo (1802–74) because they tried to justify the use of Tuscan based on its elegance and clarity; that for Manzoni missed the point.

15. Bruno Migliorini, *The Italian Language* (London: Faber and Faber, 1966), pp. 362–6.

16. Reynolds, *Manzoni* and Moss, 'Language and Identity', pp. 98–123.

17. Migliorini, *Italian Language*, pp. 403–94; Devoto, *Languages of Italy*, pp. 282–324.

18. Antonio Gramsci, *Quaderni del carcere* (4 vols), edited by Valentino Gerratana (Turin: Einaudi, 1975); pp. 5, 82, 351, 2237. Also in Antonio Gramsci, *Prison Notebooks* (vol. 1), edited by Joseph A. Buttigieg, translated by Joseph A. Buttigieg and Antonio Callari (New York: Columbia University Press, 1992), pp. 99 and 179; Antonio Gramsci, *Prison Notebooks* (vol. 2), edited and translated by Joseph A. Buttigieg (New York: Columbia University Press, 1996), p. 70; and Antonio Gramsci, *Selections from Cultural Writings*, edited by David Forgacs and Geoffrey Nowell Smith, translated by William Boelhower (Cambridge, Mass.: Harvard University Press, 1985), p. 173. Hereafter cited as SCW.

19. While Piedmont and its capital Turin played a more significant role as the political and economic centre for unification, its language did not have the historical literary prestige of Tuscany. As will be explored in Chapter 3, one of the major themes within hegemony is how the North–South axis becomes the fundamental division in Italy through galvanizing specific social groups in the North.

20. De Mauro, *Storia*, p. 95.

21. See Alastair Davidson, *Antonio Gramsci: Towards an Intellectual Biography* (London: Merlin Press, 1977), pp. 22–23; Guiseppe Fiori, *Antonio Gramsci: Life of a Revolutionary*, translated by Tom Nairn (London: Verso, 1980), p. 17. Germino argues that none of the versions of this story are credible, and that Gramsci suffered from Pott's disease, which caused deformities that his family needed to explain to themselves and others, pp. 1–2.

22. Fiori, *Antonio Gramsci*, p. 55.

23. SPWI, p. 84.

24. Fiori, *Antonio Gramsci*, p. 67. As Davidson notes, Gramsci's attention to the miners, of whom he had no actual experience, is curious but perhaps explicable due to his resistance towards identifying with peasants who had treated him cruelly as a hunchback and the son of a discredited administrator.

25. Fiori, *Antonio Gramsci*, p. 71.
26. Fiori, *Antonio Gramsci*, pp. 73–4, 80–81.
27. Fiori, *Antonio Gramsci*, p. 88.
28. This point is emphasized by, among others, Richard Bellamy and Darrow Schecter, *Gramsci and the Italian State* (Manchester: Manchester University Press, 1993).
29. Lo Piparo, *Lingua*; and 'Studio', pp. 167–75.
30. Manzoni would not define his 'solution' in these terms of imposition. He was adamant that the prestige already enjoyed by Florentine was an indication that it had already been chosen as the natural common language. He also was not a 'purist' but argued that where Florentine was deficient it should be augmented by the more general Tuscan dialects and other Italian dialects. However, he did seem to move from a position that he held earlier in his life that a common Italian should be created by using vocabulary and phrases from many Italian dialects and even French (a position comparable to Gramsci's as we shall see). He rejected this in favour of elevating Florentine as 'standard' Italian. See Reynolds, *Manzoni*.
31. SCW, p. 178.
32. This method has similarities with Saussure's borrowed notion that 'Geographical diversity can be translated into temporal diversity'. *Course in General Linguistics*, translated by Roy Harris (Lasalle, Illinois: Open Court, 1983), p. 197 [271].
33. Early on he did use a more Crocean-influenced language of the 'superior spirit' but by 1925 he had consistently shifted away from this terminology.
34. See for example, Anna Morpurgo Davies, 'Karl Brugmann and late nineteenth-century linguistics', in Theodora Bynon and F.R. Palmer (eds), *Studies in the History of Western Linguistics* (Cambridge: Cambridge University Press, 1986), pp. 160–61. See also Ernst Cassirer, 'Structuralism in Modern Linguistics', *Word* 1 (1945), pp. 99–120. Cassirer locates the birth of structuralism in nineteenth-century linguistics and its adoption of Cuvier's method for palaeontology and comparative anatomy. Interestingly enough, Gramsci's criticisms of Cuvier run parallel to his critique of positivism in general and Neogrammarian linguistics in particular.
35. As quoted by R.H. Robins, *A Short History of Linguistics* (third edition) (London: Longman, 1990), p. 205.
36. Hermann Osthoff and Karl Brugmann, 'Preface to *Morphologische Untersuchungen auf dem Gebiete der indogermanischen Sprachen*', in *A Reader in Nineteenth-Century Historical Indo-European Linguistics*, edited and translated by Winfred P. Lehmann (Bloomington: Indiana University Press, 1967), pp. 197–209. See also Morpurgo Davies, 'Karl Brugmann' p. 154; and Robins, *Short History*, pp. 201–3, where he emphasizes how much the Neogrammarians attempted to follow the natural sciences, especially geology.
37. Antonio Gramsci, *Letters from Prison*, edited and translated by Lynne Lawner (London: Harper & Row, 1973), pp. 79–80. Corroborating Gramsci's point here is the fact that Bartoli dropped the term 'neolinguistics' in favour of areal or spatial linguistics in 1934 because,

according to Bartoli, 'among other things it was irritating to esteemed colleagues of the older schools.' Lo Piparo, *Lingua*, p. 59.

38. Angelo d'Orsi, 'Lo Studente che non divenne "Dottore" Gramsci all'Università di Torino', *Studi Storici* 40(1) (January–March 1999), p. 67.
39. Gramsci actually wrote, 'One ought to write a critical demolition of Bertoni as a linguist'. SCW, p. 173.
40. SCW, pp. 173–6, 185.
41. Antonio Gramsci, *Further Selections from the Prison Notebooks*, edited and translated by Derek Boothman (Minneapolis: University of Minnesota Press, 1995), p. 355. Hereafter cited as FSPN. As Gramsci notes, this famous image of Marx's is better understood when we remember it is derived from Hegel's comments about the French Revolution changing the world so that it is walking on its head, that is, that the world is now guided by reason, FSPN, p. 318; see also Boothman's endnote 56, FSPN, p. 563.
42. Benedetto Croce, *The Aesthetic as the Science of Expression and of the Linguistic in General*, translated by Colin Lyas (Cambridge: Cambridge University Press, 1992), p. 156.
43. Karl Vossler, *The Spirit of Language in Civilization*, translated by Oscar Oeser (London: Kegan Paul, Tench Trubner, 1932), p. 15.
44. Croce, *The Aesthetic*, p. 160.
45. SCW, p. 26, n. 4.
46. Antonio Gramsci, *La Città Futura, 1917–1918*, edited by Sergio Caprioglio (Turin: Einaudi, 1982), pp. 592–5.
47. Sergio Caprioglio, in Gramsci, *La Città Futura*, pp. 673–4, n. 6.
48. SCW, p. 26, n. 4; and Gramsci, *La Città Futura*, pp. 612–13.
49. As quoted in SCW, p. 26, n. 4; and Gramsci, *La Città Futura*, p. 612.
50. SCW, p. 27. This criticism fails to address Zamenhof's initial inspiration for Esperanto to ease the ethnic conflict in Russian Warsaw. For current discussions of contemporary global language issues, see David Crystal, *English as a Global Language* (Cambridge: Cambridge University Press, 1997).
51. SCW, p. 26.
52. See G.I. Ascoli, 'Italy – Part III, Languages', *Encyclopedia Britanica* (vol. 13), (ninth edition) (New York: Henry G. Allen, 1898) pp. 497–8. Advocates of Esperanto respond by arguing that it is a 'living' language just as much as so-called 'natural' languages.
53. SCW, p. 28.
54. For example, see Perry Anderson, 'The Antinomies of Antonio Gramsci', *New Left Review* 100 (November 1976–January 1977), pp. 5–79, here pp. 20–25.
55. Lo Piparo, *Lingua*, p. 135.
56. SCW, pp. 268–9.
57. FSPN, p. 304.
58. FSPN, p. 282.
59. FSPN, p. 304.
60. SCW, p. 41.
61. SCW, p. 43.
62. SPN, p. 263.

## Chapter 3   Language and Hegemony in the *Prison Notebooks*

1. For a more detailed overview of the historical precedents to Gramsci's hegemony, see Jeremy Lester, *Dialogue of Negation: Debates on Hegemony in Russia and the West* (London: Pluto Press, 2000), pp. 1–51.

2. See Perry Anderson, 'The Antinomies of Antonio Gramsci', *New Left Review* 100 (November 1976–January 1977), pp. 5–78, especially pp. 15–16; and Lester, *Dialogue*, pp. 33–40.

3. While I disagree with many of his conclusions, John Hoffman provides a detailed account of Gramsci's importance to Marxism due to his posing of the question of how coercion and consent are related. *The Gramscian Challenge: Coercion and Consent in Marxist Political Theory* (Oxford: Basil Blackwell, 1984).

4. Ludwig Wittgenstein, *Philosophical Investigations*, second edition, translated by G.E.M. Anscombe (Oxford: Basil Blackwell, 1958), p. 20. It is Wittgenstein's earlier work that makes the distinction between telling and showing that I allude to here, *Tractatus Logico-Philosophicus*, translated by D.F. Pears and B.F. McGuinness (London: Routledge, 1974), pp. 18–26.

5. Anne Showstack Sassoon, 'Gramsci's Subversion of the Language of Politics', *Rethinking Marxism* 3(1) (Spring 1990), pp. 14–25, here p. 16.

6. Kate Crehan, *Gramsci, Culture and Anthropology* (London: Pluto Press, 2002), p. 20.

7. The most famous and intricate version of this position is Anderson, 'Antinomies'.

8. Joseph Buttigieg, 'Introduction', in Antonio Gramsci, *Prison Notebooks* (vol. 1), edited by Joseph Buttigieg (New York: Columbia University Press, 1992), p. 31.

9. Anne Showstack Sassoon, 'Subversion', p. 15.

10. Joseph V. Femia, *Gramsci's Political Thought: Hegemony, Consciousness, and the Revolutionary Process* (Oxford: Clarendon Press, 1987), p. 46.

11. The notion of 'organic', especially as connected to 'organic intellectuals', is crucial to Gramsci's thought and will be discussed below.

12. As we shall see below, even this is potentially misleading. Gramsci's writings on language are an excellent source for his detailed considerations of how conceptually coercion and consent should not be defined in contrast to one another.

13. Thomas Hobbes, *Leviathan*, revised edition, edited by Richard Tuck (Cambridge: Cambridge University Press, 1996), p. 120.

14. For Hobbes, consent is not exclusive of coercion. He argues that it is reasonable for an individual to grant consent to the sovereign precisely due to the sovereign's power and potential use of force and violence. Hobbes, *Leviathan*, pp. 97; 117–124.

15. Max Weber, 'Politics as a Vocation', in *From Max Weber*, edited and translated by H.H. Gerth and C. Wright Mills, (New York: Oxford University Press, 1946), p. 78.

16. Antonio Gramsci, *Selections from the Prison Notebooks*, edited and translated by Quintin Hoare and Geoffrey Nowell Smith (New York: International Publishers, 1971), p. 323, emphasis added. Hereafter cited as SPN.

17. SPN, p. 9. *Homo faber* is the human maker, fabricator and *homo sapien* is the thinking human. We should not read this as a rejection of Marx's notion that capitalism alienates workers by, among other dimensions, separating their physical labour from intellectual activity.
18. SPN, p. 8.
19. See SPN, p. 323, n. 1.
20. Gramsci is using his standard method of beginning with someone else's concept or phrase and then redefining it. Gramsci attributes the idea that 'all men are philosophers' to Croce, who argued that 'the "common sense" of the "man of common sense" is the heritage left by the philosophies preceding him, an inheritance continually increased by the capacity it has for absorbing the net products of new thought'. Benedetto Croce, *The Conduct of Life*, translated by Arthur Livingston (New York: 1924). Gramsci gives the phrase an almost opposite meaning, that 'philosophers' philosophy' is just the singling out and granting prestige to particular conceptions of the world. SPN, p. 422, see also pp. 9, 323–43.
21. SPN, p. 422. See also pp. 324–5, where Gramsci describes 'common sense' as a collective noun, a product of history and historical process, and argues that philosophy coincides with 'good sense' since through criticism it supersedes religion and 'common sense'.
22. SPN, p. 8.
23. SPN, p. 37.
24. SPN, p. 326.
25. SPN, p. 7.
26. SPN, pp. 177–8, and n. 79.
27. SPN, p. 7.
28. SPN, p. 8.
29. SPN, p. 12.
30. SPN, p. 327.
31. Antonio Gramsci, *Prison Notebooks* (vol. 2), edited and translated by Joseph A. Buttigieg (New York: Columbia University Press, 1996), p. 139.
32. Marcus Green, 'Gramsci Cannot Speak: Presentation and Interpretation of Gramsci's Concept of the Subaltern', *Rethinking Marxism* 14(3) (Spring 2002), pp. 1–24.
33. SPN, p. 324. The last sentence is omitted in this translation. See Antonio Gramsci, *Quaderni del carcere* (4 vols), edited by Valentino Gerratana (Turin: Einaudi, 1975), p. 1376, translation my own. Hereafter cited as QC.
34. SPN, pp. 327–8.
35. SPN, p. 327.
36. This 'passivity' is central to Gramsci's 'passive revolution', see Chapter 4, pp. 102–12.
37. Eduard Bernstein, *Evolutionary Socialism*, edited by Edith C. Harvey (New York: Schocken, 1961).
38. Antonio Gramsci, *Selections from Cultural Writings*, edited by David Forgacs and Geoffrey Nowell Smith, translated by William Boelhower (Cambridge, Mass.: Harvard University Press, 1985), pp. 167–73. Hereafter cited as SCW. For discussions of the concept of the national–popular in Gramsci, see David Forgacs, 'National–Popular: Genealogy of

a Concept', in *Formations of Nation and People* (London: Routledge & Kegan Paul, 1984), pp. 83–98 and Geoffrey Nowell Smith, 'Gramsci and the National–Popular', *Screen Education* 22 (1977), pp. 12–15.

39.  SCW, p. 168.
40.  SCW, p. 170.
41.  SCW, pp. 183–4.
42.  SPN, p. 325. We shall discuss below, at greater length, Gramsci's evaluation of dialects, to show that he was not simply critical of their shortcomings.
43.  SPN, p. 349.
44.  SPN, p. 349. The parenthetical qualification is presumably to prevent the obvious need to distinguish culture and philosophy from language.
45.  SPN, p. 450.
46.  Gramsci was probably familiar with the French translation of this work, SPN, p. 378. The English translation, *Historical Materialism: A System of Sociology*, 1926, is based on the third edition.
47.  Nikolai Bukharin, *Historical Materialism: A System of Sociology* (Ann Arbor: University of Michigan Press, 1969), p. 26. Gramsci seems to be blowing Bukharin's almost incidental point out of proportion given that Gramsci agrees with his basic argument against 'teleology'. However, this type of reductionism and superficiality is for Gramsci symptomatic of his more general arguments about the laws and objective predictability in the social sciences.
48.  SPN, p. 400; also see Antonio Gramsci, *Further Selections from the Prison Notebooks*, edited and translated by Derek Boothman (Minneapolis: University of Minnesota Press, 1995), pp. 307–18.
49.  SPN, p. 450.
50.  SPN, p. 450.
51.  This is why, Gramsci explains, we cannot think of translation as finding equivalents within language. See SCW, pp. 384–5.
52.  SCW, p. 180. Gramsci retains a distinction between how words create meaning in language and other systems of meaning studied by semioticians, for example a siren or picture.
53.  SPN, p. 452.
54.  SPN, p. 452, emphasis added.
55.  SCW, p. 180.
56.  SCW, p. 187 and p. 180.
57.  SCW, p. 181. As explained below, this theoretical statement is too extreme, for reasons raised by Wittgenstein's private language argument. Wittgenstein, *Philosophical Investigations*, pp. 91–6.
58.  SCW, p. 124.
59.  Isaiah Berlin, 'Two Concepts of Liberty', in *The Proper Study of Mankind* (London: Pimlico, 1997), pp. 191–242.
60.  Benedetto Croce, *The Aesthetic as the science of Expression and of the Linguistic in General*, translated by Colin Lyas (Cambridge: Cambridge University Press, 1992), pp. 158–61.
61.  Ferdinand de Saussure, *Course in General Linguistics*, translated by Roy Harris (La Salle, Illinois: Open Court, 1983), p. 82 [118]. Noam Chomsky also claims the Port Royal Grammar as a precursor to his approach to linguistics.

62. SCW, p. 180.
63. SCW, p. 180.
64. SCW, pp. 180–81.
65. SCW, pp. 179–80.
66. For Saussure's more nuanced discussion of the impossibility of separating a language system from its history, see Saussure, *Course*, p. 9 [24]; but he concludes by prioritizing and separating linguistic structure from actual speech, pp. 9–15 [23–32].
67. SCW, p. 181.
68. SCW, p. 185.
69. SPN, p. 196. See also p. 198–200, where he distinguishes between the regressive and progressive examples of the spontaneity of the subaltern classes.
70. SPN, p. 324, except the last sentence that is omitted in the translation. QC, p. 1376.
71. SCW, p. 182.
72. SCW, p. 182. He notes that the fight against illiteracy is an important part of creating a common national language.
73. See Antonio Gramsci, *Selections from Political Writings (1921–1926)*, edited and translated by Quintin Hoare (Minneapolis: University of Minnesota Press, 1990), pp. 446–56.
74. SCW, p. 183. By 'tradition' here, he clearly means the various traditions of the language users themselves, not an elitist tradition of traditional intellectuals.
75. SCW, p. 183.
76. SCW, pp. 26–8.

## Chapter 4    Gramsci's Key Concepts, with Linguistic Enrichment

1. Antonio Gramsci, *Selections from the Prison Notebooks*, edited and translated by Quintin Hoare and Geoffrey Nowell Smith (New York: International Publishers, 1971), p. 59. Hereafter cited as SPN. Elsewhere Gramsci notes that he has 'completely modified and enriched' Cuoco's concept of the 'passive revolution', SPN, p. 108.
2. SPN, pp. 58, 97–8.
3. For a succinct overview, see the introduction and concluding essays in Dagmar Engels and Shula Marks (eds), *Contesting Colonial Hegemony: State and Society in Africa and India* (London: British Academic Press, 1994); and Stuart Hall, 'Gramsci's Relevance for the Study of Race and Ethnicity', in *Stuart Hall: Critical Dialogues in Cultural Studies*, edited by David Morley and Kuan-Hsing Chen (London: Routledge, 1996), pp. 411–40.
4. SPN, p. 105.
5. SPN, p. 59. See John Davis (ed.), *Gramsci and Italy's Passive Revolution* (New York: Barnes & Noble, 1979).
6. A non-historical or economistic approach might expect the dialect of Turin to be chosen as the national language, but at least since Dante and the fourteenth century, the affinities between Tuscan and the literary Italian of the intellectuals made it the prime candidate. See Chapter 3.

7. It may seem troubling to equate feudal economic relations with peasant dialects. Gramsci wishes to eradicate feudalism but incorporate at least some aspects of the dialects. But the point is that the everyday practices and understandings of the world in both the economic and cultural realms need to be engaged and transformed.

8. The linguistic resonances come through clearly when Gramsci writes about how during a passive revolution, 'a State ... "led" the group which should have been "leading" and was able to put at the latter's disposal an army and a politico-diplomatic strength'. SPN, p. 105. That is, it took the governmental apparatuses such as funding for books and training of school teachers to impose Florentine on Italy, as opposed to the prestige and attraction of the language and its speakers themselves. Gramsci's interest in Ascoli's theory of the linguistic substratum mirrors his argument about Italy's 'passive revolution'; see Chapter 3.

9. SPN, pp. 102–4.

10. See 'Introduction: Antonio Gramsci and Italy's Passive Revolution', in Davis, *Gramsci*, pp. 11–30.

11. SPN, pp. 125–33. Especially in the current context of debates around nationalism and the future of the nation-state, it is important to ask about Gramsci's focus on the nation as the (presupposed?) unit of political community. Dante Germino's biography emphasizes the extent to which Gramsci was committed to his identity as a Sardinian even more than an Italian, and how his focus on Italy was not at the expense of his internationalism. See Dante Germino, *Antonio Gramsci: Architect of a New Politics* (Baton Rouge: Louisiana State University Press, 1990), especially pp. 5–24, 43–51.

12. SPN, pp. 77–79.

13. SPN, pp. 103–4.

14. SPN, pp. 103–4.

15. However useful such metaphors are, Gramsci cautions that '[P]olitical struggle is enormously more complex' than military warfare, and military metaphors must be taken with a 'grain of salt'. SPN, pp. 229, 231. It is also noteworthy that an important section defining these terms discusses the struggle for Indian independence, attributing war of position, manoeuvre and underground warfare to different phases of Ghandi's activities. He also uses the Balkans and Irish struggle against the British to delimit these terms. SPN, pp. 229–31.

16. Gramsci includes strikes, that is withholding one's labour power, as a form of war of manoeuvre, whereas boycotts are part of the war of position. SPN, p. 229.

17. SPN, p. 234.

18. For a succinct summary of such changes, see Eric Hobsbawm, *Age of Extremes: The Short Twentieth Century, 1914–1991* (London: Abacus, 1995), pp. 21–54.

19. As Anne Showstack Sassoon explains, he utilized this concept to combat the mistakes of economism. See her *Gramsci's Politics* (second edition) (London: Hutchinson, 1987), pp. 193–204.

20. Antonio Gramsci, *Quaderni del carcere* (4 vols), edited by Valentino Gerratana (Turin: Einaudi, 1975), p. 973, hereafter cited as QC; as discussed in Sassoon, pp. 199–200.

21. SPN, p. 236.

22. Antonio Gramsci, *Selections from Cultural Writings*, edited by David Forgacs and Geoffrey Nowell Smith, translated by William Boelhower (Cambridge, Mass.: Harvard University Press, 1985), p. 182.

23. SPN, p. 108.

24. SPN, p. 108.

25. Quintin Hoare and Geoffrey Nowell Smith, for example, explain it by positing that Gramsci used 'war of position' in two partially conflicting ways, as the struggle during periods of stable equilibrium that prevent war of manoeuvre and as the type of warfare possible in the West with a strong civil society. SPN, pp. 206–7.

26. SPN, p. 421.

27. SPN, p. 204.

28. SPN, pp. 125–36.

29. Antonio Gramsci, *Letters from Prison*, edited and translated by Lynne Lawner (London: Harper & Row, 1973), p. 80. I have used Lynne Lawner's translation here since it uses 'popular creative spirit' rather than 'the creative spirit of the people', used by Rosenthal in *Letters from Prison* (2 vols), edited by Frank Rosengarten, translated by Raymond Rosenthal (New York: Columbia University Press, 1994), p. 84.

30. Renate Holub, *Antonio Gramsci: Beyond Marxism and Postmodernism* (London: Routledge, 1992), pp. 54–55.

31. SPN, pp. 365–6; see also pp. 377, 418, 137 and p. 421 n. 65. On 'historic bloc', see Sassoon, *Gramsci's Politics*, pp. 119–25 and Walter Adamson, *Hegemony and Revolution: A Study of Antonio Gramsci's Political and Cultural Theory* (Berkeley: University of California Press, 1980), pp. 170–79.

32. Roger Simon, *Gramsci's Political Thought: An Introduction* (London: Lawrence & Wishart, 1991), p. 25.

33. Mary O'Brien has criticized Gramsci from a socialist feminist position; see *Reproducing the World: Essays in Feminist Theory* (Boulder: Westview Press, 1989), pp. 223–44. As we shall see in Chapter 5, Ernesto Laclau and Chantal Mouffe criticize Gramsci from a very different perspective but find him similarly guilty of focusing too much on the working class.

34. Michael Hardt and Antonio Negri have theorized about how revolution can be formed by creating a unity, not by mixing nations and peoples indifferently, but rather by creating a 'new city'. *Empire* (Cambridge, Mass.: Harvard University Press, 2000), p. 395.

35. Gobetti was a liberal and friend of Gramsci's who founded the journal *La Rivoluzione Liberale* and was assassinated by Fascists in 1926. Gramsci discusses the importance to communism of liberals like Gobetti in 'Some Aspects of the Southern Question', Antonio Gramsci, *Selections from the Political Writings (1921–1926)*, edited and translated by Quintin Hoare (Minneapolis: University of Minnesota Press, 1990), pp. 441–62. See also Piero Gobetti, *On Liberal Revolution*, edited by Nadia Urbinati, translated by William McCuaig (New Haven: Yale University Press, 2000).

36. For a good discussion, see Joseph Buttigieg, 'Gramsci on Civil Society', *Boundary 2* 22(3) (Fall 1995) pp. 1–32; Jan Rehmann, '"Abolition" of Civil Society?' *Socialism and Democracy* 13(2) (Fall/Winter 1999),

pp. 1–18; and Ellen Meiksins Wood, 'The Uses and Abuses of "Civil Society"', in Ralph Miliband, Leo Panitch and John Saville (eds), *Socialist Register 1990* (London: Merlin Press, 1990), pp. 60–84.

37. SPN, p. 235.

38. Indeed, what Gramsci lauds in the Moderate Party's actions are that they secured power within civil society. See Buttigieg, 'Gramsci on Civil Society', p. 21.

39. G.W.F. Hegel, *The Philosophy of Right*, translated by T.M.Knox (London: Oxford University Press, 1973), p. 110.

40. The classic exchange on this issue was in 1969 between Norberto Bobbio and Jacques Texier, both articles translated in Chantal Mouffe (ed.), *Gramsci and Marxist Theory* (London: Routledge Kegan Paul, 1979), pp. 21–47 and pp. 48–79. This debate is intertwined with various readings of the influence of Croce (a follower of Hegel) as opposed to Marx on Gramsci; see Walter Adamson, *Hegemony and Revolution*, pp. 215–22.

41. QC, p. 704; as cited in SPN, p. 208.

42. At one point, Gramsci defines 'civil society' as 'the ensemble of organisms commonly called "private" ... ' SPN, p. 12.

43. Joseph V. Femia, *Gramsci's Political Thought: Hegemony, Consciousness, and the Revolutionary Process* (Oxford: Clarendon Press, 1987), p. 24.

44. Adamson, *Hegemony and Revolution*, p. 218.

45. It is important to note that in works such as *The Eighteenth Brumaire* and *The Civil War in France*, that is, Marx's more political and less economic works, he comes closer to Gramsci's concerns.

46. Antonio Gramsci, *Further Selections from the Prison Notebooks*, edited and translated by Derek Boothman (Minneapolis: University of Minnesota Press, 1995), pp. 315–18. Gramsci does not note the sexism of such an attitude, but for today's reader the power of his critique rests on this notion, making one wonder at the appropriateness of his comparison.

47. Perry Anderson, 'The Antinomies of Antonio Gramsci', *New Left Review* 100 (November 1976–January 1977), pp. 5–79; Robert Bocock, *Hegemony* (Chichester: Ellis Horwood, 1986); and Hoare and Nowell Smith, in SPN, p. 207.

48. SPN, p. 238.

49. V.I. Lenin, *State and Revolution*, translated by Robert Service (London: Penguin, 1992), pp. 7–15.

50. SPN, p. 182. Gramsci first raises this point in a letter of 7 September 1931, Antonio Gramsci, *Letters from Prison* (vol. 2), edited by Frank Rosengarten, translated by Raymond Rosenthal (New York: Columbia University Press, 1994), p. 67. For a discussion of Gramsci's pre-prison development of his critique of the liberal state, see Germino, pp. 82–85.

51. This point separates Gramsci from many other Marxists, including Althusser, Adorno and others, who seem to suggest that modern capitalist societies are 'totally administered' and thus subaltern groups have been successfully blocked out of influence on the social development. Michael Hardt and Antonio Negri take up Gramsci's position here, emphasizing the extent to which subaltern groups (or what they call the 'multitude') continually play a role in shaping the form of the state, *Empire*, pp. 93–113. See also Gramsci's discussion of 'separation of powers', SPN, p. 245, n. 46.

52. SPN, p. 244. Gramsci is raising the issue of sociology here, because he is criticizing Bukharin's book subtitled, *A Popular Manual of Marxist Sociology*. He argues that the decline of the study of politics in the nineteenth century is due to its narrowing focus on purely parliamentary activity and politicians. He is critical of sociology because in its name the positivist methods of the natural sciences are being used by the likes of Bukharin to study political issues.
53. SPN, p. 239.
54. SPN, p. 263.
55. Anderson, 'Antinomies', pp. 12–14, 33–39. He then argues that this fusion is taken up by Althusser's position that the state in bourgeois society includes everything, and Gramsci's distinctions are really between 'ideological state apparatuses' and 'repressive state apparatuses'.
56. Sassoon, *Gramsci's Politics*, pp. 112–13. See SPN, p. 12 for Gramsci's discussion of the limited definition of the state and pp. 262–3 for his more expanded notion.
57. Simon, *Gramsci's Political Thought*, p. 72. He also argues that for Gramsci capitalist society is made up of three sets of social relations; those of production, those of the state and those of civil society. By separating the relations of production from civil society, Simon reads Gramsci as departing quite drastically from Marx's location of the economy within civil society, p. 70.
58. Buttigieg, 'Gramsci on Civil Society', p. 26, p. 19.
59. The epitome of such explicit coercion is the history of residential schools for aboriginal and native peoples in Canada and the United States, some of which expressly forbade the use of native languages enforced by physical punishment. See Ruth Spack, *America's Second Tongue: American Indian Education and the Ownership of English, 1860–1900* (Lincoln: University of Nebraska Press, 2002); J.R. Miller, *Shingwauk's Vision: A History of Native Residential Schools* (Toronto: University of Toronto Press, 1996), pp. 199–216; and John Milloy, *A National Crime: The Canadian Government and the Residential School System, 1879–1986* (Winnipeg: University of Manitoba Press, 1999), especially pp. 38–39.

## Chapter 5  Postmodernism, New Social Movements and Globalization: Implications for Social and Political Theory

1. For example, Stuart Hall, 'The Problem of Ideology: Marxism Without Guarantees', and 'Gramsci's Relevance for the Study of Race and Ethnicity', both in *Stuart Hall: Critical Dialogues in Cultural Studies*, edited by David Morley and Kuan-Hsing Chen (London: Routledge, 1996), pp. 25–46 and 411–40.
2. For a rather different approach from Laclau and Mouffe's, to be discussed at length below, see T.J. Jackson Lears, 'The Concept of Cultural Hegemony: Problems and Possibilities', *American Historical Review* 90(3) (June 1985), pp. 567–93.

3. Antonio Gramsci, *Selections from the Prison Notebooks*, edited and translated by Quintin Hoare and Geoffrey Nowell Smith (New York: International Publishers, 1971), p. 465.
4. Jean-François Lyotard, *The Postmodern Condition: A Report on Knowledge*, translated by Geoff Bennington (Minneapolis: University of Minnesota Press, 1984).
5. This is one of the few elements that really ties together Baudrillard's diverse writings, from his rejection of Marxism in the early 1970s to his inflammatory arguments that the 1991 war in Iraq did not take place and that the attack of 11 September 2001 was worse than 'real', it was symbolic. See *Jean Baudrillard: Selected Writings*, (second edition), edited by Mark Poster (Stanford: Stanford University Press, 2001); Jean Baudrillard, *The Gulf War Did Not Take Place*, translated by Paul Patton, (Bloomington: Indiana University Press, 1995); and Jean Baudrillard, *The Spirit of Terrorism: And Requiem for the Twin Towers* (London: Verso, 2002).
6. David Harvey, *The Condition of Postmodernity* (Oxford: Basil Blackwell, 1989); and Fredric Jameson, *Postmodernism, or, the Logic of Late Capitalism* (Durham: Duke University Press, 1991).
7. See Richard Rorty, *Philosophy and the Mirror of Nature* (Princeton: Princeton University Press, 1979); and *Contingency, Irony, and Solidarity* (Cambridge: Cambridge University Press, 1989).
8. One of the best arguments for how these two notions of 'modern' relate is Marshall Berman, *All That is Solid Melts into Air: The Experience of Modernity* (New York: Penguin, 1988).
9. Steven Best and Douglas Kellner, *The Postmodern Turn* (New York: Guilford, 1997), especially pp. 24–5, and Steven Best and Douglas Kellner, *Postmodern Theory: Critical Interrogations* (New York: Guilford, 1991), pp. 29–32.
10. Friedrich Nietzsche, 'On Truth and Lie in an Extra-Moral Sense', in *The Portable Nietzsche*, translated by Walter Kaufmann (New York: Viking, 1954), pp. 46–7.
11. Derrida essentially redefines 'writing' to be much broader than 'phonetic writing' and to include any form of coding or inscription. Jacques Derrida, *Of Grammatology*, translated by Gayatri Chakrovorty Spivak (Baltimore: Johns Hopkins University Press, 1974), pp. 101–40.
12. Derrida, *Of Grammatology*, especially pp. 1–94.
13. See Victor B. Shklovsky, *Theory of Prose*, translated by Benjamin Sher (Elmwood Park: Dalkey Archive Press, 1991).
14. Esteve Morera, *Gramsci's Historicism: A Realist Interpretation* (London: Routledge, 1990) and Jonathan Joseph, *Hegemony: A Realist Analysis* (London: Routledge, 2002).
15. Karl Marx, *Capital: A Critique of Political Economy*, translated by Samuel Moore and Edward Aveling (New York: New Modern Library, 1906), p. 198.
16. SPN, p. 448.
17. This argument resonates with ordinary-language philosophy, inspired by Wittgenstein, which insists that most philosophical problems arise only because philosophers use language incorrectly and if we analyse how ordinary people understand the terms involved, the philosophical

problems cease being problems. But in this case, these philosophical or theological positions have pervaded common sense.
18. SPN, pp. 440–41.
19. See for example his discussion of whether 'Americanism' should be understood as constituting a new epoch, SPN, pp. 279–318.
20. See, for example, Michel Foucault, *The Order of Things: An Archaeology of the Human Sciences* (New York: Vintage, 1973), especially pp. 34–45, 78–124, 280–306; and 'What is an Author?', in *Language, Counter-Memory, Practice*, translated by Donald Bouchard and Sherry Simon (Ithaca: Cornell University Press, 1977), pp. 113–38.
21. Foucault, *Order of Things*, p. xv.
22. For example, Renate Holub, *Antonio Gramsci: Beyond Marxism and Postmodernism* (London: Routledge, 1992) pp. 13, 29–30, 191–203; Joan Cocks, *The Oppositional Imagination: Feminism, Critique and Political Theory* (London: Routledge, 1989). For critical readings of Gramsci, see Barry Smart, 'The Politics of Truth and the Problems of Hegemony', in David Conzens Hoy (ed.) *Foucault: A Critical Reader* (Oxford: Basil Blackwell, 1986), pp. 157–73; and Michèle Barrett, *The Politics of Truth: From Marx to Foucault* (Stanford: Stanford University Press, 1991), especially pp. 49–80 and 121–68. For a response to Smart, see R. Radhakrishnan, 'Toward an Effective Intellectual: Foucault or Gramsci?' in Bruce Robbins (ed.) *Intellectuals: Aesthetics, Politics, Academics* (Minneapolis: University of Minnesota Press, 1990), pp. 57–100.
23. Foucault explicitly notes that he uses the term 'discursive formation' so as to avoid the 'already overladen' designations such as ideology, theory or domain of objectivity. *Archaeology of Knowledge*, translated by A.M. Sheridan Smith (London: Routledge, 1989), p. 38.
24. Manfred Frank, 'On Foucault's Concept of Discourse', in *Michel Foucault Philosopher*, translated by Timothy Armstrong (New York: Routledge, 1992), pp. 99–116.
25. See n. 22.
26. Nancy Hartsock, 'Foucault on Power: A Theory for Women?' in Linda Nicholson (ed.), *Feminism/Postmodernism* (New York: Routledge, 1990), pp. 157–76, here p. 165.
27. In addition to Hartsock, 'Foucault on Power', see Cocks, *The Oppositional Imagination*, pp. 45–62.
28. Alan Keenan, *Democracy in Question* (Stanford: Stanford University Press, 2003), p. 108.
29. For example, see Ellen Meiksins Wood, *Retreat from Class: A New 'True' Socialism* (London: Verso, 1986), especially pp. 47–89; and Norman Geras, 'Post-Marxism?' *New Left Review* 163 (May/June 1987), pp. 40–82, reprinted in his *Discourses of Extremity: Radical Ethics and Post-Marxist Extravagances* (London: Verso, 1990). For a more favourable criticism of Laclau and Mouffe from a different perspective see Keenan, *Democracy in Question*, pp. 102–43.
30. See Ernesto Laclau, *New Reflections on the Revolution of Our Time*, pp. 198–201. For overviews, see Jacob Torfing, *New Theories of Discourse: Laclau, Mouffe, and Žižek* (Oxford: Blackwell Publishers, 1999), pp. 15–35; and Anna Marie Smith, *Laclau and Mouffe: The Radical Democratic Imaginary* (London: Routledge, 1998).

184    Language and Hegemony in Gramsci

31. See especially Ernesto Laclau, *Politics and Ideology in Marxist Theory* (London: Verso, 1977), which includes essays analysing Argentina, the debate between Nicos Poulantzas and Ralph Miliband, and Fascism.
32. See especially her edited collection *Gramsci and Marxist Theory* (London: Routledge, Kegan Paul, 1979) including her essay, 'Hegemony and Ideology in Gramsci', pp. 168–205.
33. Ernesto Laclau and Chantal Mouffe, *Hegemony and Socialist Strategy: Towards a Radical Democratic Politics* (London: Verso, 1985), p. 3. Hereafter cited as HSS.
34. In an interview in 1988, Laclau explained the first two chapters of HSS by noting that class struggle is the 'supplement' – in Derrida's sense explained above – to Marxism's critique of capitalism as an economic system. See Laclau, *New Reflections*, pp. 180–81.
35. HSS, p. 12.
36. Laclau and Mouffe's most extensive discussion of 'overdetermination' is on pp. 97–105, where they emphasize that, as Althusser noted, overdetermination has no meaning outside the 'field of the symbolic', in other words it is not just multi-causality, or a plurality of structures that determine something. Rather, it deconstructs any distinction between 'essence' and 'appearance' – where appearances are determined by essences, even a multiplicity of essences. Laclau and Mouffe then favour this conception as presented by Althusser in *For Marx* (translated by Ben Brewster, New York: Vintage, 1970) over what they see as Althusser's relapse into economism apparent in his work with Etienne Balibar, *Reading Capital*.
37. Louis Althusser, 'Contradiction and Overdetermination', in *For Marx*, pp. 97–106.
38. HSS, p. 30.
39. HSS, p. 59.
40. HSS, p. 67.
41. HSS, p. 65. Later in that work they define 'articulation' as 'any practice establishing a relation among elements such that their identity is modified as a result of the articulatory practice'(p. 105).
42. HSS, p. 85.
43. HSS, p. 69.
44. Wendy Brown criticises Laclau and Mouffe for their inadequate analysis of the economy. Anna Marie Smith attempts to redress this admitted insufficiency in an astute (if not totally convincing) account of practical and political applications of Laclau and Mouffe's work. Wendy Brown, *States of Injury: Power and Freedom in Late Modernity* (Princeton: Princeton University Press, 1995); and Smith, *Laclau and Mouffe*, p. 19. This issue is also raised in the various empirical studies that apply Laclau and Mouffe's theory in David Howarth, Aletta Norval and Yannis Stavrakakis (eds), *Discourse Theory and Political Analysis: Identities, Hegemonies and Social Change* (Manchester: Manchester University Press, 2000).
45. Laclau and Mouffe are weary of Foucault's suggestion of a distinction between discursive and non-discursive practices, arguing that he is inconsistent and while objects exist 'outside' of discourse and thought, their meaning or any symbolic awareness of them is, by definition, discursive. HSS, p. 108; and Ernesto Laclau and Chantal Mouffe,

'Post-Marxism Without Apologies', in Ernesto Laclau, *New Reflections on the Revolution of Our Time* (London: Verso, 1990), pp. 100–103. (originally published in *New Left Review* 166 (November–December 1987)).
46. Chantal Mouffe, *The Democratic Paradox* (London: Verso, 2000), p. 21.
47. HSS, p. 105.
48. HSS, p. 105. They explain that a 'discourse' will include linguistic and non-linguistic elements, in this case the mechanisms for audible traffic signals and the notion that there are some advantages to being blind. They borrow significantly from Foucault's notion of discourse, but find that he is inconsistent in maintaining a distinction between discursive and non-discursive practices. HSS, p. 107.
49. HSS, p. 113.
50. HSS, p. 134.
51. HSS, p. 108.
52. See for example, Geras, 'Post-Marxism?', pp. 66–67.
53. Laclau's later work relies increasingly on Lacan's psychoanalysis; see Ernesto Laclau, *Emancipation(s)* (London: Verso, 1996). Smith is quite critical of this move, arguing that it must be supplemented with a more Gramscian approach to historicity. She also suggests that the differences between Gramsci and Laclau are not as irreconcilable as they may appear. *Laclau and Mouffe*, p. 82, p. 165.
54. See Elizabeth Grosz, *Jacques Lacan: A Feminist Introduction* (London: Routledge, 1990), especially pp. 31–49.
55. Laclau first offered this argument in 1983 in his short article, 'The Impossibility of Society', included in *New Reflections*, pp. 89–92.
56. HSS, p. 111.
57. HSS, p. 88, n. 1.
58. HSS, p. 125.
59. HSS, p. 125.
60. HSS, p. 125.
61. As will be discussed in the final section of this chapter, there is an issue, not raised by Laclau and Mouffe, of whether Gramsci presupposes that the nation should play an essential role in the creation of a progressive language or hegemonic formation. Gramsci addresses this to some degree in his discussion of translation and the 'translatability'of cultures and world-views.
62. For a succinct overview see Andreas Bieler and Adam David Morton, 'Theoretical and Methodological Challenges of Neo-Gramscian Perspectives in International Political Economy', available at <www.italnet.nd.edu/gramsci/resources/online_articles/index.html>. See also Stephen Gill, *Power, Resistance and the New World Order* (New York: Palgrave, 2003); Stephen Gill (ed.), *Gramsci, Historical Materialism and International Relations* (Cambridge: Cambridge University Press, 1994); and Robert Cox, *Production, Power and World Order: Social Forces in the Making of History* (New York: Columbia University Press, 1987).
63. SPN, pp. 277–318.
64. Their classic, though problematic, essay is Max Horkheimer and Theodor Adorno, 'The Culture Industry: Enlightenment as Mass Deception', in *The Dialectic of Enlightenment*, translated by John Cumming (New York: Continuum, 1969), pp. 120–67.

65. Robert Dombroski, *Antonio Gramsci* (Boston, Twayne, 1989), p. 132.
66. I have addressed the differences between Gramsci's conception of language and that of Horkheimer and Adorno in my *Gramsci's Politics of Language*, Chapter 4.
67. Dombroski discusses this drawback with reference to Gramsci's approach to literature.
68. SPN, p. 416. There is a note of criticism in this passage, but Gramsci nowhere entirely rejects this 'Hegemony of Western Culture over the Whole World'.
69. The by now classic work here is Benedict Anderson, *Imagined Communities* (second edition) (London: Verso, 1991). Similarly to Anderson's contention that 'nationalism' is significantly a product of interactions between the 'old' world European powers and 'new' world colonies, Donna Gabaccia has also argued that the creation of Italian national identity in the nineteenth century needs to take account of the role played by emigration. *Italy's Many Diasporas* (Seattle: University of Washington Press, 2000).
70. I have discussed this and the comparisons with Benjamin at length in Chapter 3 of my *Gramsci's Politics of Language*.
71. Joseph Buttigieg, 'Gramsci on Civil Society', *Boundary 2* 22(3) (1995), pp. 1–32; Jan Rehmann, '"Abolition" of Civil Society? Remarks on a Widespread Misunderstanding in the Interpretation of "Civil Society"', *Socialism and Democracy* 13(2) (Fall/Winter 1999), pp. 1–17.
72. For example, David Held, *Democracy and the Global Order: From the Modern State to Cosmopolitan Governance* (Stanford: Stanford University Press, 1995); and Jürgen Habermas, 'Crossing Globalization's Valley of Tears', *New Perspective Quarterly* 17(4) (Fall 2000), pp. 51–57. For a rather different analysis of culture and globalization that also accepts the demise of the nation-state and hopes that it can result in diasporic public spheres of a more progressive postnational politics, see Arjun Appadurai, *Modernity at Large: Cultural Dimensions of Globalization* (Minneapolis: University of Minnesota Press, 1996).
73. For example, Timothy Brennan, 'Cosmopolitanism and Internationalism', *New Left Review* 7 (January–February 2001), pp. 75–84.
74. David Crystal, *English as a Global Language* (Cambridge: Cambridge University Press, 1997).
75. See my 'Language, Representation and Supra-State Democracy: Questions Facing the European Union', in David Laycock (ed.) *Representation and Democratic Theory* (Vancouver: UBC Press, 2004), pp. 56–91.

# Bibliography

Adamson, Walter L. *Hegemony and Revolution: A Study of Antonio Gramsci's Political and Cultural Theory*, Berkeley: University of California Press, 1980
Althusser, Louis 'Ideological State Apparatuses', in Slavoj Žižek (ed.) *Mapping Ideology*, London: Verso, 1994: 100–140
—— *For Marx*, translated by Ben Brewster, New York: Vintage, 1970
Ambrosoli, Luigi 'Nuovi contributi agli "Scritti giovanile" di Gramsci', *Rivista Storica del Socialismo* 3 (1960): 545–50
Anderson, Benedict *Imagined Communities* (revised edition), London: Verso, 1991
Anderson, Perry *In the Tracks of Historical Materialism*, London: Verso, 1983
—— 'The Antinomies of Antonio Gramsci', *New Left Review* 100 (November 1976–January 1977): 5–79
Ascoli, Graziadio Isaia 'Italy – Part III, Languages', *Encyclopedia Britanica*, (vol. 13) (ninth edition), New York: Henry G. Allen, 1898, 497–8
Balakrishnan, Gopal (ed.) *Mapping the Nation*, London: Verso, 1996
Barrett, Michèle *The Politics of Truth: From Marx to Foucault*, Stanford: Stanford University Press, 1991
Baudrillard, Jean *The Spirit of Terrorism: And Requiem for the Twin Towers*, translated by Chris Turner, London: Verso, 2002
—— *Selected Writings* (second edition), edited by Mark Poster, Stanford: Stanford University Press, 2001
—— *The Gulf War Did Not Take Place*, translated by Paul Patton, Bloomington: Indiana University Press, 1995
Bellamy, Richard and Darrow Schecter *Gramsci and the Italian State*, Manchester: Manchester University Press, 1993
Berlin, Isaiah 'Two Concepts of Liberty', in *The Proper Study of Mankind*, London: Pimlico, 1997, 191–242
Berman, Marshall *All That is Solid Melts into Air: The Experience of Modernity*, New York: Penguin, 1988
Bernstein, Eduard *Evolutionary Socialism*, edited by Edith C. Harvey, New York: Schocken, 1961
Best, Steven and Douglas Kellner *The Postmodern Turn*, New York: Guilford, 1997
—— *Postmodern Theory: Critical Interrogations*, New York: Guilford, 1991
Bieler, Andreas and Adam David Morton 'Theoretical and Methodological Challenges of Neo-Gramscian Perspectives in International Political Economy' <www.italnet.nd.edu/gramsci/resources/online_articles/index.html>
Bocock, Robert *Hegemony*, Chichester: Ellis Horwood, 1986
Brandist, Craig 'Gramsci, Bakhtin and the Semiotics of Hegemony', *New Left Review* 216 (March/April, 1996): 94–109
—— 'The Official and the Popular in Gramsci and Bakhtin', *Theory, Culture and Society* 13(2) (1996): 59–74

Braverman, Harry *Labor and Monopoly Capital: The Degradation of Work in the Twentieth Century*, New York: Monthly Review Press, 1975

Brown, Wendy *States of Injury: Power and Freedom in Late Modernity*, Princeton: Princeton University Press, 1995

Bukharin, Nikolai *Historical Materialism: A System of Sociology*, Ann Arbor: University of Michigan Press, 1969

Burawoy, Michael *The Politics of Production: Factory Regimes under Capitalism and Socialism*, London: Verso, 1985

Buttigieg, Joseph 'Introduction', in Antonio Gramsci, *Prison Notebooks* (vol. 1), edited by Joseph Buttigieg, New York: Columbia University Press, 1992

—— 'Gramsci on Civil Society', *Boundary 2* 22(3) (Fall 1995): 1–32

Cameron, Deborah (ed.) *The Feminist Critique of Language: A Reader* (second edition), London: Routledge, 1998

Carrannante, Antonio 'Antonio Gramsci e i problemi della lingua italiana', *Belfagor* 28 (1973): 544–56

Cassirer, Ernst 'Structuralism in Modern Linguistics', *Word* 1 (1945): 99–120

Centre for Contemporary Cultural Studies *On Ideology*, London: Hutchinson, 1978

Cocks, Joan *The Oppositional Imagination: Feminism, Critique and Political Theory*, London: Routledge, 1989

Cox, Robert *Production, Power and World Order: Social Forces in the Making of History*, New York: Columbia University Press, 1987

Crehan, Kate *Gramsci, Culture and Anthropology*, London: Pluto Press, 2002

Croce, Benedetto *The Aesthetic as the Science of Expression and of the Linguistic in General* translated by Colin Lyas, Cambridge: Cambridge University Press, 1992

—— *The Conduct of Life*, translated by Arthur Livingston, New York: 1924

Crystal, David *English as a Global Language*, Cambridge: Cambridge University Press, 1997

Culler, Jonathon *Saussure* (sixth edition), London: Fontana Press, 1988

Davidson, Alastair *Antonio Gramsci: Towards an Intellectual Biography*, London: Merlin Press, 1977

Davis, John (ed.) *Gramsci and Italy's Passive Revolution*, New York: Barnes & Noble, 1979

Davis, John B 'Gramsci, Sraffa, Wittgenstein: Philosophical Linkages', *European Journal of the History of Economic Thought* 9(3) (Autumn 2002): 384–401

De Felice, Renzo 'Un corso di glottologia di Matteo Bartoli negli appunti di Antonio Gramsci', *Rivista Storica del Socialismo* 7 (1964): 219–21

De Mauro, Tullio *Storia Linguistica Dell'Italia Unita*, Rome: Editori Laterza, 1986

Derrida, Jacques *of Grammatology*, translated by Gayatri Chakrovorty Spivak, Baltimore: Johns Hopkins University Press, 1974

Devoto, Giacomo *The Languages of Italy*, translated by V. Louise Katainen, Chicago: University of Chicago Press, 1978

Dombroski, Robert *Antonio Gramsci*, Boston: Twayne, 1989

d'Orsi, Angelo 'Lo Studente che non divenne "Dottore" Gramsci all'Università di Torino', *Studi Storici* 40(1) (January–March, 1999): 39–75

Engels, Dagmar and Shula Marks (eds) *Contesting Colonial Hegemony: State and Society in Africa and India*, London: British Academic Press, 1994

Femia, Joseph V. *Gramsci's Political Thought: Hegemony, Consciousness and the Revolutionary Process*, Oxford: Clarendon Press, 1987

Fiori, Guiseppe *Antonio Gramsci: Life of a Revolutionary*, translated by Tom Nairn, London: Verso, 1980

Fontana, Benedetto 'Politics, Philosophy and Modernity in Gramsci', *Philosophical Forum* 29(3–4) (Spring–Summer 1998): 104–18

Forgacs, David 'National–Popular: Genealogy of a Concept', in *Formations of Nation and People*, London: Routledge & Kegan Paul, 1984, 83–98

Foucault, Michel 'What is an Author?' in *Language, Counter-Memory, Practice*, translated by Donald Bouchard and Sherry Simon, Ithaca: Cornell University Press, 1977, 113–38

—— *The Order of Things: An Archaeology of the Human Sciences*, New York: Vintage, 1973

—— *Archaeology of Knowledge*, translated by A.M. Sheridan Smith, London: Routledge, 1989

Frank, Manfred 'On Foucault's Concept of Discourse', in *Michel Foucault Philosopher*, translated by Timothy Armstrong, New York: Routledge, 1992, 99–116

Gabaccia, Donna *Italy's Many Diasporas*, Seattle: University of Washington Press, 2000

Gensini, Stefano 'Linguistica e questione politica della lingua', *Critica Marxista* 1 (1980): 151–65

Germino, Dante *Antonio Gramsci: Architect of a New Politics*, Baton Rouge: Louisiana State University Press, 1990

Gill, Stephen *Power, Resistence and the New World Order*, New York: Palgrave, 2003

—— (ed.) *Gramsci, Historical Materialism and International Relations*, Cambridge: Cambridge University Press, 1994

Gobetti, Piero *On Liberal Revolution*, edited by Nadia Urbinati, translated by William McCuaig, New Haven: Yale University Press, 2000

Gramsci, Antonio *Prison Notebooks* (vol. 2), edited and translated by Joseph A. Buttigieg, New York: Columbia University Press, 1996

—— *Further Selections from the Prison Notebooks*, edited and translated by Derek Boothman, Minneapolis: University of Minnesota Press, 1995

—— *Letters from Prison* (2 vols), edited by Frank Rosengarten, translated by Raymond Rosenthal, New York: Columbia University Press, 1994

—— *Prison Notebooks* (vol. 1), edited by Joseph A. Buttigieg, translated by Joseph A. Buttigieg and Antonio Callari, New York: Columbia University Press, 1992

—— *Selections from Political Writings (1921–1926)*, edited and translated by Quintin Hoare, Minneapolis: University of Minnesota Press, 1990

—— *Selections from Political Writings (1910–1920)*, edited by Quintin Hoare, translated by John Matthews, Minneapolis: University of Minnesota Press, 1990

—— *Selections from Cultural Writings*, edited by David Forgacs and Geoffrey Nowell Smith, translated by William Boelhower, Cambridge, Mass.: Harvard University Press, 1985

Gramsci, Antonio *Quaderni del carcere* (4 vols), edited by Valentino
Gerratana, Turin: Einaudi, 1975
—— *Letters from Prison*, edited and translated by Lynne Lawner, New York:
Harper & Row, 1973
—— *Selections from the Prison Notebooks*, edited and translated by Quintin
Hoare and Geoffrey Nowell Smith, New York: International Publishers,
1971
—— *La Città Futura, 1917–1918*, edited by Sergio Caprioglio, Turin: Einaudi,
1982
Green, Marcus 'Gramsci Cannot Speak: Presentation and Interpretation of
Gramsci's Concept of the Subaltern', *Rethinking Marxism* 14(3) (Spring
2002): 1–24
Grosz, Elizabeth *Jacques Lacan: A Feminist Introduction*, London: Routledge,
1990
Haddock, Bruce 'State, Nation and Risorgimento', in Haddock and Bedani
(eds) *Politics of Italian National Identity*, Cardiff: University of Wales Press,
2000, 11–49
Haddock, Bruce and Gino Bedani (eds) *Politics of Italian National Identity*,
Cardiff: University of Wales Press, 2000
Hall, Stuart 'The Problem of Ideology: Marxism Without Guarantees', in
David Morley and Kuan-Hsing Chen (eds) *Stuart Hall: Critical Dialogues in
Cultural Studies*, London: Routledge, 1996, 25–46
—— 'On Postmodernism and Articulation', in David Morley and Kuan-
Hsing Chen (eds) *Stuart Hall: Critical Dialogues in Cultural Studies*, London:
Routledge, 1996, 131–50
—— 'Gramsci's Relevance for the Study of Race and Ethnicity', in David
Morley and Kuan-Hsing Chen (eds) *Stuart Hall: Critical Dialogues in
Cultural Studies*, London: Routledge, 1996, 411–40
Hall, Stuart et al. *Culture, Media and Language*, London: Hutchinson, 1980
Hardt, Michael and Antonio Negri *Empire*, Cambridge, Mass.: Harvard
University Press, 2000
Harris, David *From Class Struggle to the Politics of Pleasure*, London: Routledge,
1992
Hartsock, Nancy 'Foucault on Power: A Theory for Women?' in Linda
Nicholson (ed.) *Feminism/Postmodernism*, New York: Routledge, 1990,
157–76
Harvey, David *The Condition of Postmodernity*, Oxford: Basil Blackwell, 1989
Hegel, G.W.F. *The Philosophy of Right*, translated by T.M.Knox, London:
Oxford University Press, 1973
Helsloot, Niels 'Linguists Of All Countries …! On Gramsci's Premise of
Coherence', *Journal of Pragmatics* 13 (1989): 547–66
Hobbes, Thomas *Leviathan* (revised edition), edited by Richard Tuck,
Cambridge: Cambridge University Press, 1996
Hobsbawm, Eric *Age of Extremes: The Short Twentieth Century, 1914–1991*,
London: Abacus, 1995
Hoffman, John *The Gramscian Challenge: Coercion and Consent in Marxist
Political Theory*, Oxford: Basil Blackwell, 1984
Holub, Renate *Antonio Gramsci: Beyond Marxism and Postmodernism*, London:
Routledge, 1992

Horkheimer, Max and Theodor Adorno 'The Culture Industry: Enlighten-
ment as Mass Deception', in *The Dialectic of Enlightenment*, translated by
John Cumming, New York: Continuum, 1969, 120–67
Howarth, David, Aletta Norval and Yannis Stavrakakis (eds) *Discourse Theory
and Political Analysis: Identities, Hegemonies and Social Change*, Manchester:
Manchester University Press, 2000
Irigaray, Luce *Speculum of the Other Woman*, translated by Gillian G. Gill,
Ithaca: Cornell University Press, 1985
Ives, Peter *Gramsci's Politics of Langauge: Engaging the Bakhtin Circle and the
Frankfurt School*, Toronto: University of Toronto Press, 2004
—— 'The Grammar of Hegemony', *Left History* 5(1) (Spring 1997): 85–104
(reprinted in James Martin (ed.) *Antonio Gramsci: Critical Assessments*
(vol. 2), London: Routledge, 2001, 319–36)
Jackson Lears, T.J. 'The Concept of Cultural Hegemony: Problems and
Possibilities', *American Historical Review* 90(3) (June 1985): 567–93
Jameson, Fredric *Postmodernism, or the Logic of Late Capitalism*, Durham:
Duke University Press, 1991
Joseph, Jonathan *Hegemony: A Realist Analysis*, London: Routledge, 2002
Keenan, Alan *Democracy in Question*, Stanford: Stanford University Press, 2003
Kristeva, Julia *The Kristeva Reader*, edited by Toril Moi, New York: Columbia
University Press, 1986
Laclau, Ernesto *Emancipation(s)*, London: Verso, 1996
—— *New Reflections on the Revolution of Our Time*, London: Verso, 1990
—— *Politics and Ideology in Marxist Theory*, London: Verso, 1977
Laclau, Ernesto and Chantal Mouffe 'Post-Marxism Without Apologies', *New
Left Review* 166 (November–December 1987) (reprinted in Ernesto Laclau,
*New Reflections on the Revolution of Our Time*, London: Verso, 1990, 97–134)
—— *Hegemony and Socialist Strategy: Towards a Radical Democratic Politics*,
London: Verso, 1985
Lacan, Jacques *Écrits: A Selection*, translated by Alan Sheridan, New York:
W.W. Norton, 1977
Lenin, V.I. *State and Revolution*, translated by Robert Service, London:
Penguin, 1992
Lester, Jeremy *Dialogue of Negation: Debates on Hegemony in Russia and the
West*, London: Pluto Press, 2000
Lichtner, Maurizio 'Traduzione e Metafore in Gramsci', *Critica Marxista* 39(1)
(January/February, 1991): 107–31
Limbaugh, Rush *See, I Told You So*, New York: Pocket Star Books, 1993
Lo Piparo, Franco *Lingua intellettuali egemonia in Gramsci*, Bari: Laterza, 1979
—— 'Studio del linguaggio e teoria gramsciana', *Critica Marxista* 2(3) (1987):
167–75
Lumley, Robert and Jonathan Morris (eds) *The New History of the Italian
South: The Mezzogiorno Revisited*, Exeter: University of Exeter Press, 1997
Lyotard, Jean-François *The Postmodern Condition: A Report on Knowledge*,
translated by Geoff Bennington, Minneapolis: University of Minnesota
Press, 1984
Marx, Karl *The Eighteenth Brumaire of Louis Bonaparte*, Moscow: Progress, 1934
—— *Capital: A Critique of Political Economy*, translated by Samuel Moore and
Edward Aveling, New York: New Modern Library, 1906

Migliorini, Bruno *The Italian Language*, London: Faber and Faber, 1966
Miller, J.R. *Shingwauk's Vision: A History of Native Residential Schools*, Toronto: University of Toronto Press, 1996
Milloy, John *A National Crime: The Canadian Government and the Residential School System, 1879–1986*, Winnipeg: University of Manitoba Press, 1999
Morera, Esteve *Gramsci's Historicism: A Realist Interpretation*, London: Routledge, 1990
Morley, David and Kuan-Hsing Chen (eds) *Stuart Hall: Critical Dialogues in Cultural Studies*, London: Routledge, 1996
Morpurgo Davies, Anna 'Karl Brugmann and Late Nineteenth-Century Linguistics', in Theodora Bynon and F.R. Palmer (eds) *Studies in the History of Western Linguistics*, Cambridge: Cambridge University Press, 1986
Moss, Howard 'Language and Italian National Identity', in Bruce Haddock and Gino Bedani (eds) *Politics of Italian National Identity*, Cardiff: University of Wales Press, 2000, 98–123
Mouffe, Chantal *The Democratic Paradox*, London: Verso, 2000
—— (ed.) *Gramsci and Marxist Theory*, London: Routledge & Kegan Paul, 1979
Naldi, Nerio 'The Friendship Between Piero Sraffa and Antonio Gramsci in the Years 1919–1927', *European Journal of the History of Economic Thought* 7(1) (March 2000): 79–114
Nietzsche, Friedrich *The Portable Nietzsche*, translated by Walter Kaufmann, New York: Viking, 1954
Nowell Smith, Geoffrey 'Gramsci and the National–Popular', *Screen Education* 22 (1977): 12–15
O'Brien, Mary *Reproducing the World: Essays in Feminist Theory*, Boulder: Westview Press, 1989
Osthoff, Hermann and Karl Brugmann 'Preface to *Morphologische Untersuchungen auf dem Gebiete der indogermanischen Sprachen*', in *A Reader in Nineteenth-Century Historical Indo-European Linguistics*, edited and translated by Winfred P. Lehmann, Bloomington: Indiana University Press, 1967, 197–209
Passaponti, M. Emilia 'Gramsci e le questioni linguistiche', in Stefano Gensini and Massimo Vedovelli (eds) *Lingua, Linguaggi e Società: Proposta per un aggiornamento* (second edition), Florence: Tipolitografia F.lli Linari, 1981, 119–28
Radhakrishnan, R. 'Toward an Effective Intellectual: Foucault or Gramsci?', in Bruce Robbins (ed) *Intellectuals: Aesthetics, Politics, Academics*, Minneapolis: University of Minnesota Press, 1990, 57–100
Rehmann, Jan ' "Abolition" of Civil Society?' *Socialism and Democracy* 13(2) (Fall/Winter 1999): 1–18
Reiter, Ester *Making Fast Food: From the Frying Pan into the Fryer*, Montreal: McGill–Queen's University Press, 1991
Reynolds, Barbara *The Linguistic Writings of Alessandro Manzoni*, Cambridge: W. Heffer & Sons, 1950
Rifkin, Jeremy *The Age of Access: The New Culture of Hypercapitalism, Where All Life is a Paid Experience*, New York: Putnam, 2000
Robins, R.H. *A Short History of Linguistics* (third edition), London: Longman, 1990
Rorty, Richard *Contingency, Irony and Solidarity*, Cambridge: Cambridge University Press, 1989

—— *Philosophy and the Mirror of Nature*, Princeton: Princeton University Press, 1979

—— *The Linguistic Turn: Recent Essays in Philosophical Method*, Chicago: University of Chicago Press, 1967

Rosiello, Luigi 'Linguistica e marxismo nel pensiero di Antonio Gramsci', In Paolo Ramat, Hans-J. Niederehe and Konrad Koerner (eds) *The History of Linguistics in Italy*, Amsterdam: John Benjamins, 1986, 237–58

—— 'Problemi linguistici negli scritti di Gramsci', in Pietro Rossi (ed.) *Gramsci e la cultura contemporanea* (vol. 2), Rome: Editori Riuniti, 1970, 347–67

Salamini, Leonardo *The Sociology of Political Praxis: An Introduction to Gramsci's Theory*, London: Routledge, 1981

Sassoon, Anne Showstack 'Gramsci's Subversion of the Language of Politics', *Rethinking Marxism* 3(1) (Spring 1990): 14–25

—— *Gramsci's Politics* (second edition), London: Hutchinson, 1987

Saussure, Ferdinand de *Course in General Linguistics*, translated by Roy Harris, La Salle, Illinois: Open Court, 1983

Schneider, Jane (ed.) *Italy's 'Southern Question': Orientalism in One Country*, Oxford: Berg, 1998

Shklovsky, Victor B. *Theory of Prose*, translated by Benjamin Sher, Elmwood Park: Dalkey Archive Press, 1991

Simon, Roger *Gramsci's Political Thought: An Introduction*, London: Lawrence & Wishart, 1991

Smart, Barry 'The Politics of Truth and the Problems of Hegemony', in David Couzens Hoy (ed.) *Foucault: A Critical Reader*, Oxford: Basil Blackwell, 1986, 157–73

Smith, Anna Marie *Laclau and Mouffe: The Radical Democratic Imaginary*, London: Routledge, 1998

Smith, Anthony D. *The Ethnic Origins of Nations*, Oxford: Oxford University Press, 1986

Spack, Ruth *America's Second Tongue: American Indian Education and the Ownership of English, 1860–1900*, Lincoln: University of Nebraska Press, 2002

Spender, Dale *Man Made Language*, London: Routledge & Kegan Paul, 1980

Tilly, Charles *Coercion, Capital and European State, AD 990–1990*, Oxford: Basil Blackwell, 1990

Torfing, Jacob *New Theories of Discourse: Laclau, Mouffe and Žižek*. Oxford: Blackwell Publishers, 1999

Urbinati, Nadia 'The Souths of Antonio Gramsci and the Concept of Hegemony', in Jane Schneider (ed.) *Italy's 'Southern Question': Orientalism in One Country*, Oxford: Berg, 1998, 135–56

Vossler, Karl *The Spirit of Language in Civilization*, translated by Oscar Oeser, London: Kegan Paul, Tench Trubner, 1932

Weber, Eugen *Peasants into Frenchmen: the Modernization of Rural France, 1870–1914*, Stanford: University of California Press, 1976

Weber, Max 'Politics as a Vocation', in *From MaxWeber*, edited and translated by H.H. Gerth and C. Wright Mills, New York: Oxford University Press, 1946, 77–128

Williams, Raymond *Marxism and Literature*, Oxford: Oxford University Press, 1977

Wittgenstein, Ludwig *Tractatus Logico-Philosophicus*, translated by D.F. Pears and B.F. McGuinness, London: Routledge, 1974
—— *Philosophical Investigations* (second edition), translated by G.E.M. Anscombe, Oxford: Basil Blackwell, 1958
Wood, Ellen Meiksins 'Modernity, Postmodernity or Capitalism', *Monthly Review* (July–August 1996): 21–39
—— 'The Uses and Abuses of "Civil Society" ', in Ralph Miliband, Leo Panitch and John Saville (eds) *Socialist Register 1990*, London: Merlin Press, 1990, 60–84
—— *Retreat from Class: A New 'True' Socialism*, London: Verso, 1986

# Index

*Compiled by Graham M. Smith*